# NARRATIVES OF DESIRE

# NARRATIVES OF DESIRE

## Nineteenth-Century Spanish Fiction by Women

*Lou Charnon-Deutsch*

The Pennsylvania State University Press
*University Park, Pennsylvania*

Publication of this book has been aided by a grant from The Program for Cultural Cooperation Between Spain's Ministry of Culture and United States' Universities.

The author thanks the publishers and agents for permission to quote passages from the following: "On Desire and Domesticity in Spanish Nineteenth-Century Women's Novels," *Revista Canadiense de Estudios Hispánicos* 14.3 (Spring 1990); "Desire in Rosalía de Castro's *El caballero de las botas azules*," in *Estudios sobre escritoras hispánicas en honor de Georgina Sabat-Rivers*, ed. Lou Charnon-Deutsch (Madrid: 1992); "Bearing Motherhood: Issues of Maternity in *Los Pazos de Ulloa*," in *New Hispanisms: Literature, Culture, Theory*, ed. Mark Millington and Paul Julian Smith (London: Dovehouse, 1993); "Social Masochism and the Spanish Domestic Novel," *Indiana Journal of Hispanic Studies* 2.1 (1993).

Library of Congress Cataloging-in-Publication Data

Charnon-Deutsch, Lou.
    Narratives of desire : nineteenth-century Spanish fiction by women / Lou Charnon-Deutsch.
        p.      cm. — (Penn State studies in romance literatures)
    Sequel to: Gender and representation.
    Includes bibliographical references and index.
    ISBN 0-271-01007-X (alk. paper). — ISBN 0-271-01008-8 (pbk. : alk. paper)
    1. Spanish fiction—19th century—History and criticism.
    2. Spanish fiction—Women authors—History and criticism.  3. Women in literature.  4. Sex role in literature.  5. Literature and society—Spain—History—19th century.  I. Title.  II. Series.
PQ6144.C427   1994
863'.509352042—dc20                                    93-17102
                                                          CIP

Published by The Pennsylvania State University Press,
Barbara Building, Suite C, University Park, PA 16802-1003

It is the policy of The Pennsylvania State University Press to use acid-free paper for the first printing of all clothbound books. Publications on uncoated stock satisfy the minimum requirements of American National Standard for Information Sciences—Permanence of Paper for Printed Library Materials, ANSI Z39.48–1984.

*To Dale,*
*for his loving support.*

# *Contents*

# List of Illustrations

# Acknowledgments

My thanks to the members of the various faculty reading groups of the Humanities Institute at the State University of New York at Stony Brook, and its director, Elizabeth Ann Kaplan, who has provided so many useful suggestions and such thoughtful encouragement over the past few years. I am especially grateful for the comments and suggestions of my colleague Helen Cooper whose ideas have been central to this project from its inception.

I am also indebted to the following for their readings of early portions of my manuscript: Barbara Morris, Maria Luisa Nunes, Adrienne Munich, Susan Squier, Elias Lynch Rivers, and Georgina Sabat Rivers. Others whose technical assistance I wish to acknowledge are María Carmen Simón Palmer and María Isabel Barbeito, and my thanks as well to Donna McGiboney and Amelia Salinero both for their reading of my work and for saving me so many trips to the library. I wish to thank the State University of New York for granting me a sabbatical leave during which the major portion of this manuscript was written, and to the National Endowment for the Humanities for a Travel to Collections Grant.

It is a pleasure to express my appreciation to the group of women who, through our constant interchanges, have influenced my ideas about the texts that I study here, among them: Noël Valis, Rosemary Geisdorfer Feal, Harriet Turner, Catherine Jagoe, Diane Urey, Kathleen Vernon, Maryellen Bieder, Stephanie Sieburth, Susan Kirkpatrick, Alda Blanco, Bridget Aldaraca, and Jo Labanyi.

Finally, I thank James Mandrell both for his encouragement and for his intelligent and painstaking readings of the various versions of my manuscript.

# *About the Translations*

All citations to primary literary sources appear in their original form followed by my own translation. In the case of both nineteenth- and twentieth-century criticism in Spanish, I have included only my translation. Titles of novels appearing for the first time are in their original followed by a translation. Thereafter, all titles appear in the original Spanish or Catalan only. All dates refer to the original date of publication.

# Introduction

IN A PREVIOUS STUDY on the representation of women in male-authored texts *(Gender and Representation: Women in Nineteenth-Century Spanish Realist Fiction)*, I described the masculinist practice of unmasking women, demonstrating to a presumed male reader either that women, despite appearances, cannot be what men want or need them to be, or that, in their excess, they pose a dangerous threat to the fragile male psyche. This unveiling of the monstrous female is often followed by a therapeutic disappearance, purging, chastisement, disfiguration, or some kind of narrative forgetting or abandonment (for example, in part 2 of Leopoldo Alas's *La Regenta* when Ana Ozores falls into silence and collapses beneath the weight of her undistinguished womanhood). Alternatively, the less engaging but no less common women characters (for example, those of José María de Pereda) rarely exceed their modest role as pliant, silent sister, mother, or spouse who has to know or learn very little, since *being* rather than *becoming* a woman requires an absence of being necessary for man's successful self-contemplation and aggrandizement.

In Spanish women-authored texts, on the contrary, growth and learning are always problematic, and being or becoming a woman is subsequently never taken for granted. Women may be perceived as disposed to good, but because the world is not, goodness must be constantly rethought or retaught to women in the form of trials that often require great suffering or personal sacrifice. In their various tutelary roles as husband, father, confessor, or brother, men are respected as an authority, but less often portrayed as a companion or comforter in times of adversity. They may ask for submission, preach resignation or other feminine virtues, transgress and beg for forgiveness, but it is the responsibility of the female characters, or if not, the narrator as female *mentor*, to comfort women, offer them solace, and suggest compensations and methods of coping with the sometimes dreary business of being a woman. We could describe this narrative practice as an aesthetics of compliance, shared sentiment, and perhaps even of solitude and abandonment, as I shall argue in the first few chapters of the present study. Women's literature of the nineteenth century accepted as its mission that of preparing its readers for a world without men, not where men exerted no influence whatsoever, but where they were not expected to share the love, emotions, domestic duties, childrearing, and even the beds of women, and where women were obliged to accept, masochistically, abandonment, abuse, neglect, and even punishment.

Grappling with the notion of a poetics for Aristotle's sister, Lawrence Lipking remarks that the literature that through the centuries has meant the most to women may seem repulsive to modern tastes because women "have tended to see themselves in heroines who suffer loss before they find their way" (77), thus colluding in their own victimization. Our repugnance for this behavior should not, he argues, obscure the role that literature has played in helping women to cope with a world that does indeed hold much sorrow and abandonment for them (77). By abandonment Lipking means not only the abandonment by a husband, lover, or friend that we customarily associate with women's narratives, but abandonment by history, by the *poesis* or words that validate men as subjects. To say that women are abandoned by history, of course, does not mean that they are not somehow *in* history, only that their words and their ideas have not become part of our cherished literary canon; and so, through systematic neglect, Western culture has both failed to stimulate the production of their words and ideas or even to preserve such as have been handed down to us.

This brings me to the subject of this book. To write a book about Spanish women writers demands an explanation that would be superfluous when one writes about Spanish men: we expect books to be written about groups of authors whom we could (not that we would ever have to) argue *happen* to be men but who are not grouped together because of their sex, while books about women writers are expected to be justified in the first place on the basis of gender and second, on the basis of previous exclusion from literary history, the latter an effect of the former. Consequently, one of the most common justifications for writing about women who have been previously excluded from the canon has been to explore the desirability of rehabilitating certain forgotten or undervalued texts, another to throw into question the sexual ideology of canon formation itself. A word about both is in order here.

The notion of the canon in any literary tradition and any period is an unstable concept determined by political and social contingencies, religious and moral beliefs, literary and aesthetic tastes, and, especially, the dynamics of a literary economic system.[1] The question of whether a work was extolled during the age it was written is only one of many factors, and sometimes not a factor at all, in determining whether it finds a place in a subsequent canon: if a book forms part of a canon we recognize, it has something to *say* to us; that is, it has something to say *about* us, which is why we treat it as our bible.[2] *Us* used to mean white European or American males who had every reason to champion what Hazel Gold in her article on the canon calls the "well-bearded" tradition (185).[3] Not that women or people of color did not read the same great books as white men, but the modern canon of American and European works came into being at the end of the nineteenth century and the beginning of the twentieth century, when the percentage of women readers and readers from other marginalized groups was still quite low in comparison to that of their white male counterparts. What counts as the contemporary Spanish canon bears the unmistakable ideological stamp of its formulators, and this tradition is steeped in patriarchal values and prejudice.[4]

As reading populations change, so, too, the canon, to a greater or (in the case of the Spanish canon) lesser degree, fluctuates to accommodate new contingencies. Evidence of this is the recent astounding success of the Enduring Works of Women Novelists series (Virago Modern Classics) published by Dial (and then Penguin) Press, which has broadened the selection of books available for the increasingly popular courses on women authors in the United States. In Spain, such fledgling series as Castalia's Biblioteca de Escritoras (Library of Women Writers) may eventually give rise to the same phenomenon.[5] At the same time that new texts are becoming more available to a readership now disposed to reconsider marginal and popular literary traditions, critical studies such as Susan Kirkpatrick's excellent *Las románticas* [The women Romantics] have begun to raise new questions about the viability of the Spanish canon. In fact, it was partially because of Kirkpatrick's example that I determined that a critical study on women novelists was overdue.

In addition to the great *public* canons we know from our school days, we all have our private canons that are also, whatever we may believe, received canons that participate in a complex literary economy.[6] These works compete for our attention despite (or perhaps even because of) their exclusion from generally revered canons. They can be divided into two groups depending on how they fit into our personal intellectual economy. The first satisfies some narrative or lyrical exigency (such as a need for catharsis, closure, acute sensitivity, sexual release, etc.), transforming some of us into closet consumers of romance, spy, or science fiction novels. The second are the texts we study as cultural products that we argue have transcendence not as literary works of *art*, but as manifestations of countercultural trends and subversive impulses at work on the fringes of any conservative canon. In them we look for, and inevitably find, the voice of repressed or underrepresented groups and the evidence of the unsavory underside of a classical, inflated, canon that must always be in dialogue with whatever is excluded from it.

In the case of our closet fictions, we read for pleasure, not because they challenge us to become better or to think differently. They ask only for the momentary suspension of our disbelief, appealing to our desire for pattern and repetition; they simply ensure our return to the bookstore. The second category of books, that were originally read for pleasure as well as edification by earlier readers, comprises the texts studied here. Today these texts are of interest only to a somewhat specialized group of Hispanists, still mostly women to or for whom the canon too often fails to speak or to those who use literature to critique and explore nonliterary issues and who I imagine rarely read these texts with pleasure. Though we (women Hispanists) agree among ourselves that some of the titles of our private canon do not deserve to be so utterly excluded from the conventional canon we teach in our classes, we have not begun to address the issues, both ideological and aesthetic, involved in the Spanish literary economy. This will certainly change with time. Gold argues that the Spanish canon is essentially unchanged despite recent debates. While I believe this is largely the case, I am less convinced that the Spanish canon is the impregnable fortress that Gold argues will emerge unscathed from the English canon debates.

The vexing question in discussions of the canon regards quality, often deployed blindly to defend the sacred core of works from the threat of infiltration. The question of what makes a great book great usually inaugurates any debate about exclusions from the canon. Addressing this, Gold gives one important key to the primacy of some nineteenth-century texts over others. We can often understand more about the canon by examining the *flaws* of works that don't make it, "texts that may have violated principles of unity or closure typically associated with realist novels and so disappointed the expectations of earlier critics" (191). I would substitute "need" for "expectation" here and argue that the time has come to ask the hard questions about gender and the canon. The search for coherence, complexity, unity, and for structural or ideological integrity still dominates discussions about literary worth, and we still do not understand exactly why this is so. The texts lacking in these qualities, including most of those studied in this book, too often fall outside the realm of literary criticism into an area of sociohistorical documentation.[7] But, in the face of mounting challenges both from inside and outside the academy, Hispanists will soon have to address the following questions: do we broaden the canon affirmative-action style to guarantee a more pluralistic (or more need-fulfilling) reading experience for our students, or do we abandon the canon altogether and broaden instead the notion of literary criticism so that *all that's writ* is equally worthy of critical comment? Do we preserve the present canon and shift our focus from the notions of integrity and complexity of the work to our fascination with the integrity of the work? Do we defend the canon as an object of study by searching deconstructively for whatever we can find in it that ruptures the symmetry or destroys the canonical work's proclaimed logic? These are only a few of the issues that we will have to confront in the coming decade.

To answer these questions requires a thorough understanding of what is at stake in canon formation, a question increasingly debated in times of literary instability like our own.[8] First we must recognize (more fully than even he does) the implications of Charles Altieri's statement that "canons are not natural facts" (40), echoed in Herrnstein Smith's contention that "[a]ll value is radically contingent, being neither an inherent property of objects nor an arbitrary projection of subjects, but, rather, the product of the dynamics of an economic system" (11). While we want to believe that the values promoted by canons are somehow transcendent, in fact they are just as historically contingent as every other facet of culture (see also Gold 199). Many critics are still in the grip of nostalgia, a kind of post-Cartesian longing for great texts that will speak about their own greatness, complex texts that validate their complexity, texts with profound integrity by which to measure their subjectivity and their difference, affirm their uniqueness, and ultimately sustain the hegemony of whatever dominant groups gave birth to the canon in a different age. Over the centuries, arguments have been put forth that how we perceive something as beautiful "can be related to 'forms' and 'qualities' that gratify human beings 'naturally' " (Herrnstein Smith 16, paraphrasing Hume), but these "naturally" gratifying categories also interact with many variables, as Herrnstein Smith argues (16). Understanding that the anxiety to sustain canons is a profoundly conservative impulse tied more to power than to excellence is the necessary prelude to challenging the existing canon and deciding what position to take on the questions posed in this introduction.[9]

The next step, exploring exclusions from the canon, entails painstaking archival research and book editing, new historical approaches to help explain literary canons as economic systems and, I believe, psychosocial analysis of class and gender systems as interrelated power structures.[10] This last enterprise requires an uneasy coalition of Foucaultian discourse theory and Lacanian and post-Lacanian psychoanalytic theory in conjunction with recent feminist theories of difference, all of which form the critical basis for this study. I say "uneasy" here not only because of feminism's ambivalent relation to Lacan and Foucault,[11] but because the use of French psychoanalytic theory when addressing discrete Spanish texts must be carefully contextualized. Yet I argue that it is no longer sufficient to engage a text from an uncritical historical perspective that underpins both liberal theories of sovereignty and Marxist analysis without taking into account Foucault's theories of power and sexuality. It is also naive to engage in Freudian or archetypal criticism that often unwittingly reinscribes woman into the essentialist or mythic figure that the new feminisms are struggling to avoid. Without recourse to the new theories of subjectivity and gender that have followed in the wake of Lacan's psychoanalytic research, we simply study women's texts as a projection of their mysterious, dark, nature. It is also my belief that feminist theory, not in its more widely known humanistic guise that, as Jana Sawicki argues, "employs a juridico-discursive model of power and appeals to a quasi-biological, universal practice, namely, mothering as explanatorily basic" (51), but as a complex theory of the historical contingency of gender relations, offers the most viable program for studying women's fiction.

The purpose of this book, then, is not to challenge the canon, but to explore what gender may have to do with writing practices that are commonly marginalized to the periphery of dominant realist discourses. Without a feminist approach to nineteenth-century writing practices, we would be at a loss to explain not only exclusions from canons, but the relevancy of political, social, and religious discourses to cultural work. Clearly formal excellence is no longer a sufficient explanation for the conspicuous absence of women writers in the Spanish canon. In the latter half of the nineteenth century, a relatively small group of mostly upper-middle-class women began to consume and write large quantities of novels that were popularly dubbed "women's literature." These novels were and are often assumed to be sentimental claptrap lacking in literary excellence. A brief glance at María del Carmen Simón Palmer's monumental *Escritoras españolas del siglo XIX: Manual bio-bibliográfico* lends overwhelming support to Cristina Enríquez de Salamanca's contention that women wrote much more than the sentimental poetry commonly attributed to them in literary histories. But, for a variety of reasons, these writers are scarcely represented in the canon of nineteenth-century novelists, important but rare exceptions such as Emilia Pardo Bazán aside. Historically, women, not for biological reasons but for a host of other factors that are not *indifferent* to biology, have not only been absent from most literary canons, but excluded from the entire economy of canon production and consumption (Winders 12).[12] In the second half of the nineteenth century, when most of the works studied in the following chapters were written, female literacy fluctuated from between 9 percent and 20 percent in Spain, compared to a male literacy rate that Cristina Enríquez de Salamanca puts at 38 percent.[13] At a time when the appropriate occupations for bourgeois women were being hotly debated (whether women should be allowed to obtain degrees was one of many issues), the literary marketplace did not encourage women writers, many of whom used pseudonyms to avoid embarrassment or scorn, and most of whom published their novels in serial form that for lack of a publisher were never later reedited.[14] Women who did manage to edit their works were often married to men who facilitated this enterprise (Rosalía de Castro, Concepción Gimeno de Flaquer, Faustina Sáez de Melgar, Josefa Estévez, among others). Despite the extensive presence of women in journalism (Enríquez de Salamanca 91), book writing was defined as a manly occupation; if a woman made a mark in the literary world, it was for her *virile* style, a distinction that always bore a price.[15] Finally, the various custodians of female morality—priests, fathers, husbands, and others—largely condemned the reading of novels as a perfidious occupation for women. They recommended instead spiritual texts, not insignificantly, works written by men such as Fray Luis de León's *La perfecta casada*, a permanent fixture of the feminine *canon* of spiritual readings since its publication in 1583.

This is not to say that a literary poetics we could provisionally call *feminine* did not exist, even before women began to stake out an area in literary journalism in the nineteenth century; women have always been good composers and tellers of stories.[16] But to appreciate this poetics we have to understand that, as Lipking says, "for many women literature itself served in place of a community—not as an occasion to affirm the general voice of the state or the will of the Gods but as an interlude in which private feelings are shared" (71). This is the case with the texts studied here, some of which seem narratively primitive and dogmatic, but all of which are imbued with a deep sense of urgency about what it means or should mean to be a woman. The virtues extolled in them are not admittedly the virtues we would be apt to instill in our daughters or students, so a feeling of moral as well as aesthetic estrangement may accompany us in our reading and, to a degree, cut us off from consuming it with pleasure. The point is, however, that much of our reading is not for pleasure. For example, when we read about mass murderers, notorious rape trials, or accounts of child- or wife-abuse many of us experience a distinct displeasure and resentment. Yet we do avidly read these *stories* in our daily newspapers because they narrate our sexual malaise, our deep alienation, and our "gender trouble." Similarly, many of us sympathize with the struggles of women writers to define spaces where male power may hold sway but where feminine sensibility, refinement, and affiliations are prized, not denigrated or trivialized.

My purpose for writing this book, nevertheless, is not to recuperate a group of authors who have fallen into silence, although it would be gratifying to think that after reading the discussions of *El caballero de las botas azules* [The gentleman with the blue boots], *Dulce Dueño* [Sweet master], or *Memorias de un solterón* [Diary of a bachelor] someone might be tempted to read or reread these texts. Rather I want to explore the poetics of women's literature, especially the relation between women's literature, women's desire, and the discourses involved in gender indoctrination in order to reach a tentative understanding of how Spanish bourgeois society configured its fictions of gender. My subject, in other words, is not simply literature, but the ideas about sex and gender that found their way into literature, especially popular or marginal literature, including almost all women's literature, in which gender ideology finds its most extreme expression.[17] However, for the purpose of limiting the vast amount of what Ellen Messer-Davidow calls "cultural bricolage" (90) that could form part of a study of sex/gender systems in Spanish culture, I have restricted my study to novels with the hope of publishing a second monograph on gender and other forms of popular culture (periodical literature, cartoons, graphic illustrations, essays, etc.) at a later time.

In recent years feminists are discovering that literature is an ideal medium for probing the intersections between power and gender formation.[18] The cruder and more dogmatic the gender representations, the easier for us to see how "[t]he representation of gender *is* its construction" (de Lauretis, *Technologies of Gender* 28).[19] All of the writers included in this study, even the least dogmatic such as Rosalía de Castro or Emilia Pardo Bazán, discovered in the novel an ideal vehicle for imagining a way for women to become the best they could be, and, in turn, I find in them an ideal source for exploring the connections among gender ideology, gender oppression, and canonical and cultural prestige. Providing an antidote to masculinist literature in which women merely wore a *mask* of beauty or goodliness, their novels of female moral development imagine a more perfect spiritual beauty and serenity, obtainable only through sacrifice, but accessible to even the most downtrodden and unexceptional of women. They ask women to strive for goodness that is a result of complex struggles, a hundred starts and setbacks, registered in a full consciousness of how these mundane steps and sacrifices are important to the lives of women. Because of this defining moral purpose, women's literature is fertile ground not for empirically describing gender relations in nineteenth-century society, but for understanding how gender ideology differed for men and for women in the Spanish literary tradition.[20]

Obviously, this ideological gender difference can be studied in both male- and female-authored texts. In this one sense, at least, the sex of the author makes no *difference,* and besides, postmodernists tell us, the author is dead. But the death knell for the author does not preclude introducing the issue of gender into discussions of writing practices for strategic purposes.[21] I agree with Nancy Miller that, in the case of women writers, who "have not had the same historical relation of identity to origin, institution, production" ("Changing" 6) that men have had, it may be premature to pronounce the "death" of the author and begin speaking instead of anonymous writing that somehow transcends sexual identity.

Today, feminists often feel caught in the dizzying course of modern criticism with its constantly shifting reading strategies. For example, Jane Gallop traces the swings in critical theory between which "this moment of feminist inquiry is torn: the literary and the political" ("Writing" 289). Naomi Schor distinguishes between the two fundamental strategies of feminist reading: "reading for specificity" ("Reading" 249) in which women's works are assumed to be *different,* and reading "beyond difference" (250) in which the gender of the author is less important than that of the text. Cora Kaplan cautions against two other extremes of feminist criticism, the psychoanalytic approach and social feminism, favoring an "interpretative integration" of the two (169). Which method we choose is sometimes dictated by the texts we select for study. For example, the quest of the problematic of *Woman-beyond-representation* is especially mandated by postmodern art and literature. But before such a quest could be fruitfully undertaken with nineteenth-century texts it is necessary to unpack some of the binary logic on which nineteenth-century Spanish authors based their notions of gender and better understand the concept of female subjectivity and social development in those texts that are subversive or supportive of the norm. This explains why I have limited my study to novels written by women. I am not a radical proponent of "gynocritics" in Elaine Showalter's sense of the term, that is, the study of socioeconomic conditions of women writers and how they expressed feminine self-awareness, but I am interested in learning how women writers configured gender, what patriarchal gender and class biases they *translated* for their readership, and, lastly, how their gender representations either alleviated or exacerbated the oppression of their readers (and their readers' maids or other groups of affiliated nonreaders).

After reading for several years almost exclusively male-authored texts (an extension of my graduate training), I was somewhat distressed to realize that novels written by women during the same period differed little in regard to their manifest gender ideology. But the more I read, the more I began to realize that there were also profound differences between men's and women's treatment of women characters, differences that needed to be scrutinized and sorted out.[22] Both traditions tend to silence women characters; nonetheless, I found myself thinking more about voyeurism and sadism when analyzing male-authored texts, while, as this book will testify, masochism, as a type of collective consciousness shaped by sexual and social relations, is an overriding issue in women-authored texts. I would never have had this insight had I restricted my analysis to the canonical writers, and had I not looked separately at men's and women's texts as a staging area for conflicts of gender and changing social relations. In this respect my monograph could be read as a sequel to *Gender and Representation*, which deals exclusively with male writers, at least for those interested in comparing representational modes of men and women writers.

This book, then, attempts a reading of women's texts as a staging area for conflicts of gender, as they relate to the changing social relations of a Spanish bourgeoisie that are reflected in its domestic ideology. As a complement to this study I believe it will prove useful to include a handful of popular graphic representations of women in nineteenth-century periodical literature. These illustrations, by male graphic artists—some Spanish, others German, British, Italian, and French—accompanied the equally prolific essays on women's family roles, ideal occupations, and appropriate education that were a mainstay even in Spanish periodicals dedicated primarily to national news and foreign events. Looking at them, we find it easy to understand how seductive stereotyped gender roles can be made to seem to the casual eye.

The ethereal loveliness of Barraud's photograph "Conformidad" (conformity) (Fig. 5), the happy rewards promised in Luigi Nion's and Eduardo Bisson's sketches of waiting women (Figs. 8 and 3), the peaceful satisfactions derived from serving men (Fig. 4), caring for or educating children (Figs. 2 and 9), or doing household chores (Fig. 7) all contributed to the collective vision of loveliness based on the bourgeois virtues of feminine service and self-abnegation. Far from the fallen women or "idols of perversity" that Bram Dijkstra found in fin-de-siècle European art, these engravings idolize the fantasy of feminine subservience: lowered eyes, extended arms; quiet, simple, honorable virtues; the promise of home comfort for the beleaguered husband, son, or father. I include some of these engravings here because they help to explain not only the obsession with sexual conformity that many have noted in Spanish women's domestic fiction, but the restlessness and contradictions that also found their way into women's narratives of feminine growth and feminine dissatisfaction, perhaps as a reaction against the impossibility of these pious images. During the last two decades of the century, when engravings such as these still proliferated in the immensely popular *La Ilustración Ibérica*, *La Ilustración Española y Americana*, and *La Ilustración Artística*, women writers were finding it increasingly difficult to imagine their heroines as the lovely rose of Figure 1. Impossibly beautiful mirrors, these illustrations were bound to produce distortions and fractured subjects when the women gazing at them *translated* what they saw into their domestic discourse. At the very least the illustrations point both to the radical disjuncture between the ideal representations of femininity as constructed by the male-dominated institution of the weekly magazine, and the sadly lacking female subject of women's fiction who finds she cannot sustain that ideal.[23] As Bridget Aldaraca has noted, idealization is a form of control over the desired object ("El ángel" 83). In no other cultural manifestation is this idealization of the woman more evident than in the weekly illustrated journal. On the other hand, domestic fiction as a desirable feminine goal was not so much a challenge to the ideal, as a documentation of the near impossibility of its realization.

# LA ILUSTRACION Ibérica

SEMANARIO CIENTIFICO, LITERARIO Y ARTÍSTICO

Año XII | Barcelona, 2 de junio de 1894 | Núm. 596

Fig. 1. "La rosa."

# The Bonds of Love

*La felicidad está en nosotros y depende
absolutamente de nosotros, de nuestro carácter, de
nuestra educación y de nuestra fuerza moral.*

*[Happiness resides within us and depends entirely
upon us, our character, our education and our
moral strength.]*

—María del Pilar Sinués de Marco, *La mujer
en nuestros días* [The woman of today]

THIS CHAPTER STUDIES two of the most popular nineteenth-
century Spanish novelists in relation to the themes of desire, love, and
domesticity. Both belong to that period when, as Alda Blanco puts it,
"women writers veered from the enabling Romantic tradition and allowed the constraining angel of the domestic woman to enter into
their homes" (372). The first, Cecilia Böhl de Faber (1796–1877), is a
precursor to the generation of women writers who wrote "under the

sign of domesticity" (Blanco 372). Moving away from the Romantic tradition's enthrallment with the troubled male subject, her narratives focus on the problematic of female development and the quest for enduring bonds of love.

The second author, the prolific María del Pilar Sinués de Marco (1835–93), properly belongs to the group of writers that we associate with the domestic novel including, among others, Angela Grassi (1826–83) and Faustina Sáez de Melgar (1834–95). Contrasting the predicaments that these women devise for their female heroines, it is possible to see a common thread of longing to define what fulfillment can mean for a woman who is willing to struggle for it. The goal is not to imagine women as free from the social structures associated with family rearing or domestic responsibilities, but to grant them a say in the decisions that bind them to others either through love or duty, and, especially in the case of Sinués de Marco, to help them imagine their work and their bonds of love as a consolation and the path to glory. Although woman was made to suffer, according to Sinués de Marco, her success lies in that she is a lover by nature, "she adores the slavery of all forms of love: as a daughter, sister, wife, mother; her glory, her greatest happiness, is to be useful, necessary to those she loves: sacrifice is more pleasing to her than triumph" (*El Imparcial* 4).

"The powers of the weak," comments Elizabeth Janeway, "are, finally, more powerful than we think" (109). This truism is relevant on the one hand, to these women's novels as an effect of power as well as a discourse that affected the lives of real women, and, on the other, to the material relations of power that novels describe, explore, and sometimes challenge. However, my goal in this chapter is not to celebrate hidden spheres of feminine influence and power; the hunt for subversion often has the unintended effect of validating unequal power relations, which, in turn, perpetuates essentialist or bio-originary conceptions of the feminine and diminishes the consequence of male dominance or repressive social structures. At issue here is feminine desire, which, nevertheless, ultimately relies upon power relations resulting from psychological as well as sociocultural determinants, this last an issue that will be taken up in Chapter 2.

Recently, feminist scholars have become increasingly suspicious of the gender bias of contemporary narratology. Tania Modleski argues in her discussions of mass-produced, popular women's culture, that given "the differences in the way men and women experience their lives, it is not surprising to find that narrative pleasure can sometimes mean very different things to men and women" (104). Perhaps we have not yet discovered the pleasures proper to domestic fiction, she suggests, and we ought to "look for clues to women's pleasure which are already present in existing forms, even if this pleasure is currently placed at the service of patriarchy" (104). Similarly, Susan Winnet reminds us that narratologists even today often look to narrative to help them remember "what men want, [and] how they go about trying to get it" (506). As a consequence of our pursuit of the fictions of male sexuality, we ignore what feminine pleasures might or might not be exercised or repressed in the Oedipal stories we often project onto literary texts. As Winnet puts it, "the pleasure the reader is expected to take in the text is the pleasure of the man" (506), and if we do not share in that pleasure, we are inclined to believe something is amiss or lacking, either in us or the texts we read.

Although this chapter focuses on female subjectivity, the aim is not to isolate specific instances of female agency in order to show that a secret desire for autonomy lies at the heart of women's dilemmas. Clearly, Spanish women writers did not use literature, at least not overtly, to promote their independence or to denounce their power-lessness in a male society (Simón Palmer, "Escritoras" 484). Feminist critics often mistakenly study the domestic novel as a history of femi-nine rebellion that somehow recaptures feminine subjects "against a prevailing ideology that seeks to crush them" (Marantz Cohen 7). The sense of feminist consciousness, in the way the term is understood today as an "awareness of one's own relationship to a society heavy with the weight of its own contradictions" (Bartky 21) is decidedly slight in Spanish women's novels in the nineteenth century. The task of the domestic novel was to increase awareness of women's ideal rela-tion to the family, not to society at large.

Yet it is equally naive to conclude that the cult of self-effacement and subservience yields no liberatory possibilities, or has no sociopolitical import and is therefore of only scant interest to the feminist critic. It is often through their pain and sacrifices that women assert an identity and become agents of change in the world around them. The very fact that the domestic novel went to such great lengths to neutralize women's worldly ambitions and to make home life seem beautiful, fulfilling, or at least tolerable and instructive, signals that something was amiss in bourgeois family life, as Emilia Pardo Bazán often argued.

The novel, like other ideological apparatuses, was helping to prop up values that were evidently not universally enforceable because there was nothing *natural* about them; its mission was to record and attempt to resolve the complex and conflictive changes that were occurring in family life as a result of Spain's tentative moves into a market economy. In Bridget Aldaraca's words, "The strident tones used to defend the inviolability of home and motherhood may be said to serve as a linguistic barometer which measures the gap between the projected male ideal of the perfect wife and mother, and the inevitable failure of women to realize it" (*El ángel* 66).

In its promotion of the nuclear family, the domestic novel had to imagine ways to contain feminine agency in order to be compatible with patriarchal family ideology dependent upon asymmetrical sexual roles. Nevertheless, sometimes feminine desire accommodates itself within the most repressive, unequal power relations. Even the justly despised "ángel del hogar" (domestic angel) opens up a space for desires that we do not have to admire to understand; even in a space as confined as the private sphere, "strange and subtle renegotiations can take place" (Massé, *In the Name* 42). Women's conformity to the ideology of women's sphere, ultimately, can be explained only partially by the various economic and moral crises that gave it its peculiar historical standing in nineteenth-century society (Lowder Newton 18–19).[1] Among the diverse factors that, if not generated, at least perpetuated the cult of domesticity are a few that can be best understood in the context of modern theories of feminine intersubjectivity based on the psychological or sociological models of Carol Gilligan, Nancy Chodorow, Nancy C. M. Hartsock, and, especially, Jessica Benjamin, that constitute the critical basis of this chapter on desire and domestic fiction.

Thanks to Aldaraca's recent study on the Spanish domestic angel and Susan Kirkpatrick's analysis of Romantic women writers, we now have a better understanding of how domesticity came to define Spanish women in fiction as in real life. What we still lack is a sense of the relation between power and desire and a definition of the spaces within which desire operates despite, or because of, unequal power relations to shape feminine subjectivity. To arrive at such an understanding as this it is necessary to analyze the relation between physical spaces (such as the home and whatever lies beyond it) and various psychological spaces that are causally linked to the limitations proscribed by spatial boundaries. That is, we need to ascertain "how domination is anchored in the hearts of the dominated" (Benjamin, *Bonds* 5). I attempt here to understand the relationship between love and the restrictions and bonds that have to be taken into account in any discussion of feminine subjectivity in nineteenth-century Spain.

## The Home as Fortress, The Home as Prison

Kirkpatrick locates the dawn of Spanish women's written discourse around 1841, when a new language for representing gender became accessible to women writers (*Las románticas* [The women Romantics] 1). Gertrudis Gómez de Avellaneda broke new ground in the 1840s by constituting herself as a writing subject whereupon emerged "Spain's first full-fledged narrative image of the Romantic self as female" (Kirkpatrick, "Gómez de Avellaneda" 165). But in her feminization of the romantic subject Avellaneda is careful to intermingle the paradigms of Romantic literature with the bourgeois strictures on female subjectivity (oppressive social conventions, marginalization, the powerlessness of the weak) that will conscribe for decades the desire of female protagonists of women's literature. Although Avellaneda wrote the first novels in which feminine agency is seriously explored in relation to family duty, the domestic novel begins in earnest with the works of Cecilia Böhl de Faber, written in the 1830s but not published until the late 1840s and early 1850s. In Böhl de Faber's fiction the cult of domesticity is enforced by women themselves, men playing the role primarily as intruders who entice women away from duty. In *La familia de Alvareda* [The Alvareda family] (1849, *El Heraldo*), for example, a direct correlation exists between virtue and reward and how a woman conforms to other women's ideal of domesticity and conduct. Women must be educated to the joys of domesticity through discipline and hard work. A mother's indulgence or lack of discipline will produce a daughter who fails to develop domestic and maternal instincts and who lives a life of dissatisfaction and sorrow. Merely showering love on a daughter or providing her with good role models does not suffice; a mother must possess "carácter y vigor suficiente" (sufficient character and vigor) to tame an unruly girl.

For Rita of *La familia*, succumbing to illicit desire implies forfeiting what the walls of a house provide women in terms of protection and respectability. In other words, a correlation exists between sexual desire and danger. Paradoxically, the home is also associated with danger because it is often the site of female illness. Of the two types of danger in women's novels, moral and physical, the latter is clearly preferable to the former. Across the road from María and her rebellious daughter Rita live the ailing Elvira and her mother Ana, models of domestic serenity achieved through subservience, suffering, and self-denial. Rita's scandalous rejection of domesticity inspires Ana's husband Pedro to remind his long-suffering womenfolk of the relationship between feminine goodness and illness: "la mujer honrada, la pierna quebrada, en casa" (142) (the honorable woman, a broken leg and homebound). As long as a woman is too passionate and unruly—and healthy—she will be unworthy of a home's protection. Better to be in Elvira's shoes (or rather bed): home-bound and ill, but virtuous and cherished. When Rita repents, she becomes as good as Elvira and, it follows, as ill. Having witnessed her lover's death she is struck with a virulent fever and must be transported home on a mattress in the back of a cart, for all the town to witness. From her sickbed she can see Elvira's body lying in state, a woman's body offered up as a holy sacrifice, arms entwined with palm branches, crossed modestly over the breast, hands "en actitud de orar" (191) (in prayerful gesture). There is no better way to die.

The repentant Rita humbly begs the town's forgiveness and the town, approving her public gesture, finally looks upon her "con caridad" (169) (charitably). Imbued with a sense of Christian charity, it is the public sphere that determines that Rita is a *pobrecita* (victim) as much as an *infame* (170) (reprobate). Unlike the theme of later domestic novels, the point here is not to salvage the female figure for *herself*, but rather to offer her up as a model for *public* edification. When Rita and her mother flee their town it is reported that Rita "no parece la misma" (193) (is no longer the same); tears have left deep furrows under her eyes; and "está más delgada que la guadaña de la muerte y no goza salud" (193) (she is thinner than death's scythe and frequently ill). This state of flight and illness mark the end of Rita's story. At last she is in a position, literally and figuratively, to inherit Elvira's virtue. A full description of her transformation and the inner contentment that her acquiescence to a greater power might have produced—topics that are explored more earnestly in the later domestic novel—here remain unreported. Again, the issue is not a woman's peace or her finding a space in the domestic sphere where she can behold herself as good. Rather, she serves as a story for the consumption of others, in this case the residents of Dos Hermanas, the travelers to whom the townspeople report their tales of feminine misbehavior, and, of course, Böhl de Faber's edified readers.

Other temptations besides sexual fulfillment lure underdomesticated women from the safety of the home. The pursuit of a career, for example, tempts some of Böhl de Faber's heroines to place personal satisfaction above family duty and pride. The results are always disastrous both for the woman so bold as to dream of a career and the family she forsakes. A popular example is the ambitious "Gaviota" (*La gaviota* [The seagull], published 1849), who dreams of becoming an opera singer. Her rise to fame and subsequent fall into oblivion are effected by a rapid series of narrative wand-wavings, but no attempt is ever made to describe her worldly satisfactions and triumphs, or even her misfortunes and failures, as felt experiences. *La Gaviota* is but one in a long and prestigious list of Spanish novels that refuse to imagine feminine satisfaction outside the home and that define desire as anathema to the female spirit. More than a story about a woman's life in the world, *La Gaviota* is a morality play about the dangers— instead of the excitement—of feminine passion. On the heels of worldly success quickly follow the seductions, scandals, and failures that are the public woman's lot. If the "gaviota" would just be content to display her operatic skills in the confines of her home, she could be the most admired of society ladies, but once she crosses the highly demarcated line between public and private entertainer, she forfeits access to the private spaces of respectable society ladies.

Ironically, when she loses her voice, María is denied the "tragic dignity of a Romantic death" (Kirkpatrick, *Las románticas* 267) and condemned to become the dreaded housewife as a kind of personal hell. The raw ingredients for domestic bliss are everywhere about her: the charming town of Villamar, a husband, children, a house, and admirers who overlook her flaws. But María's despair and dissatisfaction demonstrate an essential concept that bourgeois women were increasingly challenged to believe in the decades following the publication of this novel: that being locked in the fortress is not the same as choosing it as a protection. Seclusion must be voluntary or at least seem so. The gender strategy behind this message is clear, especially when viewed from a modern feminist perspective familiar with the mechanics of patriarchal power. But it must also be stressed that allowing women readers a glimpse of a failed female subject may have constituted as subversive a gesture as imagining a successful and satisfied public woman. Readers who approached Böhl de Faber's fiction in search of the best examples of feminine virtue and models of conduct for bourgeois women came to the wrong place.

However scant the attention explicitly paid to the female protagonist as a desiring subject, *La Gaviota* does indirectly address the issue of women's desire, as do many Spanish women's novels, through its celebration of idealized male facilitators. The men conjured up to be María's helpers share the remarkable capacity to recognize a woman as a subject of inestimable worth even when everyone else has rejected her. The tender and trusting Stein, and later the generous and noble Duke, show a marked capacity to be supportive and attuned to María's every need and feeling, however contradictory or self-defeating. They are the prototypes for what will be in later women's fiction that indulgent, nonjudgmental other (most often a woman) who is virtuous beyond reproach and yet who recognizes something to salvage in even the most flawed female subject. Despite her betrayal of their trust and rejection of their ideals, these men remain so sensitive to María's desires that they even allow her to fail since that is what she is bent upon doing. Both are explicitly identified as a feminine presence who does not seek to control, only to understand, nurture, and love. The sentimental Stein possesses "un corazón tierno y suave, y en su temple una propensión a la confianza que rayaba en ceguedad" (133) (a tender and gentle heart, with a nearly blind propensity to trust others); the Duke searches endlessly for the good in others "con la misma satisfacción pura y sencilla que siente la doncella al recoger violetas" (44) (with the same simple and pure satisfaction that the young maid feels while gathering violets). Significantly, the very *feminine* qualities of tenderness and empathy are some of the main attributes that Spanish women authors, beginning with Böhl de Faber, imagine in the ideal marriage partner.

## Home Alone

As the novel gained ascendancy in the latter half of the nineteenth century, women writers came to embrace the ideal of the bourgeois home watched over by a self-sacrificing wife and mother. But even as the cult of domesticity became the axis on which revolved the lives and happiness of fictional characters it became increasingly important to explain what, exactly, satisfied women's desire in their arrested growth and domestic captivity. While this rationalization for the cult found its typical expression in the later works of María del Pilar Sinués de Marco and others, it is already operative in several of Böhl de Faber's lesser-known novels, such as the underappreciated *Clemencia* (1852). While in *La Gaviota* and *La familia de Alvareda* a link is established between domesticity, sexual normalcy, and women's earthly punishments or rewards, in *Clemencia* the problems of love, marriage, and wifely duty intersect and are amply explored in relation to a woman's happiness and sense of achievement. By allowing a woman to explore her options in a much more self-determined way, the relationship between agency and desire could be broached, and the contradictions between female desire and female duty resolved. If happiness can be lost through blindness and unrestrained passion as in *La Gaviota* or *La familia*, it can also be earned through judicious decision-making during the critical moments of a woman's life.

Despite its saccharine morality, *Clemencia* is a tribute not only to patience and prudence, but to the importance of allowing a woman to reach important decisions about her future alone and unadvised, with only reason and the lessons of experience to guide her.[2] In the later novels of Sinués de Marco a guiding voice, usually a maternal figure (grandmother, mother-in-law, or priest, for example) helps women enter into a dialogue with their desires and disappointments.[3] In Böhl de Faber's novels, this figure is largely absent, or available but unavailed, such as Ana of *La familia* or la tía María of *La Gaviota*.[4] Clemencia, however, is fortunate to have a guide, an inner voice that permits her to distinguish between passion and reason. It is not so much what the voice instructs her to do that is significant (it seems offensively sanctimonious today), but the fact that it allows her to weigh the consequences of her actions herself instead of having them put forth for her by a husband, confessor, or father. In this respect, the much-ignored *Clemencia* could be considered an important benchmark in the evolution of female subjectivity in women's novels.

Like the later novels of Sinués de Marco and Concepción Gimeno de Flaquer, *Clemencia*'s attraction lies in its explorations of ideal love. All manner of cultural, social, and religious restrictions can be cheerfully accepted, all forms of neglect, abuse, and disdain suffered because, it is reckoned, the shining ideal of perfect love allows women to transcend authority and deprivation. Women are redeemed by their belief in this ideal, which makes forbearance not merely a virtue but a path, like the path of the mystic who strives ultimately to transcend all earthly pain. To obtain the ideal, Clemencia passes through several stages that ironically call on her to disregard her desires and to accept victimization, submission, and self-domination as a way of life. Unless we momentarily overlook the degradation these stages imply in terms of Clemencia's relationship with the other, we may not be able to gauge how they empower her with the understanding necessary to redirect her life once she has passed through them. It is only when Clemencia is nearly devoid of self that she possesses the sagacity to see behind the veils of deception that society draws around her. This knowledge of self-degradation may have held a special attraction for the novel's readers, who would have read in their popular magazines hundreds of short parables about the joys of self-sacrifice—such as the one by Sinués de Marco that I quoted on page 15—that only hinted at the darker side of domestic life, or the desires that were forbidden to women.

Desire in the Spanish domestic novel revolves around one of two paradigms. What is desired often is the *other:* adventure, agency, culture, the outside world, all those things that, according to Jessica Benjamin, the maturing woman associates with the forbidden father (*Bonds* 100–107). Such is the model for the novels discussed above in which women's desire usually leads to disappointment, degradation, or death. The ideal in many domestic novels, conversely, is the *same*, whatever is a reinforcement of the love women were expected to embody, whatever accommodates feminine sensibility, simplicity, and reciprocity or intersubjectivity. By this I mean that nineteenth-century heroines often seek recognition from an other whose love best mirrors their own: they search endlessly for a husband who is sensitive, sincere, humble, and generous. And when that ideal proves impossible, they fall back on relationships in which the ideal of sharing provides positive rewards, such as those fostered by motherhood or religion, and other social institutions that invite women to see themselves not as separate, unique identities, but as part of a community in which caring and self-abnegation are not only valued but necessary.

Because, as Benjamin argues (*Bonds* 25), Western culture so values individualism, we may cringe at the self-regulation promulgated in these women's novels. But this self-abnegation not only represents a loss of assertiveness, regarded by social psychologists as crucial to the male's differentiation phase, but a passport to a world in which loss is equivalent to gain. At best, what can emerge is an identity (arguably equated with female development) keyed into the intersubjectivity that Benjamin suggests should be the developmental norm for both sexes. This can be seen by comparing Clemencia's first husband, Fernando Ladrón de Guevara, and the group of suitors from among whom she chooses her second marriage partner. Fernando plays a critical role in Clemencia's development because loving him is the first difficult task she has to perform as part of her ascension to true femininity.[5] Their relationship embodies the paradox that a woman's happiness depends not so much on the suitability of the marriage partner as upon the stage of a woman's maturity. For her husband's every vice—cruelty, indifference, irreverence—Clemencia learns an opposite virtue. Thus satisfaction is achievable through the practice of virtue, even in a void where all virtue is unrewarded (ironically, diminishing the importance of the husband, a figure so critical to the Gothic romance). The implication is that while the world crowds a woman's subjectivity and destroys her individuality, within the feminine space of caring or intersubjectivity, a woman can disengage herself from the specifics of her relation with another in order to produce her happiness *herself.* Clemencia's survival depends on this knowledge. A consciousness of her victimization does not translate into resistance as it may for twentieth-century heroines, but this does not mean that she paints her existence in bleak terms:

> en medio de tantos sufrimientos, no se creyó la mujer, *incomprendida,* ni la *heroína inapreciada,* ni la *víctima de un monstruo;* creyó sencillamente que Fernando era un mal marido como otros muchos, que tenía que sobrellevarle como hacían otras muchas mujeres. (130)

> [in the midst of so much suffering, she did not consider herself the *misunderstood* woman, the *unappreciated heroine,* the *victim of a monster;* she believed simply that Fernando was a bad husband like so many others, and that she had to tolerate him like so many other women tolerated their husbands.]

The words italicized by Böhl de Faber represent popular literary expressions describing women's relationships with their husbands. Refusing to align herself with the cliché of the "misunderstood heroine," Clemencia opts instead to circulate herself into a mass of sister sufferers who bear their pain in silent communion with other women, as a duty that, paradoxically, converts a woman into a kind of hero after all, for accepting to be what she does not want to be. In this way, presumably, her passivity was also rewarded by the readers' recognition of her goodness. Readers would also be relieved to find that, as a reward for her endurance, Clemencia's first husband magically dies, providing her the opportunity to choose her next partner, either the urbane and materialistic Sir George Percy or the humble and quixotic Pablo. Past suffering makes it possible for Clemencia to understand that the kind of relationship Pablo offers her will make the self-delusive satisfactions of the teenage bride unnecessary. Pablo will be that rare man capable of supporting a woman's subjectivity. Rather than consuming her, his love will be a recognition of her right to full agency. He assures her: "No seré yo el que abuse de tu condescendencia porque eres sumisa, que oprime tu voluntad porque eres dócil, ni avasalle tu libre albedrío porque eres débil" (232) [I won't be one to abuse your compliance because you are submissive, who oppresses you because you are docile, nor who restricts your free will because you are weak]. Between them there will be no secrets or mysteries; their communication will be perfect. In the presence of another who understands the abuse of gender power, docility, feminine weakness, and submission are *safe* virtues.

Having bent her will so totally to others, Clemencia understands the importance of being allowed to make decisions on her own behalf. The text may be full of pious exhortations to young girls to accept whatever marriage partners parents select for them but, in fact, it is only because Clemencia is left alone for a lengthy period that she comes to see clearly that what she wants for a husband is a duplicate of her (docile) self, someone capable of turning his back on the deceptions of "gran cultura" (high culture). Pablo curses the time wasted between his proposal and Clemencia's decision, but Clemencia appreciates fully what the dimensions of time and space mean in terms of female agency. She has come to recognize the emptiness and corruption so cleverly and seductively masked by good breeding and to see the true nobility of the soul, "con la rectitud de un entendimiento no contaminado con los vicios de la sociedad, con un carácter franco y entero que sigue con valor la senda del bien, . . . para el que son instintivos la generosidad, el heroísmo, la virtud y la delicadeza" (353) (with the righteousness of an intellect unsullied by social vices, a frank and upright character who courageously follows the path of good, . . . for whom generosity, heroism, virtue and sensitivity are instinctive).

The message of Böhl de Faber's fiction is that women can only be fulfilled when defined as a part of a relationship. There is nothing startling about this conclusion. What is significant is that a woman's bonds of love do not erase her. If she loves properly, a woman can be happy whether she is married to a man who cares to see her happy or not. The role of the man, thus, is primary to a woman's role definition and yet secondary to it, since any relationship may be transcended by the *right* woman. The problem of unmutuality may be the fault of men but becomes the moral responsibility of women to remedy or surmount,[6] and women's worth is measured by the "subtle nuances of behavior" that attach "precise moral value to certain qualities of mind" (Armstrong, *Desire* 4); in other words, women who embrace a life of sacrifice and love are compensated with a sense of self-worth. A moral regime carried out with rigor can substitute for the sought-after mutuality. The ideal of mutuality is often held forth as the shining possibility in women's fiction to the character who learns, ironically, to subsist in a state of utter solitude.[7] In a space where she is entirely alone, all things become possible to the patient female subject. This space of self-containment, sometimes figured as illness, abandonment, confinement, convent seclusion, spiritual delirium, or artistic reverie, will become a more common feature in women's novels such as those of Sinués de Marco in decades to come. But in novels that genuinely problematize a woman's existence, like *Clemencia* and *Elia* (1849) (unlike *La familia de Alvareda* or *La Gaviota*), there are brief glimpses of it. Clemencia clears her head only when she clears her house of others. Even though she would define her happiest moments as those times spent in the midst of a family, the only instances in which she thinks and makes decisions that lead to her happiness occur when she extricates herself from family and friends and goes into voluntary seclusion.

During these periods Clemencia evaluates her suitors and, as I have said, comes to recognize what qualities make Pablo her best choice.[8] Similarly, the heroine of *Elia* makes the decision not to marry from her convent retreat. In this case, the convent provides the space in which the heroine can transform herself into the ethical subject of her behavior. Most of Elia's acquaintances define the convent, as we are tempted to define Böhl de Faber's fiction in general, as a place where love is denied or cut off from its object (Carlos in this case). But the convent paradoxically provides a space for self-contemplation, a place where resignation is not forced but awarded as a prize to the women who seek its solitude. What seems to be a capitulation to patriarchy turns out to be "a refusal to submit to the law that makes women the object of male desire" (Kirkpatrick, *Las románticas* 260). Thus the convent offers what it has always offered the characters of women's writings, a place where love is not dependent upon the vicissitudes of men's passions, where freed of the physical, it dwells in some very safe and rare form that women need not fear since it is of their own invention.[9] In the convent, Elia's love for Carlos is distilled into some unalterable abstraction over which time and space have no sway:

> en este íntimo e infinito amor que te tengo no hay presencia ni ausencia, presente, pasado ni futuro. . . . Es un amor que no teme la ingratitud, porque se da sin exigir correspondencia; es un amor inalterable, que se mezcla en las oraciones y se lleva consigo al cielo. Es un amor que en la noche terrestre brilla como una estrella de otras religiones, que se ama cual ellas sin querer asirlas, porque subiremos a ellas. (*Elia* 207)

> [in this intimate and infinite love I feel for you there is neither presence nor absence, no present, past or future. . . . It is a love that fears no ingratitude, because it asks not to be corresponded; it is an inalterable love that we combine with our prayers and carry to heaven with us. It is a love that in the terrestrial night shines like a star of other religions, that we love without trying to seize because we know we will rise to them.]

To the beleaguered heroine, there is always the promise of a better life after this, where a woman's love is corresponded in exactly the right way. As Catherine MacPherson Bremon put it in her early domestic novel *El hilo del destino* [The thread of destiny] (1853):

> hay una existencia, en la que no tienen entrada los pequeños males que afligen esta vida humana y transitoria: que aquella

otra vida, la única segura y duradera, nos ofrece mil halagos, mil felicidades en compensación de los males que hayamos sufrido en esta; y que por cada prueba sufrida con resignación y valor, mil goces inefables y que no tienen fin nos esperan allí. (2:51)

[there is another life, in which the petty afflictions of this human and transitory life do not enter: that other life, the only secure and lasting one, offers us a thousand caresses, a thousand happy moments in compensation for the wrongs we have suffered in this life; and for each test that we suffer with resignation and courage here, a thousand ineffable pleasures await us there.]

## Intersubjective Space

In the bourgeois novel it is usually the home, rather than the convent, that provides the safe harbor for sublimations such as Elia's. Especially in the novels of Sinués de Marco domesticity is not only a positive virtue but a reward. The home represents not merely a duty, or a fortress to contain dangerous or weak women, such as in *La gaviota* or *La familia de Alvareda,* but a privileged space where mutuality is possible because such things as reproduction, a sense of sharing and caring, work and self-sacrifice are best prized and fostered there. In most of Sinués de Marco's novels such mutuality is rarely achieved between a husband and a wife, even though the ideal of the companionate marriage certainly dominates many a character's waking thoughts. Rather, it exists between an older and a younger woman, between two sisters or cousins, or between a father and a daughter, often as a compensation for not giving in to despair, or for not failing in duty to a husband who, by all accounts, deserves to be despised instead of loved. A woman is helped or helps someone less fortunate than she on nearly every page of Sinués de Marco's novels, and this capacity to help the needy, crossing all barriers of class, age, and sex, is what defines the feminine experience more than the desired companionate marriage.

For example, in *Una hija del siglo* [A woman of the century] (1873), most of the many women whose troubled existence the novel traces and combines are offered comfort and peace at the hearth of another woman after they are orphaned or abandoned by a callous lover or husband. Even as single parents living alone, they are comforted in their loss by their love for their children or that of their children for them. After her lover Andrés abandons her, Elvira is taken in first by her aunt and then by Madame Duval. Resigning herself to her solitude, she is granted the solace of a quiet domestic existence with her daughter by her side. When she dies suddenly, her daughter Elvira is taken in by a sympathetic shopkeeper who offers her a home and security. Meanwhile Isabel, another victim of Andrés, is granted the consolation of a quiet life caring for her son. The son cares only for his mother who has helped him avoid the "pasiones desoladoras" (desolate passions) that are the scourge of youth: "una madre hermosa, buena e inteligente; una madre, que era a la vez su hermana y su amiga; una madre que le entendía, que le adivinaba, que estaba siempre a su nivel, y con la cual podía conversar, pensar y sentir" (54) (a beautiful good and intelligent mother, a mother who was at once a sister and a friend, someone who understood him, who knew his mind, who was always at his level and with whom he could converse, think and feel). Isabel will be rewarded for her sacrifices at the end of the novel when Andrés finally marries her and makes her a baroness. She, in turn, sets about rescuing other women whose misfortunes resemble her own.

The neglected Gracia, another of the novel's female foundlings, is taken in by the long-suffering Clemencia who later marries her brother Carlos. Gracia and Clemencia develop for each other the most common form of love in Sinués de Marco's novels, the love of one victim for another. After Clemencia is abandoned by her husband, she finds solace in her love for Gracia, her home duties, and her children at whose side, "se despojó de su dolor como de una vestidura incómoda, y se vistió de su fisonomía más feliz y más bella" (73) (she cast off her sorrow like an uncomfortable dress, and she donned her happiest and most radiant face).

What is constant in all of these shifting relations in which the fortunes of a woman swing wildly from great wealth and class status to utter destitution, or vice versa, is the presence of pain, that the narrator (quoting Victor Hugo) says is woman's most faithful companion (98) regardless of her status or fortune. But the pain is mitigated by the

Fig. 2. "La mejor maestra."

solace of children, work, and the rescuing companions who everywhere appear in the good woman's life. Woman's happiness is also
dependent on her capacity to cope, materially and spiritually, with a
husband's neglect or abuse. This last, according to the narrator of *Una
hija*, is properly a wife's work, as common and necessary as mending
socks and tending children in an age when, as Sinués de Marco's
narrators are fond of explaining, marital bliss is the exception not the
rule. One begins by fabricating an image of the husband that aggran-
dizes his virtues while minimizing the faults of the real-life model:
"Entonces empieza para la mujer un trabajo sublime, y que solo a ella
pertenece: el de fabricar dentro de su pensamiento galas . . . para
adornar el objeto de su cariño" (116) (That is when woman's sublime
task begins, one that is hers alone, that of mentally fashioning finery
. . . to adorn the object of her love). From whatever raw material
provided her, the wife must fashion a kind of "semidiós del que solo
es un pobre mortal lleno de debilidades y a veces también de vicios"
(116) (semigod from a mere mortal full of weaknesses and sometimes
vices). If a woman is lucky, this "sublime ceguedad" (117) (sublime
blindness) can last a lifetime. Her "blind benevolence" allows Clemencia to forgive the defects and faults not only of her husband and his
sister Gracia, but her husband's previous lover. In fact, Clemencia
must go on and on forgiving everyone until the end of this lengthy
novel of men's endless guilt and expiation, and women's endless pain
and forgiveness and feminine consolation. As long as there is one child
or one man for a woman to love and care for, her life can have meaning
and as long as she is willing to forgive even the most indifferent or
cruel man, she will find peace within herself. *Una hija*, like many of
Sinués de Marco's novels, ends with a synopsis of these lessons in
achieving feminine peace through suffering and love. Kissing her
daughter on the forehead, Clemencia wishes for her a life free from
sorrow, but her friend, the baroness who has been schooled in sorrow,
adds the following recommendation: "enséñale, sobre todo, a *amar*, a
*creer* y a llevar con paciencia la cruz que el cielo le haya destinado. En
todos tiempos ha habido mártires y opresores, y no es poco fecundo
en unos y otros el siglo XIX" (216) (Above all teach her to *love*, to
*believe* and to bear patiently whatever cross heaven has destined for
her. There have always been martyrs and oppressors, and the nineteenth century is not lacking in either).

   To begin to reappraise Sinués de Marco's novels, as well as those of her generation now largely ignored by the critical establishment, we have to reevaluate domesticity together with Freudian assumptions regarding normal childhood development. For classical psychoanalysis the fundamental developmental task of the child is separation. To assert independence, the subject needs to control the object, in order to ensure that her "alien otherness is either assimilated or controlled, that her own subjectivity nowhere asserts itself in a way that could make his dependency upon her a conscious insult to his sense of freedom" (Benjamin, "A Desire" 80). While this might adequately describe the norm for the male child seeking separation from its mother, it is insufficient to describe female development, at least in its nineteenth-century configurations. For instance, to begin to think about female subjectivity as it evolved in Spanish literature, it is necessary to recognize Spanish women's appreciation of the delicate "balance of separation and connectedness, of the capacity for agency and for relatedness" (82). Most of Sinués de Marco's female characters learn to cultivate the joys of dependency, clearly a negative force as far as male development is concerned, when it becomes clear that separation and self-determination translate into loss of the power to relate meaningfully and productively to others. Thus dependency is valued as a positive, uniquely feminine attribute.

As a complement to the image of the phallus as the symbol of desire, Benjamin proposes a metaphor to allow for the expression of the feminine paradox of separation and connectedness. The metaphor must serve to explain the deep causes of women's lack of sexual subjectivity and the reasons why women's desires become "alienated into forms of submission and dependency" (*Bonds* 85). Addressing the question "How does it come about that femininity appears inextricably linked to passivity, even to masochism, or that women seek their desire in another, hoping to have it recognized and recognizable through the subjectivity of an other?" (*Bonds* 85), Benjamin evolves the concept of intersubjectivity. A special metaphor, the intersubjective mode denotes a locus "where two subjects meet, where both woman and man can be subject" and where woman's "relationship to desire is not represented by the phallus" (*Bonds* 93), in other words by the thing she lacks. And yet, it acknowledges that the other person really exists in the here and now, not merely in some symbolic dimension typically conceptualized by psychoanalytic paradigms.

In Sinués de Marco's novels the space of the home is connected to this interior, intersubjective space. Receptivity, or the knowing and taking in the other, which home-bound women come to prize, becomes a mode of activity in its own right. This is how, presumably, Spanish women trained themselves to see acquiescence to patriarchal restrictions of their freedoms in a positive light, that is, as an activity, not simply a radical nonparticipation. Understanding the positive values of intersubjectivity perhaps would allow us to reevaluate the rhetoric of passivity in the novels of Sinués de Marco and her many contemporaries. According to Benjamin, "[a]n important component of women's fantasy life centers around the wish for a holding other whose presence does not violate one's space but permits the experience of one's own desire, who recognizes it when it emerges of itself" (*Bonds* 96).[10] This is the space of holding, of the semiotic, of the mother, but not the phallic mother of psychoanalytic discourse. This semiotic space has its literary representations in the homes and fabulous facilitators that beckon young female characters back to the hearth, such as those mentioned from the novel *Una hija del siglo*. Other examples abound: the countess del Vilar of *La abuela* [The grandmother] (1878), the baroness of *La amiga íntima* [The intimate friend] (1857), Cecilia of *Morir sola* [To die alone] (1890), Felicia of *La mujer en nuestros días* [The woman of today] (1878), Luisa of *El sol de invierno* [Winter's sun] (1863), and the dozens of Sinués de Marco's other maternal mediators who help young women to care about and for the other but also to subsist in an emotional vacuum when the occasion warrants.

The cult of feminine solitude in the midst of feminine companionship is the paradox that pervades the domestic fiction of Sinués de Marco. It represents a challenge to pursue spiritual growth even in the face of severe hardship. Studying this "benign aloneness" (Gilligan 97), Benjamin explains that what is experientially female is the association of desire with a space within the self, configured not only as a refuge or escape, but a fertile womb. This inner space connects with the space of a relation between the self and the other. The one really is a continuum of the other. These two spaces are contiguous and their borders are, I argue, flexible in Spanish women's literature. Clemencia's passion for Carlos in *Una hija* quickly translates into her desire to be *all* to a man which is really a figment that inhabits her private space of desire. When her self-sacrifice to the real-life man is rejected, she does not abandon her desire; rather, she allows it to be manifested in her material relation with the others for whom she cares.

To explain women's ethic of submission, Benjamin offers this interpretation: "The fantasy of submission in ideal love is that of being released into abandon by another who remains in control. . . . The freedom and abandon called for by this powerful, controlling other represent an alienated version of the safe space that permits self-discovery, aloneness in the presence of the other" ("A Desire" 97). As they endlessly pursue the strategy to idealize their less-than-ideal mates, the heroines of Sinués de Marco's novels carve out a space in which, ironically, self-discovery is possible, as it was for·Böhl de Faber's Clemencia. At the same time, they are remembering and re-creating the space of special care, bounty, and suffering that is the remembered mother, "la imagen más perfecta de la providencia, porque ella es el amparo de todos nuestros dolores y la que cuida de nosotros en todos los momentos de la vida"·(214) (the most perfect figure of providence, a refuge in all our sorrows, the one who cares for us in all moments of our life) (*El ángel de los tristes* [The angel of the downtrodden], published 1864). In view of this, we should not only study subversion as women's momentary spurts of independence, autonomy, or separation from a powerful other. Rather, we should explore female desire as a dual mechanism to be both with and distinct from the other: "This relationship can be grasped in terms of intersubjective reality, where subject meets subject. The phallus as emblem of desire has represented the one-sided individuality of subject meeting object, a complementarity that idealizes one side and devalues the other. On the contrary the spatial metaphors for female desire help to suspend and reconcile such opposition, and conceive a dimension of recognition between self and other" (Benjamin, "A Desire" 98).

Contemporary theories of the subject may help us to reinterpret the "ángel del hogar" as not just a distasteful anomaly but a powerful notion of space that fosters the notion of feminine intersubjectivity that, I suggest, it is now incumbent upon us to reassess even as we weigh the negative effects of familist literature. The home was not just a prison (although this it certainly was in a physical sense for many *bad* heroines), but a place where a feminine ideal of intersubjectivity could be striven for if not obtained. In this sense, the cult of domesticity fostered a kind of recognition that placed a high value on women's activities and problems. It recognized and valued the mother for her sacrifice to her children, as much as the children's sacrifice for the good of others.

In her landmark study *Money, Sex and Power*, Nancy C. M. Hartsock proposes that when considering the issues of sexuality and power, we shift our attention away from the narrower paradigms widespread in Western cultures to eros in order "to develop a cultural construction of sexuality that need not depend on hostility for its fundamental dynamic" (166). In her positive conception, eros would first be a fusion of many into one, but without the destruction of the other. Second, the body and sensuality would be at home in the concerns of larger social life, not banned from it as if it were a pollutant; in other words woman's body would not be feared as the evil other. Third, creativity and generation would be celebrated for producing "the pleasure of competent activity." All three positive aspects of eros depend on the absence of hostility and violence that form barriers to what women often defined as a better society.

In the context of this conception of eros, Sinués de Marco's domestic novel has some positive things to say to its women readers. The gratification of conquest and subjugation in her fiction is always of the self, not the other. The self must recognize the other without controlling it and without losing itself totally in the process; Sinués de Marco's women characters are challenged to *become* their children or devote themselves to a husband and in turn enjoy an intimacy and communion that recognizes their worth only *through* the others they care for. When this ideal proves unobtainable, they learn to forego the sought-after mutuality. In either case they do not need to devour those around them in order to feel a sense of satisfaction or pleasure. Unlike many male-authored texts, in which great bodily restrictions are placed on women because they pose a threat for society, in the domestic novel it is often society that threatens and restricts women's bodies, and it is in the private sphere where women can most easily escape this threat, often by learning to use their bodies as a site for a struggle for self control.

In brief, Sinués de Marco imagines female moral creativity and reproduction in a positive light, as part and parcel of the everyday that it is the writer's mission to recommend and praise. Men are isolated from this creativity and therefore the general estimation of women. They do not even *naturally* love their children, as Pablo demonstrates in *La virgen de las lilas* [The virgin of the lilies] (1863), or Carlos in *Una hija del siglo*. The relation between artistic creativity and reproduction or woman's role as caretaker is still antagonistic, as is evident in *La senda de la gloria* [The path to glory] (1863), but the fact of women as producers is not in itself threatening but a consolation for the general lack of esteem accorded to them by men.[11] The phallocratic, agonal society, according to Hartsock, is "obsessed with revenge and structured by conquest and domination" (177), which puts men and women in opposition to one another because the gain of one is predicated upon the loss of the other. The domestic novel, which we despise for its apparent shackling of the female spirit, perhaps deserves a better fate, if merely for its rejection of revenge, aggression, and subjugation of the other. Women are not free to experience eros any way they choose but they do participate in it in a more positive sense than we usually imagine, especially if we apply Benjamin's notion of intersubjectivity to their experiences, or study eros in the context of Hartsock's definition.

Intersubjectivity between a man and a woman usually remained an impossible ideal in the Spanish domestic novel. Women survived by believing in it and aspiring to it, not by obtaining it exactly, or they achieved it through great personal sacrifice, or, alternatively, through their care and love for others. During the later decades of the century domesticity gradually lost its appeal as the primary medium of the intersubjective relationship, even though the domestic novel still enjoyed great popularity in bourgeois publications and women's self-sacrifice continued to be promoted as a first step on the path to wholeness. One needs only to read Pardo Bazán's *Una cristiana* [A Christian woman] (1890) or *La prueba* [The test] (1890) to understand both the tenacity of the ideal of feminine self-sacrifice and domesticity, and also the perversity of the ideal as it was sometimes represented in the latter decades of the century.

With the advent of Naturalism, it was becoming increasingly naive to ask readers to imagine the domestic scene as the great incubator of feminine virtue and happiness. In Pardo Bazán's *Memorias de un Solterón* [Diary of a bachelor] (1896), for example, the protagonist Fe Neira does not confront her subjectivity until she briefly turns her back on her home and family and tries to confront the world as a somewhat more independent agent. The development of the female subject, Pardo Bazán intuitively understood, depends on the establishment of relations, including kinship relations, that are not determined by ideals but by circumstances that can interfere with ideals. Because she manages to extricate herself from her family, Fe's new knowledge allows her to see herself for the first time in relation to others, where before she was only able to see herself. Her decision to marry will only seem contradictory if we judge female development as Freud, Piaget, or Kohlberg did, as deficient because it hinges on a flawed conception of morality. Carol Gilligan, on the contrary, would define Fe as a mature woman, since, in Gilligan's words, a woman's "conception of morality as concerned with the activity of care centers moral development around the understanding of responsibility and relationships" (19). By testing what it is like to be free of responsibility to anyone but herself, Fe comes to the conclusion, which we should not simply dismiss as regressive, that relationships are primary to the individual. As a consequence she attains a stage of female maturity that sexologists are only now beginning to recognize as positive. The awareness of her responsibility to others, that is, that the "world is comprised of relationships rather than of people standing alone" (Gilligan 29), leads her to evolve an ethic of care that she, and obviously Pardo Bazán, interpreted as a positive development.

The reward for her unselfishness, as we shall see in Chapter 5, is that Fe will not be locked up alone in her home at night because, beside her, "en asociación constante" (2:510) (in constant association), will be that ideal husband, working hand in hand to solve her family's problems. Echoing Pardo Bazán's ideal of sexual complementarity, Mauro announces his willingness to suspend all claims to superiority, to proclaim that Feíta is equal in condition and right (2:510). Thus Fe is not gaining a *dueño*, but a "hermano, compañero, . . . amante" (2:510) (brother, companion, . . . lover). Whereas in her radically domestic novel *La prueba* Pardo Bazán simply rewards the selfless heroine by leaving her to her own devices (truly one of the happier conclusions of the domestic novel), *Memorias* tempts readers by allowing them to entertain an alternative both to the much-criticized *new woman* that Feíta was on her way to becoming, and the selfless domesticated angel that had lost some currency in the final decades of the century. She designs a modern romance in which it is possible to be taken care of and to take care of others at the same time, to be a wife *and* a friend to a man, and to wish away conventional gender protocol.

In summary, on the level of narrative, nineteenth-century women's novels imply that women do not want except to be wanted or serviceable, and this is the only way for women to achieve a measure of marital, social, personal, and material well-being: subjecthood through the subject's self-denial. This glorification of domesticity restricted the roles of mothers and daughters in order to maintain, functionally, the stability of the nuclear family at a point in Spain's history when a tight family structure was useful to its emerging bourgeois ideology. But, contrary to what we may believe, there are also hidden, positive aspects to the writing of so many books and articles urging women to accept the dubious role of domestic goddess. If these parables of family living seem to be showing women the path to insignificance they also recognize at some level that women are not the "nothing to write home about" implied in our misattributions of their desire. The truth that women reflect back to men to satisfy their—that is, men's—desires and needs is also always the proof of something beyond or behind that reflection that does not simply reflect male subjectivity. It is precisely this beyond the symbolic structures of the male psyche that postmodernism usually categorizes as female *jouissance*, which could be simply the mark of a failure of a dominant phallocentric master-discourse to speak for this other side of women's lives.

I do not wish to imply that women's novels recuperated some hidden female essence that men's novels overlooked or underestimated, because I do not believe there is some "beyond the veil" that is somehow readable without recourse to patriarchal, symbolic structures. Rather, domestic fiction may have helped women cope with historical realities that depended on the bourgeois woman *knowing her place*. It may have provided them with a way to prize the psychological ideal we call intersubjectivity so that the oppression they were living would be disguised and therefore livable.

# Social Masochism and the Domestic Novel

*Will is the manner of men; willingness that of women. That is the law of the sexes—truly, a hard law for women.*

—Friedrich Nietzsche, *The Gay Science*

READERS OF THE NINETEENTH-CENTURY Spanish novel know that in the shadows of the canon there exists a rich tradition of marginal fiction that was consumer-oriented and destined to serve as a "moral guidebook in favor of the status quo" (Andreu 40). This chapter focuses on the link between domestic fiction and the categories of masochism described by psychologists and other interpreters of cultural models of feminine conduct. It also addresses the problem of the domestic novel as an effect of social realities that proscribe the limits of feminine subjectivity. Finally, it briefly studies the relation of the rise of capitalism and the rise of domestic fiction, specifically the notion of bourgeois ideology as promotional to the rise of literary masochism. The premise on which the following discussion is based is that nineteenth-century Spanish women were oppressed in a variety of ways: economically, legally, educationally, physically, and, of most interest in this chapter, psychologically.[1] Domestic fiction helped disguise this oppression by encouraging women to accept oppression through a masochistic sublimation of their pain and sacrifice.

Again I turn primarily to the fiction of María del Pilar de Sinués, perhaps the maximum promoter not only of the domestic angel's rewards and consolations, but of her duties and sacrifices. Sinués de Marco's novels about women were not only immensely popular during the decades they were written (1860s–1880s), many were reedited in the last decades of the century and continued to enjoy a wide readership into the twentieth century. Just as the conservative Sinués de Marco followed in the footsteps of the ultratraditionalist Cecilia Böhl de Faber, so too the even more widely read narratives of Sinués de Marco influenced the writings of a somewhat more emancipated, but by no means radical, Emilia Pardo Bazán. Of particular interest in this chapter on sacrifice and "social masochism" are Pardo Bazán's justifiably forgotten *Una cristiana* [A Christian woman] (1890), and its sequel *La prueba* [The test] (1890). Both of these novels were the worthy successors of Sinués de Marco's domestic novels and treatises of earlier decades, among the ones discussed here: *La abuela* [The grandmother] (1878), *La amiga íntima* [The intimate friend] (1857), *El sol de invierno* [Winter's sun] (1863), *Una hija del siglo* [A daughter of the century] (1873), *La mujer en nuestros días* [The woman of today] (1878), and *La senda de la gloria* [The path to glory] (1863).

## Feminine Masochism

We owe the name masochism to the nineteenth-century German neurologist Baron Richard von Krafft-Ebing, who derived it from the surname of a popular German writer of erotica, Leopoldo von Sacher-Masoch. The most influential early classifications were put forth by Freud in his essays "A Child is Being Beaten" (1919) and "The Economic Problem in Masochism" (1924). Freud believed that masochism, like all perversions, contains traces of a breakdown of the Oedipal structures of the primary stage of psychological development. He distinguished three types of masochism. By *erotogenic masochism* he understood those certain conditions, such as pain, that cause sexual arousal; he analyzed this form mainly in the erotogenic fantasies of the child. The second type is *feminine masochism*, which he studied mostly in adult men but called feminine because the subject, like a woman, "fantasizes that he is being castrated, is playing the passive part in coitus, or is giving birth" ("The Economic Problem" 258). The third category is *moral masochism*, which represents an adult regression to the Oedipus complex. In this case the ego and superego, resexualized as a result of regression, play the role of child and father; the ego / child feels a desire to be beaten by the father. "In order to provoke punishment from this parent-substitute," writes Freud, "the masochist must do something inexpedient, act against his own interests, ruin the prospects that the real world offers him, and possibly destroy his own existence in the world of reality" (266–67).

This third category is especially pertinent to domestic fiction whose heroines so often work against their best interests. When they rebel against conventional family ideology, their "naughty" instincts to become the father—to work outside the home (María of Böhl de Faber's *La Gaviota*), to become an artist (Julia of Sinués de Marco's *La senda de la gloria*), or to love their lovers more than their children (Adriana of Sinués de Marco's *La abuela*, or Leocadia of Pardo Bazán's *El Cisne de Vilamorta* [The swan of Vilamorta] [1885])—are punished with silence, isolation, loss of talent, abandonment, a bankrupt sense of domestic fulfillment, or, conversely, imprisonment in the strictures of childrearing and housekeeping. To be loved by the father, to be a good woman in the eyes of society, means stifling the desire to take his place and instead positioning herself so as to be worthy of that love by novel's end. But Freud's category of moral masochism only provides a useful model to describe the masochism of the domestic novel and conduct book if we place the proper emphasis on social strictures as well as on unresolved Oedipal complexes relating to primary family experiences. Consequently, I call it *social masochism* in order to distinguish it from primary masochism, which finds its expression in literary forms such as the Gothic or pornographic novel, and to identify it with the large apparatuses that watched over women's lives such as Catholicism, capitalism, and bourgeois moral and social codes in general. My argument is that these social structures are the stand-in for the superego and, because they rely on female subordination for their continuance, they teach women that masochistic behavior is what *naturally* befits them.

Although Freud in his essay "Femininity" suggests that the influence of social customs has been underestimated in explaining women's passive tendencies, he largely attributed this aspect of femininity to women's "instinctual disposition." Biology accounts for women's libidinal constraint: "the accomplishment of the aim of biology has been entrusted to the aggressiveness of men and has been made to some extent independent of women's consent" (116). Freud challenged his students not to think of masculine and feminine simply in terms of passive and active adaptability (102), but he did little to further the study of sociological influences in determining femininity, and, consequently, his model for normal female psychological development "leaves women in a permanently melancholic position" (Massé, *In the Name* 88).

One of the stumbling blocks encountered when approaching the problem of masochism in domestic fiction is the confusion surrounding the psychological dimensions of female (as opposed to male) masochism. Since women are so often portrayed as biologically predisposed to masochistic behavior, certain other social determinants have been underplayed. In fact, many of the psychological studies of the perversion, both prior to Freud's (such as the case histories of Krafft-Ebing) and subsequent to his (such as the work of Theodor Reik, Gilles Deleuze, and others), cast the issue of *female* masochism as a footnote.[2] Even studies of the manifestation of masochism in contemporary culture—for example, Gaylyn Studlar's book *In the Realm of Pleasure,* which studies masochism in film, or Kaja Silverman's analysis of masochism and subjectivity in *Camera Obscura*—concentrate on male masochism. The key to explaining this missing information about female masochism can be located ironically in Freud's repeated comments about the "part of a woman" ("A Child" 193) which is to be passive. Steeped in nineteenth-century popular gender stereotypes that still influence us today, Freud believed that men were biologically determined to show sadistic instincts, while women were naturally masochistic. He based some of his theories about female sexuality on the findings of Krafft-Ebing, who, in *Psychopathia Sexualis* (1886), insisted that women had "an instinctive inclination to voluntary subordination to man. . . . Under the veneer of polite society the instinct of feminine servitude is everywhere discernible" (130; quoted in Dijkstra 101).

Freud, as nearly everyone else since, felt compelled to study male masochism because that was the unnatural, or pathological, phenomenon.

Fortunately, that position is now being challenged by researchers such as Michelle Massé, who emphasize in their projects that there is nothing "natural" about the connection between love and pain and that women's masochism is taught to them in literature and culture, for example, through such literary forms as the Gothic novel (*In the Name* 3). Nevertheless, at some level, many of us still act as if we believed women were biologically determined to be masochistic even though theoretically we argue that masochistic and sadistic tendencies are socially constructed. This is unfortunately reinforced even in the classic studies that do specifically address female masochism. For example, in her influential analyses of the "feminine woman" (1944–45), Hélène Deutsch agreed with Freud that women were by nature more masochistic, although she argued that their masochism does not express itself in perverse acts, only in masochistic fantasies and attitudes. Deutsch believed that environmental pressures to pacify women simply reinforced their biological and instinctual masochism. Even in normal development, women's narcissistic guardian has to be very vigilant in order to control their natural masochism. Female masochism reflects the situation of the "primitive conquered woman" (222), biologically determined by the passive female organ (the vagina), women's reproductive role, and their "unfavorably small" clitoris (228). To her credit, Deutsch insisted that this predisposition to masochism is constantly reinforced by environmental factors: male aggression, an overevaluation of the father, the mother's discouragement of female aggression, and the social bribes for feminine passivity. The result is a greater tendency toward moral masochism in women than in men and "an obvious tendency to suffer without compensation through love" (240). "Masochism," she concludes, "is partly an adjustment to reality through the necessary consent to pain" (278).

This decades-long *scientific* identification of women with masochism and men with aggression was bound to be reflected in European culture. Bram Dijkstra describes its influence on late nineteenth-century artists and authors such as Émile Zola, Frank Norris, Pierre Louÿs, and Thomas Hardy, concluding that many of their heroines took for granted that women expected to be abused or neglected by men (100–103). Similarly, Massé traces the masochistic fantasies that underpin the Gothic novel and its sister genre, the pornographic novel. My premise is that some of the same conclusions as Dijkstra's and Massé's can be reached from a study of nineteenth-century domestic fiction by Böhl de Faber, Sinués de Marco, Gimeno de Flaquer, Grassi, and other women writers. Even though their writing appeared long before the influence of modern psychoanalytic theories spread to Spain, they all focused to varying degrees on the meaning of women's suffering, stressing the very *feminine* practice of the sublimation of pain and sacrifice in order to achieve the prize of love. Love is the sought-after prize of the domestic angel, just as it is of the woman masochist, and both go to great lengths to obtain it.

In *The Myth of Women's Masochism*, Paula Caplan challenges the validity of the myth of women's innate masochism while showing how firmly entrenched it is in popular, collective understandings of gender. Caplan lists the behavioral responses that we commonly associate with masochism (and women) and then shows that many of them are not masochistic but ironically adaptive responses, intended to avoid suffering.[3] Edmund Bergler would call someone who presents such responses a "nice masochist" (380). A nice masochist, like a nice domesticated woman, does not engage in perverse sexual activity, and always behaves in a way that is often appreciated by or beneficial to others. Both have (1) the ability to delay gratification, wait for rewards and pleasure, or attempt to earn happiness through effort; (2) the capacity to put the needs of others ahead of one's own; (3) the belief that what one has is about all one can expect to get; and (4) the need to suffer in order to avoid punishment, rejection, or guilt. In her comprehensive survey *Female Perversions*, Louise Kaplan concludes that although the percentage of perversely masochistic women is small relative to men, women's masochism is a pathology that derives its emotional force from ingrained social gender stereotypes that foster what I call here social masochism. Young girls seek to allay anxiety by accentuating certain ideals of feminine virtue such as "passivity, cleanliness, purity, kindness, concern for others, submission. When the social order colludes with these infantile ideals of femininity by insisting on innocence and submission as ways of achieving a normal adult femininity, females learn very early to disguise their intellectual powers as 'feminine intuition' and to compromise their active sexual desires into flirtatiousness and a teasing sexual unavailability" (15).

## Social Masochism and Domestic Fiction

This "ideal of feminine virtue," with its core of social or moral masochistic behavioral tendencies such as those observed by Caplan and Kaplan, is rampant in the domestic novels and conduct books of the latter half of the nineteenth century. The key to understanding social masochism is to realize that the behavioral responses that signal it are defined by the reigning social institutions as a desirable and easily achievable part of what was advertised as *normal* feminine development.

The literature of domesticity teaches that suffering is a necessary prelude to satisfaction and that women should always try to make the best of things. It does so, moreover, by focusing very strongly on desirable gender roles: it is women who ought, for the sake of (pre)-serving society, to be self-sacrificing, nurturing, humble, and long-suffering. Whether men are rescued from crass materialism (Pardo Bazán's *La prueba* [The test] [1890]), poverty (Sinués de Marco's *La senda de la gloria* [The path to glory]), or atheism (Gimeno de Flaquer's *El doctor alemán* [The German doctor] [1880]); whether they even manage to stay alive (Grassi's *El bálsamo de las penas* [The balsam of sorrows] [1863]) often depends on women's sacrifices and their ability to withstand adversity. Women were expected to be the "nobler half of humanity whose role was to elevate man's sentiments and inspire their higher impulses" (Rogers 189). The manifest goal of most domestic fiction, with its glorification of subservience to children and spouse, to the sick and needy, is to teach women how to put the needs of others before their own.

Whether or not we count these behavioral characteristics as avoidance techniques, as Caplan, Massé, and other proponents of adaptational theories of masochism would,[4] or ways to foster intersubjectivity, as I outlined in Chapter 1, we must still try to understand their psychological sources in early development, whatever social and historical realities may have produced or fostered them, and the reasons why the novel was the genre that appropriated their representations particularly well. Diane Griffin Crowder argues that women are not repressed, but oppressed, but the case may be that they are both and that both phenomena are interrelated and should be examined in their cultural contexts.[5]

Specifically, we ought to question who benefitted from the cultivation of the ideal of *little women* who would remain little forever even as they mature to accept places in new families and create new little women. Another question is whether there is a psychological model, other than Freud's three categories mentioned above, that better describes the masochism of the domestic novel. For instance, adapting Deleuze's radical revision of the psychology of the masochistic perversion, can we discern anything subversive about the masochism of the domestic novel, related perhaps to some deep rejection of the centered, patriarchal subject? Is there a peculiar kind of feminine *jouissance* that they approach that we cannot see because we are blinded by our delusions of progress? Does masochism leave any space open for the discussion of feminine desire, for example, the desire to regress even further than the Oedipal stage to the presymbolic, allowing the subject to experience the fusion that denies the difference between the I and the not-I? Of related interest, in light of the recent speculations on desire and narrative (Leo Bersani, Peter Brooks, Christine Brooke-Rose),[6] is the relationship between the perversion we call masochism and the perversity of the novelistic genre, that is, its oft-cited propensity to make us wait for a very long time to get our rewards from it, its use of anticipation, forestalling, dilatoriness, and other formal devices that we can relate to masochistic suspense. Could it be that, with domestic fiction as a point of departure, we could study the rise of the novel as it relates to the staging of the pre-Oedipal, the realm of primary masochism, instead of always insisting (as Roland Barthes and so many others have) that the novel is by definition the reenactment of the family romance, a bildungsroman, or a reworking of Oedipal complexes?[7]

In Deleuze's monograph *Masochism: An Interpretation of Coldness and Cruelty*, masochism is described as a process that expurgates the father through punishment of his likeness in the son, the masochist. According to Deleuze, becoming a man means "to be reborn from the woman alone, to undergo a second birth" (*Masochism* 100). The expurgator par excellence is the woman torturer, while women masochists are conspicuous for their absence in his account of the perversion. Following Deleuze, in her book on cinema *In the Realm of Pleasure*, Gaylyn Studlar claims that "the masochistic narrative acts out pre-oedipal wishes associated with the socially disruptive, polymorphous sexuality of masochistic desire" (112). In this way it successfully undermines "the Oedipal trajectory of unveiling the father's truth," by repudiating the father and the superego, and shattering the "expected progress toward the idealized, stable patriarchal family structure" (112). This compelling notion, based on Deleuze's theory of masochism, deserves careful consideration here for its similarity with social masochism. After all, what is the story of the domestic heroine if not the psychological allegiance to some pre-Oedipal stage "characterized by fusion, fluidity, continuity and lack of differentiation"? (Hirsch 14).

But, when we examine domestic fiction closely, we find very little that is socially subversive about its *ángel del hogar*. Regressing into a doll-like state, as Sinués de Marco's narrators often urge young women to do, is not an unveiling of the Father's truth, but an acquiescence to his internalized word. The domestic novel's *torturer* may be but often is not the oral, sadistic, or phallic mother but a very "phallic" father or husband, while the masochist is a young woman—no resemblance to the heroes of Sacher-Masoch's sado-masochistic classic *Venus in Furs*—who has little, if any, role in organizing the scenarios of her degradation. Furthermore, in many novels in which a woman is seen as alone, as dwelling in some space of containment where all desires are suspended, it is a patriarchal society that reaps the benefit of her self-control as much or more than she. This makes it difficult to imagine the domestic woman's masochism as an expurgation of the father. To study it as such would be to obscure the effect that these novels had on readers and whatever nineteenth-century historical reality they lived, leaving unexamined what historical women learned from these models of feminine subservience.[8] In other words, by applying Deleuze to the model of masochism deployed in domestic fiction we would be blissfully participating in the vogue of the pre-Oedipal, a respectably postmodernist preoccupation, but we could easily fall into the trap of writing out history and underestimating how the novel's readers were seduced by its social and domestic lessons.

In domestic fiction the father does not pose a threat to the subservient woman's world from *outside*, as is the case in the masochistic hero of *Venus in Furs;* rather, he supports it through his own need to foster masochistic behavior. This puts in question Deleuze's assertion that sadism and masochism are "complete in themselves" (67); that is, that they do not rely on each other in any way. In domestic fiction, there sometimes occurs a disruption of the patriarchal family structure, which may be prolonged or brief, tragic or playful, but order is always miraculously reestablished in the ending chapter, as in *La senda de la gloria* when the artist Julia abandons her career to care for her husband. The result is usually the elimination of women's demands that emotional, sexual, social, or material needs be met. What is eliminated is not the Father's Law but feminine desire, or rather feminine desire becomes synonymous with women's duty, and love divests itself of the physical sensuality that the domestic novel always sees as an evil force. As one writer of conduct books put it, "women when they love truly exclude from their love material sensuality, and they absorb, avariciously, the sensuality of the soul" (Pérez Escrich; quoted in Andreu 59).[9] It is the business of the domestic novel and conduct book to teach women that they can be happiest if they eliminate needs rather than satisfy them; that is, if they accommodate their desire to that of others.

Very often the heroine of the domestic novel is alone at novel's end (or dead, forgotten, sent away to the country or a convent, enveloped in social obscurity) but she is at peace with herself because she has suppressed her longings.[10] A popular example is the especially dreary novel called *Suplicio de una coqueta* [The flirt's penalty] (1885) by Concepción Gimeno de Flaquer, that ends with the question "¿Qué fue el amor para esta mujer, culpa o expiación?" (315) (What was love for this woman, a sin or an expiation?). The answer is, of course, both. The heroine was guilty of being a flirt and loving the wrong man, and she expiates her sin by dying from unrequited love. Whatever danger the heroine's challenge to domesticity or, conversely, her embrace of domesticity (with matriarchal overtones) posed to patriarchy is eradicated in the masochistic narratives of Gimeno de Flaquer, Sinués de Marco, Grassi, and even Pardo Bazán. Their domestic novels are not transgressive in any real sense; rather, they embrace a social masochism, a perversion at the service of the social. Women are enjoined collectively to identify with the bourgeois fantasy of the good home, watched over by the faithful wife and caring mother; presumably this ideal had real advantages for the men whose responsibility for their wives' happiness could be considerably reduced if women took full responsibility for their own emotional well-being.

At the heart of domestic fiction the procedure is "all persuasion and education" to use Deleuze's term (20), except that the heroine performs the role of pupil, not educator, which is another thing that differentiates the social masochism of the domestic novel from Deleuze's model. Sinués de Marco's women receive instruction from others about the value and possible pleasures of pain and the necessity of putting restrictions on their activities and friendships. For example, the grandmother of *La amiga íntima* [The intimate friend] teaches her granddaughter about the danger of allowing women to have intimate friendships with women other than their mothers or grandmothers, while the grandmother of *La abuela* [The grandmother] gives pious lessons to her granddaughter from her favorite play, *La cruz del matrimonio* [The cross of matrimony].

As to be expected, accepting pain and suffering does not necessarily translate into a heightened sense of feminine subjectivity as it does for the heroine of Böhl de Faber's *Clemencia*. Often it encourages women to become pure materiality, something that, being nothing, will no longer have to feel pain or be punished. In Sinués de Marco's *El sol de invierno* [Winter's sun], an abused and neglected María tries to escape to a fantasy world where all women are like the wonderful dolls, those "hijas, madres y amigas" (daughters, mothers and friends) who accompany us through childhood when "¡todas las niñas eran buenas, todas las madres tiernas y cuidadosas, todas las amigas amables y llenas de mil buenas cualidades!" (32) (all children were good, all mothers tender and caring, all friends loving and full of good qualities!). It would never occur to anyone to think that dolls were bad or deserved punishment, for dolls are as happy and good as their owners imagine them to be. Here the narrator proposes an ethics of caring and communal love by asking adult women readers to recall the love they once showered on their dolls. What the dolls are in terms of María's desire for the best world, they could also be as models for adult women. If women would just imitate the good qualities of the dolls that they played with when they were young, "si cada una fuese modesta, retirada, sufrida; si realizase en sí propia sus cándidas utopias de niña, todas serían buenas, amables, queridas y estimadas" (33) (if each one were modest, retiring, long-suffering; if each one realized in herself the candid utopia of the little girl, they would all be good, loving, loved and esteemed women).

The woman who dies peacefully, or even the one who lives *happily ever after*, in Sinués de Marco's domestic novels is the woman who, like Clemencia of *Una hija del siglo*, or Julia of *La senda de la gloria*, learns to estimate her sacrifice to patriarchy as a boon. If she fails to learn this lesson she will sacrifice herself to ideals that crush her brutally while offering her no space in return in which she can see herself as an object of worth. Sinués de Marco's *happy* ending occurs when the heroine comes to accept a sedentary, self-sacrificing role in order to earn, or more usually hold onto, the love of another or to redeem a man who has been led astray. The frequently *sad* ending marks the heroine's failure to accept her domestic destiny, again leading to death or self-cancellation.

## Feminine Suspense

Despite the basic differences between Deleuze, Silverman, and Studlar's model for masochism, on the one hand, and the "nice masochism" of the domestic novel, on the other, there are some similarities related to the way pain and pleasure are perceived to be causally linked events in the fulfillment of desire. What is analogous between perversely masochist texts like Pauline Réage's *The Story of O* or Sade's *Justine*, in which masochism is eroticized, and masochistic domestic texts, by which I mean narratives that foster the ideals I mentioned above (46), are the unmistakable similarities in the ways both treat female agency and submission. In both the ego must be repressed and the sublimation of instincts to higher aims complete. Also, an essential point of masochistic pain is that it must be repeated or prolonged to be significant, thereby creating suspense. Suspense, concludes Silverman, is at the "center of all forms of masochism" (44), connected with "uncertainty, dilatoriness, pleasurable and unpleasurable anticipation, apparent interminability, and—above all—

excitation" (44). Masochism seeks to prolong rituals that provide suspense, "at the expense of climax or consummation" (44). Similarly, waiting must be prolonged to be of use to the domestic angel and the domestic plot. It is not that the subject "lusts after pain," as Freud claimed in his definition of masochism, but that she lusts after pleasure that only occurs through its deferral. This notion of suspense is of particular importance to the plot of the domestic novel that is often agonizingly suspenseful in regards the heroine's happiness. In *Una hija del siglo*, for example, the heroine waits a lifetime (and the reader two implausibly eventful and repetitive volumes) for the moment when the heroine's emotional and economic stability is finally earned.

For some heroines the wait becomes endless when the narrator loses interest in what was being awaited and instead focuses on the conditions of the wait, on waiting as a properly feminine nonactivity. No conclusion to waiting is guaranteed or necessarily desirable, and readers' desire to know it has ended is sometimes even frustrated. It is important to question the meaning of this feminine suspension. When waiting becomes an ideal instead of a stage, what are the perceived gains and for whom? Is it, as Deleuze claims for the male masochist, being allowed to be born again parthenogenetically, all traces of the father obliterated, a fundamental disavowal of the pressures of the superego (*Masochism* 127)? I suggest that the answer is not, in the case of under- or overdomesticated women, a "rebirth of an ideal ego that is pure, autonomous and independent of the superego" (127). Nor should we imagine the disavowal at the end of the domestic novel a refusal to recognize difference, or a "setting aside of the Oedipal Law," as Parveen Adams puts it (252). The symbolic order that we usually consecrate to the father is so powerful that it relegates the words of female disassociation to the silence of embroidery, convent walls, and diaries. If we can speak at all of a woman reborn at the end of the Spanish domestic novel, she is nearly always devoid of sexual feelings and the superego has not been destroyed but reinforced. The end of a woman's suspense does not presume a total suspension of movement, only a cessation of desire, an *arrested* desire, while her labor continues. She embroiders her way into the heart of patriarchal society, which has organized her retreat because it relies, economically and psychologically, on her fulfilling a domestic career. The ruthless husband of *La senda de la gloria*, to give one example, could never survive if his wife Julia were not willing to stay at home, working to save his soul

Fig. 3. "Esperando."

and his fortune, and canceling her name by signing her husband's name to her paintings.

Sometimes, as is the case with Julia, the heroine even gets the man she suffered and schemed and most of all waited for, against all reasonable hope. After lengthy apprenticeships of solitude and numerous trials and defeats, during which she comes to learn something about a woman's *mission*, her self-purging earns her a return to the world of fathers and children from which the novel had either temporarily allowed her to stray or exiled her. She is then turned over to that world as part of a ritual passage from either maternal governance or worldly peril to masculine protection and tutelage. A model for this is the heroine of Böhl de Faber's *Clemencia*, who, as discussed in Chapter 1, endures an unhappy childhood, abusive husband, hateful relatives, seclusion and solitude before she enters into a second, more compatible marriage. After Clemencia passes through several stages of self-annihilation during which she learns to pass over her desire and to accept victimization, submission, and self-domination as a way of life, she has earned her measure of happiness. Noël Valis, however, throws into question the *happy* conclusion to Clemencia's travails by suggesting that the heroine's second marriage is more a capitulation than a desire fulfilled. Since hers had been a "dream of chaste innocence" (254), Clemencia brings to this second marriage yet another set of lowered expectations. Similarly, nearly all of Sinués de Marco's novels have ambiguous endings: pious exhortations to accept a less than favorable lot.

One of the most common and conflictive of domestic plots tells the story of a married woman's waywardness, which, once corrected, allows her to be reinstated as a prodigal daughter who has earned a new place in the nuclear family usually with greatly lowered expectations and curtailed activities. Typical examples are the unruly Elvira of *El sol de invierno*, who is rehabilitated by her sister María; the materialistic Margarita of *La amiga íntima*, whose close friend teaches her that a wife is "la encargada por Dios de vigilar de la dicha y el bienestar de su familia" (85) (the one responsible for the happiness and wellbeing of her family); and Adriana of *La abuela*, whose physical and moral beauty are restored as a consequence of her moral reformation. A repentent Adriana, like some of Sinués de Marco's luckier heroines, sees at last the meaning of true love, "las palabras *amor, deber, sacrificio,* se esculpían en su alma con caracteres de luz" (306) (the words *love*, *duty*, *sacrifice* were chiseled onto her heart in luminous letters).

A contemporary of Sinués de Marco, Angela Grassi often modeled her heroines after these reformed sinners. For example, Clotilde of *El copo de nieve* [The snowflake] (1876) begins married life as a model wife, with no other care than her husband's happiness. Soon however, dissension enters her marriage when Guillermo gives her the key to a library filled with novels. As she begins to read tales of romantic heroines and their great passions, she loses interest in her husband and children and even begins to question the need for women to sacrifice themselves to men:

> la mujer ha dejado de ser la esclava del hombre. . . . la mujer ha sacudido el yugo brutal con que quiso dominarla en aquellos tiempos de funesto oscurantismo, en que se consideraba como un delito que supiese leer, y en que hasta se la negaba que tuviese alma. (194)

> [woman is no longer man's slave. . . . she has cast off the brutal yoke with which men tried to tame her in those terrible, dark times, when it was considered a sin to know how to read, and when it was denied she even had a soul.]

More fortunate than heroines of Böhl de Faber's *La gaviota* or *La familia de Alvareda*, Clotilde finally comes to accept the yoke of marriage and to understand that poetry resides not in books but "en el escondido hogar en donde chisporrotea el amigo fuego encendido por ella, y hasta en los remiendos que echa a los vestidos de sus hijos" (199) (in the obscure hearth where the friendly fire lit by her hands burns gaily, and even in the patches that she sews on her children's clothes). She then courageously throws the key to her husband's library into the family hearth that for her holds the true key to poetry.

For many nineteenth-century heroines, suspense is the "waiting for the door to open and a Pygmalion to bring life into limbo" (Auerbach, *Communities of Women* 39); in other words, a waiting to be transformed by a man into whatever it is he imagines a woman's destiny to be. When the domestic novel conjures up an acceptable Pygmalion, like Guillermo of Grassi's *El copo*, the door often shuts discreetly behind the newlywed or newly recovered woman as she enters or reenters her home, and the narrative closes beyond that door. Women's "purgatorial existence," as Auerbach calls prenuptial rites (*Communities of Women* 47), does not necessarily come to an end; we merely see a break in its continuity with a marriage, elopement, escape, or reconciliation. Usually, in fact, very little leads us to imagine a passage from purgatory to heavenly bliss, even when someone as right as Pablo *(Clemencia)* or Guillermo enters the picture.

If there is anything subversive about the domestic novel it is that although domestic bliss is always an imagined good, it rarely stretches beyond the imaginary world of a beleaguered woman seeking to rise above the realities of her dreary existence through the sublimation of her desires. And, unlike *Clemencia* and *El copo*, most novels leave a woman in a state of suspense, not necessarily waiting for her man, but postponing forever her earthly pleasure until some happy moment in another life. This is an especially popular scenario in Spanish domestic fiction, in which earthly desire is willingly suspended upon the promise of a greater fulfillment beyond the grave. For example, this is where Genoveva will find her reward for renouncing her marriage to Claudio in Angela Grassi's *El bálsamo de las penas* [Sorrow's balsam]. According to the best medical doctors, if Genoveva had followed her inclinations and married Claudio, he would have died from the shock of love. In her convent retreat "sus días se deslizan apacibles y tranquilos cual las aguas de un arroyo" (319) (her days slip away peacefully and tranquilly like the waters of a stream).

## The Uses of Social Masochism

Most heroines do not end up in a convent, but nearly all of the domestic novel's resolutions require some form of feminine self-cancellation, acquiescence, subservience, or stasis similar to Genoveva's silent days. Psychoanalysts interpret this as a uniquely *feminine* desire for regression reinforced, to be sure, by environmental circumstances that foster it. However, from the point of view of male psychology, it also could be related to the desire to contain the positions of women within the symbolic order, a kind of mass psychological oppression. As Sandra Lee Bartky reminds us, psychological oppression "serves to make the work of domination easier by breaking the spirit of the dominated and

by rendering them incapable of understanding the nature of those
agencies responsible for their subjugation" (23).

This leads back to the question of whether the social masochism of
domestic fiction is a female adaptation to danger, that is, a way to
practice pain and sacrifice in a controlled setting where the promised
rewards are potentially substantial (love, economic stability, educational opportunities, honor, and adulation), or whether it is rather a
male solution to the female's dangerous encroachment on male territo-
ries that seems to have occasioned such great alarm among Spanish
educated men.[11] After all, many benefits accrue to men if women are
willing to sacrifice all for them and their children. In other words, is
social masochism a device for coping or the indirect expression of some
kind of collective, unconscious male fear? My conclusion is that it is
both. According to Paula Marantz Cohen, feminine adaptability is the
single most important role for the nineteenth-century heroine, for
upon it depends the stability of the nuclear family (33). Concurring,
Bridget Aldaraca argues that placing women on a pedestal, at home,
is the most efficient way to ensure women's exclusion from the public
sphere of activity (*El ángel* 20). On the other hand, even though she
so carefully documents the various conditions for the endurance of the
domestic angel myth in Spanish society, Aldaraca also recognizes its
psychological base in primary relations: "In Spain, the iconization of
woman as an eternally young and virginal mother has much more to
do with a nostalgic longing for home, that is, with a return to the
relationship between male child and mother, than it does with the
relationship between adult men and women in marriage or outside of
marriage" (*El ángel* 20).

Since, according to Deleuze, paternal and patriarchal themes pre-
dominate in sadism, perhaps the apparent masochism of the domestic
ideal is simply a disguise for its essential, violent sadism. Such an
argument risks joining sadism and masochism into the reciprocal relation that Deleuze argued did not exist. This paradox leads me to
explore more critically Deleuze's insistence on this separation and what
historical meanings his campaign might have had. Whatever the case,
the discourse of sadism belongs to the realm of social conservatism
and the often explicit goal of the most radical domestic angel ideologue
is to conserve the existing social fabric against the chaos of moral
breakdown and decay. The result is to keep men and women in their
proper—separate but not equal—spheres, resulting in what Aldaraca

calls "sexual apartheid" (*El ángel* 28). The virtuous woman was a creature handily adapted to fit certain social and political needs. While
this woman, argues Alicia Andreu, seems to evoke in the reader the
feelings of suffering and sadness, an analysis of these sentiments reveals the manipulating force behind them (44).

The cult of feminine acquiescence was advertised as the best way
to avoid the even greater pain of homelessness, prostitution, hospital-
ization, powerlessness, or hell. Thus seen, the feminine masochism of
the domestic novel was also an adaptive response—as so many masochistic responses really are according to social psychologists like Paula
Caplan. According to the adaptive theory, a woman's regression is a
reaction to the impasse caused by the impossible demands society puts
on her conflicting with her own desires. By becoming only a body,
she fuses herself to the other and paradoxically shares the joy that
the other has in her. We could also explain women's fascination with
narratives of learned insignificance by using the now-famous Freudian
analogy of the fort/da game.[12] What women novelists explored in their
domestic fictions were painful social realities in a controlled setting.
Alternating presence and absence, activity and passivity, pleasure and
pain, they repeated situations that, because imaginary, were never so
awful or painful as what they repeated. Because we are conditioned to
despise both tragically melodramatic and sentimentally happy endings, it is easy for us to overlook the fact that domestic fiction chronicles acute family problems that certain classes of Spanish women
understood as all too real. Nineteenth-century readers of the genre
similarly would be able to distance themselves from, or vicariously
enjoy, the joys and sufferings of the domestic heroine. Every novel had
a measure of both and this permitted readers to rehearse reactions to
the pain and pleasures of domestic life, both of which were underrepresented and underestimated in many of the great canonical novels. Perhaps, as Peter Brooks points out, "the repetition of unpleasant
experiences reflects a movement from passivity to mastery" (98), meaning that the cycle of repeating is an experiment in control as much as
self-abandonment.

In Chapter 1, I discussed the utopia—rarely achieved but always
aspired to—that the domestic novel constructs as an antidote to a
changing world in which traditional values of caring for others were
eroding. The ideal self's development is based on human interaction,
and this interaction, while requiring great sacrifice, is always vastly

superior to selfishness because it places awareness of others above a woman's own sense of self-worth. Control over the body, whether this means self-control or control of it by others, is worth the price, especially since the subject can learn to find satisfaction in another's satisfaction. In general, women writers were proud of women's special resiliency in the face of poverty and adversity. As early as 1853, in her romantic novel *El hilo del destino*, Catalina MacPherson de Bremon bragged about the qualities that would later become synonymous with the domestic angel:

> [e]sa fibra concedida a la mujer para resistir los golpes de la adversidad y que, revistiéndola de una fuerza y resistencia sobrenaturales, la eleva a un grado tan sublime de resignación, paciencia y dulzura, que, convertida en espíritu angelical, desafía y desprecia la más extrema de las miserias, la más profunda de las desgracias mundanales. (1:24)

> [that fiber accorded women to resist the blows of adversity, that endows her with a supernatural strength and resistance, elevating her to such a sublime level of resignation, patience, and sweetness that she is transformed into an angelic spirit, challenging and despising the most extreme miseries, the most profound worldly misfortunes.]

In the decades that followed MacPherson's *El hilo*, the lists of domestic virtues taught to bourgeois women in the popular press, with their promised or implied rewards (either material or deferred to the afterlife), provided women readers a way to imagine the displeasure of self-containment and self-abnegation as pleasurable and productive, for on them depended the entire family's stability. As Ramón García Sánchez admonished his readers in the periodical *La mujer* [Woman], equality is not for women:

> Woman, the queen of her house, should nevertheless not aspire to be the equal of man.
> Let humanity advance all it wishes on the path to civilization; she should only desire those rights she already possesses if she wishes to preserve the adoration that man now professes for her.
> The day that she becomes equal with man, intervening in

public affairs, will be her last happy day, because she will see man as a rival for her ambition and egoism.

No; woman was born to feel and love the tranquility of the home.

The moment she abandons this sphere she will lose the category of angel. (7)

Clearly the material beneficiaries of this social masochism, even when women were said to *enjoy* it, were primarily men; female masochism in general represents patriarchy's frenzied need to locate the meaning of men's desire in the desire of others. That is, the masculine desire to dominate and be subjects requires a complementary feminine desire to be dominated and to negate feminine subjectivity. In this sense, sadism and masochism are inseparable impulses feeding on each other, and domestic literature springs from both within a tight circle of uneven power relations.

It was only in the later decades of the century that Spanish women began to discuss what ends female subordination served the dominator as opposed to the oppressed and what the modes of feminine repression had in common with political contexts. Most notably, Pardo Bazán frequently complained that women's circumstances and aptitudes were overdetermined by the directives of patriarchal institutions and collective male needs and fantasies. In an 1890 essay she complains that Spanish men had devised a way to control women by assigning God to be their Almighty Custodian: "God, then, is the nuptial bed; which offers the advantage that if the husband is distracted and seeks pleasure elsewhere, the guardian becomes the consoler and the sane adviser who, taking the wife in his loving arms, will cure her with a gentle balsam, keeping her from the path to perdition" (*La mujer española* 35). Evidently, Pardo Bazán understood what even modern feminists sometimes ignore, that the will-to-power, as Michel Foucault often argued (*Power* 97), is not the result of conscious conspiracy, but of unconscious, collective drives: "I don't wish to insinuate," she told her audience at the Pedagogical Conference of 1892, "that there has existed a vast conspiracy of one sex to dominate the other; the great instances of historical domination and submission are not the fruit of calculated combinations, but of an unconscious impulse dictated by a collective interest" (*La mujer española* 76). Female subordination served as a bulwark of patriarchy, according to Pardo Bazán, much the same way that loyalty to the king or queen was the unconscious, collective instinct required to bolster or shore up *(rebustecer)* the monarchy (77). The same impulses that produce laws to protect the rights and privileges of certain men result in what Pardo Bazán referred to often in her works as women's "destino relativo" (relative destiny) within the Spanish patriarchy: "Man's collective instinct, then, sufficed to elaborate a concept of woman's relative destiny, and to lend this gigantic error such a firm consistency that it endures even today, making him the ultimate but formidable bastion of legal inequality in modern society, which, to be sure, has proclaimed the rights of man, but neglected to recognize those of all humanity" (77).

Since the female subject's experience of herself and her relation to a community is determined by "the social division of labor and the social organization of sexual difference" (Brenkman 173), it is always finally a question of the relation between psychology and the social. In this sense I agree with Foucault, that perversions are always "drawn out, revealed, isolated, intensified, incorporated by multifarious power devices" *(History* 48). This makes it impossible to separate the sadistic, conservative impulse of domestic fiction from the masochistic pleasures it taught women to expect from the sublimation of their earthly trials. In fact, domestic fiction seems to be an ideal meeting place for these two behavioral extremes.

To address the question raised in the beginning of this chapter regarding the rise of literary masochism, it is useful to examine the structural similarities between literary masochism and capitalism before addressing the specific context of Spanish domestic literature. In capitalism the production and reproduction of material life causes some subjects to regard others as objects, for "[r]eification is the pervasive effect of the capitalist division of labour" (Brenkman 174). Both masochism and capitalism foster the creation of slave mentalities. In the case of capitalism the production of value is a violence that requires participants who believe the violence will also benefit them. Similarly, the masochist derives her value as object to another subject. Both subject and object derive profit from the relation, but never to the same degree. Given their structural similarity, it is not unreasonable to expect that a rise in capitalism (or even an anticipation of its advent) should foster a rise in the masochistic aesthetic, even though clearly women's oppression is not a product of capitalism but predates it (Scott, *Gender* 35). Although they do not usually make the political connection, most social psychologists (Baumeister, "Masochism as Escape" 49) argue that masochism is the most modern of our perversions, especially linked to highly developed Western societies that stress individualism.

As has been often argued, in Spain, the bourgeois revolution did not succeed because industrial progress and land disentitlements failed to keep pace with other European countries. And yet Spain did undergo what Adrian Shubert calls a liberal revolution (5) and the values of its dominant cultural institutions are remarkably similar to the bourgeois ideology disseminated in those European countries moving faster toward a capitalist economy. For one thing, the division of labor along gender lines was becoming more acute in the second half of the century. It was then, as Aldaraca shows, that the separation of private and public spheres was most clamorously defended, and its pleasurable benefits for women overstated. The bourgeois glorification of housework, caring for the sick and elderly, childrearing, and so forth were said to produce a special, uniquely feminine pleasure. The Romantic hero has disappeared and been replaced with a heroine who, in the words of Alicia Andreu, knows her place in popular fiction: "The hero of romantic literature has been transformed into a heroine, not an active woman anxious for passion and in search of adventures that would lead her in a process from self-realization to freedom without limits. No, the heroine of popular literature is defined precisely by the opposite qualities: obedience, passivity and happiness in resignation" (48).

Just as gender is a group illusion, the female masochism of the domestic novel and conduct book is what Deleuze and Guattari would call a group fantasy, as Pardo Bazán well understood, and it requires a collective psychosocial analysis in order to undermine "those meanings and symbolic constructions that transfigure social domination into images of transcendence and establish communal ideals that rest on the real absence of community" (Brenkman 197). Perhaps the woman who transcends all pain for the love of a child, husband, brother, or parent symbolizes society's need of a more binding communal structure.[13] But it is not just that, as John Brenkman states, the domestic angel symbolized some "idealized 'organic community' of precapitalist society," enjoying "satisfactions deriving directly from the labor process" (214). The missing ingredient in Brenkman's imagined relationship is the use-value of women's care, which, I would argue, benefits a bourgeois more than a precapitalist structure. Woman's value in the home, as Aldaraca explains, is firmly linked to the evolving notion of woman's work as the servant of the nuclear family: "The image of the Angel is never presented in isolation, but always with the necessary accoutrements that bring her into existence: the cradle, the thimble and sewing box, and if not a spinning wheel in the late nineteenth century, perhaps a sewing machine. But above all she is surrounded by the family members, for she exists *only* to serve them" (*El ángel* 64). Bourgeois society sadistically genderized its ideal roles by stipulating that women are morally and physically suited to their homebound ministry. It was women's sacred duty to save for the private sphere what in public men were allowing to slip away: commitment, sacrifice, honor, duty. It was women's responsibility to regenerate Spain because "[h]er capacity for love signals her also as the one selected by God and nature to reform the Spanish people" (Andreu 26).

This "privatization of virtue" (Aldaraca, *El ángel* 150) is a necessary stage in the development of the bourgeois state and the gradual implementation of industrial capitalism.[14] Bourgeois virtue comes to be defined as whatever good women do *for* men within the confines of their home. Or, as Eustaquio puts it in Angela Grassi's *El copo de nieve* (1876), the home is where just about every imaginable good can be found. There a man can find:

> la fuerza para luchar contra las borrascas de la vida, las suaves inspiraciones del bien, las gratas esperanzas de mejores días: en el seno de la familia, se educa el niño que luego será hombre, y acaso decidirá de los destinos de la patria; en el seno de la familia, reposa el anciano caduco y fatigado por su larga peregrinación sobre la tierra.
>
> En el bendito dintel del hogar doméstico, se estrellan los huracanes que engendra la vida pública; se detienen las pasiones tumultuosas y bastardas; allí encuentra el hombre los puros goces en los días felices; la resignación y el consuelo en los días de amargura. (196)

> [the strength to struggle against the storms of life, gentle proddings to do good, pleasant hopes for a better tomorrow. In the bosom of the family is educated the small boy who will perhaps decide the fate of the nation, in the bosom of the family the

frail and weary old man finds repose from his long pilgrimage
on this earth.

On the blessed doorstep of the family hearth, the tempests
of public life are calmed, tumultuous and bastardly passions
are tamed, there a man can enjoy pure pleasures in happy times;
receive resignation and consolation during bitter times.]

The women of domestic fiction cheerfully *forgive* men for their flaws
by being the sacred vessel in which, ideally, men can deposit for safe-
keeping all the virtues that they both want to preserve and are relin-
quishing in the public sphere. Perhaps nowhere is this mission more
clearly illustrated than in Pardo Bazán's curious novels *La prueba* [The
test] (1890) and *Una cristiana* [A Christian woman] (1890). In *La prueba*,
a male narrator recounts the edifying process of his aunt Carmiña
learning to enjoy caring for her leprous husband. The husband, portrayed as a greedy, self-serving Jew whose sense of public good is as
deficient as his family loyalties, contrasts sharply with the self-obliter-
ating Christian heroine who sacrifices her happiness to make her husband's dying hours more tolerable. In other words, what Carmiña
strives for is the ideal Victorian marriage, a "union between husband
and wife where the two merge into one, and where the husband is
the One" (Rabine 125). She copes with her bad choice of a *Jewish* (with
all the negative connotations the word usually bore in nineteenth-
century Spanish literature) husband by adopting a *Christian* attitude
and defining his materialism and his illnesses as tests intended to make
her a better wife. The harder the test, the greater the glory for passing
it. She deserves the tests, she reasons, because of her earlier, unchris-
tian distaste for her husband and her all-but-suppressed affection for
her nephew. God accommodatingly provides her with the fortitude
she needs to set things straight:

¿Frialdades tenemos? Pues yo haré que te veas en la precisión
de acercarte a tu marido . . . y que no puedas desviarte de él
ni un minuto. Yo te mandaré una enfermedad que solo tú arran-
ques para asistírsela . . . ¿No has querido admitir en tu corazón
el cariño de esposa en las condiciones naturales? Yo haré que
lo admitas por medio del sacrificio y de la prueba. (1:697)

Fig. 4. From *La Ilustración Ibérica*.


[So we are coldhearted, are we? Well, I will see to it that you
are forced to approach your husband . . . and that you can not
leave his side for a moment. I will send you an illness that only
you can bear to treat . . . You have refused to allow your heart
to feel a wifely regard for your husband? I will make you feel
it through sacrifice and tests.]

The Christian spouse's efforts are doubly crowned with success.
The dying husband, dejudaicized by his wife's Christian example,
rights some of the wrongs he committed in years gone by—after all,
what does the dying, childless capitalist have to lose? And after Car-

miña places a long, intense kiss on the leprous face of her husband, her amazed and ecstatic nephew suddenly feels as if *he* also had become a Christian "por espacio de una hora lo menos" (1:703) (at least for the space of an hour). The nephew Salustio comes to interpret his aunt as the ideal Christian woman who contains and preserves the good part of men that in public, for example, in the presence of enlightened school friends, a man must deny:

> En el fondo de mi conciencia su sacrificio me parecía unas veces hueco y vano; otras, admirable y sublime; unas veces quintaesenciado, artificioso y estéril; otras, espontáneo, heroico y provechosísimo a la moralidad de las generaciones futuras. Era mi doble naturaleza presentando me el pro y el contra de la idea del matrimonio cristiano; eran el tradicionalista y el reaccionalista que yo llevaba en mí enzarzados y arañándose. (1:663)

> [Deep in my soul her sacrifice seemed at times empty and vain; at other times, admirable and sublime; sometimes quintessential, artificial and sterile, other times, spontaneous, heroic, and important for the morality of future generations. This was my double nature presenting me with the pros and cons of the notion of a Christian marriage; it was the traditionalist and the reactionist that I bore within me locked in struggle, clawing at each other.]

What homebound women are still able to teach worldly men "al cabo de los años mil" (1:686) (at the end of the 1900s) is that the law of pain precludes death, which alone opens the door to "otra vida mejor que ésta" (1:686) (a better life than this). This message, delivered ostensibly by Carmen to worldly men like Salustio, speaks, in fact, to Spanish women about their place in a world obsessed with the bourgeois feminine ideal, "which instills in women the vocation for love, assigns them in life the almost exclusive task of loving and then makes love, or any tender emotion, impossible" (Rabine 111). *La prueba* illustrates this in its opposition between the world of philosophy, business, and politics (the world of the uncle and Salustio) in contrast to the world of pure affection, sacrifice, and ultradomesticity (represented by the mother of Salustio and Carmen).

While conduct books like the popular *Avisos saludables a las casadas* (1846) by Queen Isabel's confessor Father Antonio María Claret, Sinués de Marco's *La mujer en nuestros días* (1878), and Gimeno de Flaquer's *La mujer juzgada por una mujer* (1882),[15] endlessly pursued a technology of producing good little women, the domestic novel went a step further and allowed women to imagine indoctrination as pleasurable, linking a strong sense of self-worth with virtues that, ironically, obliterate the self and making feminine desire consist of the desire to be feminine.[16] The result was a notion of womanhood as a totally private experience that effectively disguised the fact that it had very public consequences. This produced a story of female development at odds with the bildungsroman that readers of novels are so fond of, because its subject journeys backward in time, not to be reborn, but to remain suspended in a kind of perpetual infancy. The more dangerous the public world was made to appear, the more idealized the image of the "isolated feminine domestic sphere which can be a timeless spiritual refuge and stable locus outside the turbulent flow of history" (Aldaraca, *El ángel* 56). If it is through idealization that human subjects are reified in order to achieve imaginary control over them, as Aldaraca stresses (*El ángel* 83), this imaginary control surely helped to shape the family's material existence in ways not always favorable for women.

On the other hand, some domestic novels also permit women a glimpse of the earthly as well as the spiritual rewards for their suffering and forbearance. As we have seen, the long-suffering Clemencia *(Clemencia)*, like Carmen, is rewarded when her abusive husband suddenly dies. Similarly, Carmen's self-sacrifice is rewarded when she is free the second time around to marry a man of her own choosing (or not to marry at all, worries Salustio), to be away from her father's unwholesome influence, and to dispose of her fortune as she sees fit. The stated message is that only in death does a woman's pain translate into pure bliss, yet at the end of Carmiña's "prueba," she is still very much alive. So, while *La prueba* and *Clemencia* seduce women into accepting masochistic relational systems, they also give them occasional access to interesting fantasies about what their waiting and pain could produce in the best of worlds.

It cannot be said, however, that the domestic novel, as a rule, paints the best of all worlds. Despite the benefits of these literary fantasies of reward, it is important to remember that aesthetic masochism is a social institution that maintains men and women in unequal power relations. Its psychological paradoxes should not distract us from its effects on the historical relations between men and women. It promotes a sublimation or a repression of female desire and, in so doing, ensures a certain domestic peace that facilitated bourgeois male adjustments to political instability, new philosophical currents and religious customs, as well as a changing labor force.[17] Men's overvaluation, in other words, is socially dependent upon women's devaluation. As Mary Poovey put it in her study of British domestic ideology in the decades of the 1840s and 1850s, the separation of feminine and masculine spheres, was "crucial to the consolidation of bourgeois power partly because linking morality to a figure (rhetorically) immune to the self-interest and competition integral to economic success preserved virtue without inhibiting productivity" (10). Even though Spain lagged behind England in the development of its dominant bourgeois class, its promotion of separate spheres for men and women was perhaps just as crucial to the moral component of its liberal revolution as the domestic angel was to bourgeois revolutions of Northern Europe.

In Spanish fiction written by women, violence, the kind of violence to the self that the domestic novel champions at any rate, is conferred with a spiritual quality that ironically obliterates the self for a greater good. The greater the service, the greater the spirituality, albeit at the price of sexual and social autonomy. The longer the wait, the more time to think about waiting. The more self-denial, the greater gains for a transcendent self who is able to will states of mind into being in order to overcome pain. This is the masochistic ethic that inscribes every domestic drama with the pain/pleasure paradox. It is not what Barthes called the phallic trajectory of the quest "formed in the shadow of the father" (Studlar 109) but a profound exercise in "feminine" self-containment. A woman must find her value through whatever use the other makes of her. While Leo Bersani finds sexuality to be grounded in a very personal kind of masochism, a *jouissance* that "distracts" him from historical violence (*Freudian Body* 114), I find it difficult to be distracted from the historical violence of domestic masochism and the sociohistorical realities that produced it or that it helped to produce. Just as separating the phallus from the penis or studying pornography as a purely aesthetic genre unconnected to the effects it has on women's material existence run the risk of dangerous ahistoricity,[18] it is fair to remind modern theorists of masochistic and sadistic narratives that people internalize *and* externalize their literary models. Women's self-

sacrifice, as Julia Kristeva argues in "Stabat Mater," is a form of ano-
nymity that preserves social norms. It is through women's ideal of
motherhood, especially, that patriarchal stability is maintained:

> Feminine perversion [*père-version*] is coiled up in the desire for
> law as desire for reproduction and continuity, it promotes femi-
> nine masochism to the rank of structure stabilizer (against its
> deviations); by assuring the mother that she may thus enter
> into an order that is above humans' will it gives her her reward
> of pleasure. Such coded perversion, such close combat between
> maternal masochism and the law have been utilized by totalitar-
> ian powers of all times to bring women to their side, and, of
> course, they succeed easily. (Kristeva, *Tales of Love* 260)

The remaining question is whether there is a way in which to imagine domestic masochism as a social mechanism (like the religious masochism of the flagellant) promotional to the institutions of capitalism,
and still make an analogy between fiction and sexual masochism in
Deleuze's sense, that is, masochism as a challenge to the difference
that the Oedipal law constructs and enforces between the sexes. We
should be skeptical. We can speculate that the gender polarizations
celebrated in domestic fiction express some latent desire or fundamental fear either that the woman and the man are both castrated, or
conversely, that they both have the phallus. And we can study masochism as one way for women to flee from the displeasure of overcontem-
plation of the self, as Roy Baumeister has argued in "Masochism as
Escape from Self." From the viewpoint of men, we could also examine
the suspenseful, fixed, stable, unchanging woman that a patriarchal
society constructs for itself as a kind of fetish, a fixed object to which
the subject returns "to exorcise the dangerous consequences of movement" (Adams 252). Certainly domestic literature articulates many
contradictions that lend themselves to these alternative approaches because, while seeming to be entirely conservative and promotional of
gender polarizations, it is a form that sometimes challenges those ideals
it most ostensibly cherishes. These explorations are useful as long as
we remember that masochism is always a violence with social, political,
cultural, and economic consequences. Women's suspense was a virtue
because it was beneficial to male mobility, in a material, not just an
imaginary sense. The family ideology that domestic fiction promoted

stretched well into the twentieth century as a dominant force not only in fiction but in women's lived experiences. It helped to shape the exercise of authority and privilege in the domesticated nuclear family that Marantz Cohen argues was becoming a more and more closed structure (38) throughout the nineteenth and into the twentieth century.

If it is of any use to study this at times rather tedious fiction it is because it shows how the production of sexual identity promotes the exercise of power by patriarchy. Unfortunately, the history of this promotion in relation to the history of the novel has yet to be written, although Aldaraca's book on Galdós is a promising beginning. It seems clear to me that even the least gifted, least educated, and most fanatical women writers were of great use to reigning political institutions through their stories, essays, and serialized novels on women's conduct and proper roles that count in the thousands in nineteenth-century periodical literature. This literature translated what women needed to be in order to be both desirable and useful to men, and thus provided a magnificent mechanism for the socialization of women, a prescriptive definition of their relation to male authority, and a rationalization of the relegation of their personal life to patriarchal institutions like confession and other religious activities during a period of diminishing religious observance (Shubert 163). Conditioning its readers to believe that caregiving was woman's loftiest mission, it provided ample scenarios in which women's work was essential to social well-being. While it can be argued that women's writings positively valued female experience, they also promoted the notion that a woman's individuality is contingent, that she is not an autonomous social and moral being apart from man (Aldaraca, *El ángel* 60).

The history of this promotional literature is not without significant changes throughout the century. It evolved in conjunction with larger historical contingencies as well as social changes directly affecting the family. Domestic fiction came into its own during the period from 1850 to 1880 when the most women writers wrote "under the sign of domesticity" (Blanco 372). But even during the first half of the century domestic ideology already served as an instrument to confine female desire as a prophylactic gesture to stave off changes in the relations between the sexes that Spaniards perceived were occurring in other countries, especially France. Later, starting in the middle decades, domestic literature seems to have expressed in a more primary way the conflicts between different social orders and evolving gender roles: "During the decades of disturbance and revolution (1850–1880) when Spain's propertied classes were divided to the point of fragmentation by political, economic, and regional differences, the image of the naturally domestic, virtuous, and submissive woman seemed to become particularly important as a shared cultural norm that preserved traditional gender—and class—hierarchy" (Kirkpatrick, *Las románticas* 291).

As she traced the changes in sexual ideology of the "ángel del hogar," Aldaraca noted the basic contradiction in the concept of domestic life during the second half of the nineteenth century. The domestic sphere is seen as both intrinsic to the total social structure but also in opposition to the activities of the public sphere (55). There is a growing awareness of the family as a socializing agent, and therefore of the need to improve women's education to perform her socializing mission adequately. Even though it was still generally accepted that "women exist to please men" (Aldaraca, *El ángel* 60), the issues of authority and family structure came into sharper focus. Obedience, not forced but embraced as a sign of familial solidarity, became crucial to the family's survival and conflicts were to be avoided by voluntary self-regulation on the part of women.

The most difficult stage of domestic fiction to classify is clearly the period from 1880 to 1910. Despite competing literary traditions such as the social and the Naturalist novel, the pedagogic role of domestic fiction was not diminished but enhanced. That domesticity was still a discourse with wide currency is evident from such novels as *La prueba* and *Una cristiana* (1890), which doubtless served as an antidote to the climate of change that was sensed and condemned in every political and social sector. As customs, in the urban scene at least, grew more lax, the exhortation to maintain separate spheres for men and women, and to seduce women into loving their domestic role, proliferated in the popular press. In the last quarter of the century Spain saw a marked decrease in religious observance, debates in the press about divorce and separation, pressure from such notable feminists as Concepción Arenal to reform women's legal status, and increasing dissatisfaction with an outmoded educational system. On the other hand, social scientists such as Paloma Cepeda Gómez argue that the Civil Code of 1889, that should have marked a broadening of women's legal rights, only served to reinforce an already entrenched patriarchy.[19] The traditional notion of the family as a working unit felt the pressure of the labor needs of an increasingly industrialized society that resulted in ever more radically separated feminine and masculine spheres (Cepeda Gómez 193).

This contradictory stance on women is reflected in both the popular and the high culture of the period. Although Emilia Pardo Bazán frequently barraged the press with complaints about the treatment of women, her novel *La prueba* creates a powerful argument against change by showing that a woman's home service can reap both material and spiritual benefits. On the other hand, Pardo Bazán's Feíta and other similarly *liberated* heroines rebel against the notion that women are a lump of clay only waiting to be fashioned by the right man. Increasingly novels propose romantic compatibility and companionship as indicators of an ideal marriage, deriding marriages of economic convenience and other strategic alliances. And, while in Spanish society the nuptiality rates were rising sharply (Shubert 32), some women's novels rejected marriage altogether as an ideal state. Even the self-negating heroine of *La prueba* and *Una cristiana* goes against the bourgeois ideal of the perfect family by rejecting her second suitor in favor of a life of seclusion and religious devotion. That in Pardo Bazán's *Dulce Dueño* [Sweet master] (1911) the heroine, like her predecessor Elia, chooses seclusion over family can hardly be thought of as a success of the bourgeois patriarchal discourse of the family as the soul of a society.

We are only beginning to study how the collective or social masochism of women's writings promoted or helped to maintain specific economic, political, and social policies and institutions as they evolved over time. While space does not permit me to explore this issue in depth, my assumption is that of Rosalind Coward, that the fictional subordination or liberation of women is necessarily contingent upon a complex history (278). The way fictional women defined themselves as relegated to the domestic sphere expresses preferences based on conveniences that made the household a public issue in the guise of a private experience. This kind of sexual politics, or bio-politics, secured the subordination of women by making them believe that their subjectivity was expendable, or at least contingent. Idealizing women's powerlessness secures an immobilization that is necessary in order not only for men to contemplate their plenitude in a placid, feminine mirror, but to preserve their hegemony over the public sphere that (obviously tenuous if it needs to be legislated) is not by *nature* of gender theirs. In the words of Kirkpatrick, "the emerging ideology of domesticity helped to provide the psychological and moral separation and subordination of women that was more appropriate to bourgeois culture" (*Las románticas* 59).

Teresa de Lauretis, in her work *Alice Doesn't*, recently asked whether women's films express the proof of female desire or if they only reflect dominant patriarchal forms. She concluded that even in women's films, the issue is to seek women's consent to be the object of male desire, because, "[a]las, it is still for him that women must be seduced into femininity and be remade again and again as woman" (155). Similarly, my conclusion is that in the domestic novel social masochism was first and foremost the expression of this impulse to seduce women into femininity for specific historical reasons. Recently this reciprocal relationship between sociopolitical events and literature was demonstrated by Mary Poovey in *Uneven Developments: The Ideological Work of Gender in Mid-Victorian England* and Nancy Armstrong in her ground-breaking *Desire and Domestic Fiction: A Political History of the Novel*. Poovey studies the representation of woman as a site of cultural contestation to the legal, religious, and medical institutions that presided over social conduct. Nancy Armstrong describes various stages in the rise of the British novel in relation to historical events that either explained or required the novel as a predictable outgrowth of the conduct book for bourgeois ladies. Her great insight is that the words of women, both as writers and fictional speakers of words, not only shaped familial and sexual relations but also intersected with political events in determined ways, thus challenging the notion of domestic fiction's ahistoricity. What is most startling is her suggestion that the desire for the appearance of the domestic angel actually preceded her historical reality. Similarly, I would argue that the fictional "ángel del hogar" was as productive as it was reflective of her material existence.[20] In other words, Spain produced a great "rhetorical support for the ideology of domesticity" (Aldaraca, *El ángel* 19) even before that domesticity was an absolute necessity for its workforce arrangements.[21] The discourse of domesticity, valid for the bourgeois class, could hardly be more than an ideal for the working classes. As Matilde Cuevas de la Cruz and Luis Enrique Otero Carvajal have argued, this disjunction served to further differentiate the middle from the popular classes, who, nonetheless, were heavily influenced by bourgeois values that in the end imposed themselves "as part of a lengthy process concurrent with changes in the social and material conditions of society" (255).

Armstrong's work on the British novel corroborates my findings with respect to the Spanish novel and also my readings of American novels of about the same period. This is not to suggest a transhistorical interpretation of narrative that would be a negation of its contextual specificity. Indeed, it should be emphasized that opening our inquiry to more than one national literature will probably convince us more than ever that, to learn something about desire and fantasy, we have to study specific configurations of desire as they change and evolve over time. Studying the novel is one way to advance studies on the specificity of sexual arrangements, and the historical changes in gender construction reflected in them. If, as Deleuze argues, literature provides a symptomatological shorthand for society's perversions, we have to relate the history of desire to the history of narrative. I argue, however, that these perversions are not gender-neutral, and that when we study what is perverse in literature we cannot (or cannot yet) abandon the category of gender. This was convincingly demonstrated in Adrienne Munich's recent book on gender and interpretation in Victorian culture, in which she shows how seemingly private fantasies, like the Andromeda in chains she studies, become national obsessions, "passed around as an agreed upon tale" (14). What is called for in these cases is a cultural analysis and a recognition of the collective nature of certain obsessions.

One particularly entrenched but unexplored obsession of nineteenth-century women's literature and essays is the Virgin Mary. Every Spanish woman carried about with her images of the Virgin that were her special models. Nearly every Spanish woman poet wrote poems in praise of the Virgin and some even dedicated their entire literary output to devotional hymns to her or other women saints. She was a symbol not only of subservience and sacrifice, but also, paradoxically, of women's influence, respectability, and virtue. Faustina Sáez de Melgar argued in her article "La mujer de ayer, la de hoy y la de mañana" [The woman of yesterday, today, and tomorrow] that the appearance of the Virgin marked an important stage in civilization, which, she believed, was moving slowly toward social perfection through the civilizing effects of the Virgin cult and Christianity in general. So powerful was this attraction of the Virgin Mary for Spanish women that women novelists often *blessed* their heroines with a male recognition of their Virgin-like qualities. In MacPherson's *El hilo del destino*, the artist Angelis creates a masterpiece based on his imaginary ideal of the Virgin Mary. MacPherson brings to life the portrait in the figure of the orphaned María, who perfectly embodies the divine ideal that Angelis had *imagined* but did not believe existed:

> Aquel rostro virginal que su imaginación concibiera, aquella Vírgen cuyo original imaginara, a quien en su ilusión revistió de todos los atributos que desaba para la que había de formar la felicidad de su vida, aquella, en fin, fantástica ilusión, sueño dorado, poesía encantadora con que hasta entonces alimentara su mente y su corazón, dejaba ya de ser una quimera. (2:22)

> That virginal face conceived by his imagination, that Virgin whose original he had imagined, whose face he endowed with all the attributes that he wished for the woman who would be the happiness of his life, that, finally, fantastic illusion, golden dream, enchanting poetry with which he fed his mind and heart, was no longer a chimera.]

It was certainly no easier for Spanish women to pattern themselves after such a perfect nineteenth-century version of the Madonna than it is for today's teenagers to emulate their modern Madonna. The fact is, however, that the illusion was made to seem so appealing that women endeavored to embody this divine perfection at the highest level imaginable, and this made, of course, for a very *humbling* experience that women's domestic fiction often exploited much more thoroughly than men's.

In conclusion, domestic literature, especially the more radically oriented fictions of Sinués de Marco and others directed toward middle-class women, is grounded in a number of historical realities as well as a set of very entrenched notions about women's masochistic nature. Among the historical contingencies are Spain's (albeit slow) transition to capitalism in the mid- to late nineteenth century; the Catholic church's struggle to maintain influence and visibility despite emerging secular philosophies and a decrease in religious observance of the cult, and the rise of anticlericalism and the perceived threat from European Protestantism. Women of whatever class or age were not expected to play a role in any of these historical changes nor to have any interest in doing so. Bourgeois women, with more time on their hands than the larger sectors of proletariat women, were thought to be easily corrupted by the materialism of the age and were consequently judged in need of constant training and supervision. On the other hand, women were thought to be childlike and close to nature (especially the domain of flowers and animals), and subservient. Logically, then, woman's place, her refuge and spiritual center, was the home. And yet the home, as a property, did not legally belong to her, so her role in it was one of caretaker and caregiver.[22] As far as women were concerned (the opposite held true for men), material possessions were corrupting while dependency and regressive behavior desirable. The only women who thought about sex were moral misfits.

Only a few voices counteracted the incredible tide of literature exhorting women to accept their secondary and sedentary status. One particularly virulent attack on traditional social-sexual norms came from the intrepid Pardo Bazán, whose comments on Concepción Arenal's concept of the Spanish housewife provide a fitting conclusion to this chapter on the literary representations of feminine oppression and servitude. By 1893, only three years after writing *La prueba* and *Una cristiana*, Pardo Bazán agrees with Arenal that the major obstacle to a woman's growth and transformation, is the ideal of the domestic angel, "the virtuous, prudent, economical, wife and loving mother, whose perfections are summarized in this by now classical phrase, 'the woman who thinks of nothing except her house, her husband and her children.'" Because this ideal is so universally accepted, it is difficult to recognize its pernicious effects. The future, however, will belong to a different woman. Women are not, as she had once thought, condemned to perpetual infancy, "quiet, petrified, for the rest of time": "As society and men reorient themselves, it will be impossible for women not to change along with them. The home can no longer be a woman's entire world, and the forces of her spirit should not consume her there without her having an harmonious influence on society. The housewife is already an anachronism that contributes nothing to human progress" (*La mujer española* 190–91).

Fig. 5. "Conformidad."

# Chapter 3

# Desire and Knowledge

*[E]l patrimonio de la mujer son los grillos de la esclavitud.*

*[Woman's patrimony are the chains of slavery.]*

—Rosalía de Castro, *Lieders*

IN CHAPTERS 1 AND 2 the discussion focused on the struggles of mostly middle-class women whose lives were shaped by social and religious norms that confined them to the domestic sphere for better or worse. Here and in Chapter 4, dedicated to the novels of Rosalía de Castro (1837–85) and Emilia Pardo Bazán, I explore some of the ways women authors who were less enamored of the domestic ideal represented feminine desire to their readers. The goal of this chapter is to examine how women characters' private and social existences intersected and to demonstrate that the kind of desire promoted by what Castro perceived as a *sick* society was an issue of sustained interest even though she did not, like Sinués de Marco or Gimeno de Flaquer, write essays on women's conduct, education, or condition.

Another important feature of Castro's novels that warrants attention
is the role of men and civilization in general in defining not only the
spheres in which women acceptably move, but their desires and needs.
The role of men in the figuring of feminine desire against the backdrop
of a decadent society will be examined both from a social and a sexual
standpoint. This role evolved in an unusual way from 1859 when
Castro's *La hija del mar* [The daughter of the sea] was first published,
through 1861 *(Flavio)* and 1864 *(Ruinas* [Ruins]) until the appearance
of *El caballero de las botas azules* [The gentleman with the blue boots]
in 1867, which, even though preoccupied with the theme of feminine
desire, features as its protagonist one of the most unusual male characters one is likely to come across in nineteenth-century women's fiction.

The sensitive and lovelorn soulmates that stand by María in Böhl
de Faber's *La Gaviota* [The seagull] also flourish in Rosalía de Castro's
*Flavio, Ruinas*, and *El primer loco* [The craziest man] (1881) in which
women are primarily the tyrants, materialists, or *belles dames sans merci*
that Castro inherited from her Romantic models. But the real evil in
Castro's novels, which allows us to connect her not only with Böhl de
Faber but the bourgeois novelists that were her contemporaries, such
as Sinués de Marco, is civilization, a destructive force that always
contaminates the relationship between men and women. While the
untutored woman-child of nature often represents the wild thing that
tempts heroes to the brink of reassuring convention in male-authored
texts of the period, what is wild, uncontrollable, and extremely dangerous for both men and women characters of women's novels is often
that which has been touched by the hand of civilization. A commonplace in the majority of nineteenth-century novels by women authors
is that women are good or evil, happy or miserable in proportion
to their proximity to highly organized social structures or economic
affluence. The difference in Castro's novels is that the home is not imagined as a place where escape from civilization can be effected through
feminine virtue, which explains the lack of domestic proselytizing
in her fiction that is so blatant in the writings of Sinués de Marco.

*La hija del mar* is Castro's tumultuous first novel (published when
she was only twenty-two years old) and the one in which this mistrust
of civilization is most acute. At issue for the *sea-child* and her mother
is freedom, a notion that differs radically for men and women. For
the former, it means the ability to exercise control over others; for
women, it spells free movement and control over their own bodies.

Consequently, illegitimacy, abandonment, and social castration paradoxically provide women with a pretext, not to extend their presence
or influence beyond normal family relations into a public sphere, but
at least to live a quiet home life and to roam about outside the home
wherever the effects of man's civilization do not reach. On the other
hand, contact with men translates into the severest forms of seclusion
and domination.[1] For years the heroine Teresa and her adopted daughter Esperanza wander about the shores of a fishing village. When Teresa's husband suddenly returns, mother and daughter are literally
locked up as part of a project to *gentrify* them and subjugate them to
another's will. The connection between civilization, male domination,
and sexual exploitation, so often woven into women's fictions, provokes
an unusually angry outburst in Castro's narrator, who lectures to the
future rulers of the world:

> Hombres que gastáis vuestra vida al fuego devorador de la polí-
> tica; jóvenes de ardiente imaginación y de fe más ardiente; almas
> generosas que tantos bienes soñáis para esta triste Humanidad:
> pobres ángeles que Dios manda a la Tierra para sufrir el marti-
> rio, no pronunciéis esas huecas palabras "¡civilización, liber-
> tad!": no, no las pronunciéis; mirad a Esperanza y decidme
> después qué es vuestra civilización, qué es vuestra libertad.

> [You men who waste your lives in the devouring fires of politics;
> youths of ardent imagination and even more ardent faith; gener-
> ous souls who dream so much good for this sad Humanity:
> poor angels whom God sends to this earth to suffer martyrdom,
> do not pronounce those empty words "civilization, liberty!":
> no, do not pronounce them; look at Esperanza and then tell
> me, what is your civilization?, what is your liberty?]

Men should continue to raise their voices in a "hymn of redemption"
because there may come a day when their prayers are answered, predicts the narrator, but for that day to be a boon to women, it is men
who will have to change: "¡Pero por Dios, no seáis egoístas como los
hombres que pasaron! . . . El día en que el mundo se eche en vuestros
brazos, acordaos de Esperanza . . . ; es decir: ¡de la mujer débil, pobre, ignorante!" (96) (For God's sake, don't be as egotistical as the men

before you . . . The day the world throws itself at your feet, remember Esperanza . . . ; that is, the weak, poor, and ignorant woman!).

This, obviously, is not the conservative cry of some of Castro's contemporaries who would lock up their heroines in a domestic fortress *for their own safety*. Rather, this passage betrays a fundamental mistrust of civilization, here associated with male coercion and treachery.[2] Rich finery, servants, and a well-furnished house are held out to the mother and daughter in exchange for sexual submission and obedience. When Teresa refuses to look the other way as Alberto fondles her adopted daughter, she is immediately dispossessed of her position and clothes. Unlike Galdós's tragic materialists, however, she wisely opts for the obscurity but relative safety of a fisherwoman: "Mucho me alegro que me devuelva lo que un día me ha arrebatado juntamente con mi tranquilidad. Abandono de muy buena gana, y no por obedecerle, este terciopelo cambiándolo gustosa por mi antiguo traje de pescadera" (113) (I am content to return to the life that one day you took from me together with my peace of mind. I willingly and gladly abandon, and not to obey you, this velvet for my old fisherwoman's dress). The tragic events resulting from Alberto's villainy prevent Teresa and Esperanza from ever returning to the secluded life they led as unattached women; they are only reunited in death, when Teresa finds her daughter washed up on the beach that they both loved to roam.[3] Unable to walk the fine line dividing what *La hija* construes as the shores of male influence and power and the sea of feminine expansiveness and unbounded love, Teresa and Esperanza wash up on the shore as so much flotsam of a wasteful society.

## The Impossible Man

All of Castro's novels are studies of overwhelming passion and tragic obsession with an impossible ideal of love, a love destroyed by proximity to the salon, the city, and society in general. With the exception of *La hija*, typically a nature-loving man falls in love with an over-civilized woman who causes him endless suffering. In *Flavio* the hero manages to "arrancar la dorada espina" (pull out the gilded thorn), while the heroes of both *El primer loco* and *Ruinas* are driven mad by love. The Becquerian legend provides many examples of this Romantic love story, but in *Flavio* there occurs an interesting transposition of the Romantic plot that bears indirectly on the topic of feminine desire. The protagonist Mara both embodies and contradicts the conventional Romantic love object. She is at the same time the *coqueta* (flirt) who trifles with men's hearts, and a poetess who complains bitterly when men refuse to acknowledge women's innate talent for translating into words their deepest thoughts (286). Which side of her character surfaces depends on her proximity to city life: frivolous and conventional when in *society*, Mara identifies with the misunderstood woman poet when she is away from society's influence. Similarly, Flavio both is and is not the obsessed lover of Castro's *El primer loco* and *Ruinas*. He goes through all the gestures of nearly going mad and nearly drowning himself but he eventually becomes a sad double of the solitary and cynical man he meets one night as he escapes to the country. A blueprint for his future self, the mysterious stranger reveals to Flavio the truth about the lie of women's beauty:

> no son más que el juguete que Dios ha puesto en medio de nuestro camino para amenizar nuestros momentos de ocio y de hastío. Cómo con una sola palabra, con una mirada, las arrojamos de su pedestal de barro, haciéndolas caer a nuestros pies implorando compasión. Ellas derraman entonces lágrimas que ruedan como perlas por sus mejillas; pero sus lágrimas y sus gemidos son solo una hermosa mentira. (238)

> [they are nothing more than a plaything God has placed in our way to gladden our idle or weary moments. With just a word, a look, we throw them down from their clay pedestal, causing them to fall to our feet to implore our compassion. And then they weep tears that roll like pearls down their cheeks; but their tears and groans are only a beautiful lie.]

Heeding the stranger's warning, Flavio becomes a calculating materialist who marries for money and drives other women mad with grief. Meanwhile, in an unusual displacement, Mara becomes the sad, steadfast lover who retires to a small country property to pass her youth remembering "cierta imagen que algún día había pasado ante ella sonriendo para no volver más" (472) (a certain image that one day had passed smiling before eyes never to return). Thus, the quest for the

ideal love undergoes a transformation in Castro's works that reverses
the gender of the archetypal Romantic couple. In this shift, the civilization versus nature dichotomy mentioned in connection with *La hija
del mar* plays a primary role: society, rather than any innate gender
differences, polarizes men and women. Characters whose obsession
reaches fever pitch in the salon or ballroom find solace and abatement
only when they escape the city.

There is another important difference in gender representation between *Flavio* and Castro's Romantic models that has direct bearing on
the following discussion of desire in *El caballero de las botas azules*.
Flavio's attraction (as Mara learns too late) resides in his wildness,
fierce eyes, dark skin, and bizarre behavior. Gradually, readers surrender to the visual representation of Flavio's dress and looks, which never
happens with Mara's character. In fact, there is no fetishization of the
female face or body in any of Castro's works; it is chiefly men who
are the object of a loving narrative gaze, and so it is the topic of male
attraction that inaugurates this discussion of feminine desire.[4]

In *Flavio*, the male figure represents alternately the child (Mara repeatedly refers to him as her "hijo") and the dark mysterious lover,
but it is the latter representation that most enthralls women. Flavio is
the counterpart of Montenegro of *Ruinas* whose blond beauty startles
a roomful of society ladies, or the truculent Pedro of *El primer loco*
whose face bespeaks "algo que se escapaba al análisis de los más sus-
picaces y versados en el arte de sorprender por medio de los rasgos de
la fisionomía los secretos del corazón y las cualidades del alma" (839)
(something that escaped the analysis of the most suspicious and versed
in the art of discovering the secrets of the heart and the qualities of
the soul by means of studying physical features). The physical attraction and wildness of these Heathcliffian figures stands not so much
for a sexual lure as for some spiritual, unfettered quality that may very
well have appealed to bourgeois women who spent their lives locked
in stifling social conventions.

All of these men scornfully defy the laws of science and reason and
give full rein to sentiment and impulse, qualities that Spanish society
undervalued and associated with the uncontrollable feminine nature.
What women admire in Pedro, writes the narrator, is the "exceso de
sensibilidad y de sentimiento de que ciertos individuos se hallan do-
tados, y que busca su válvula de seguridad, sus ideales, su consuelo,
no en lo convencional, sino en lo extraordinario y hasta en lo imposible

también" (846) (the excess of sensitivity and sentiment with which certain people are endowed, and which searches for its security valve, its ideals, its consolation, not in the conventional, but in the extraordinary and perhaps even in the impossible). What is desired but impossible to possess in Castro's works is not the ephemeral female specter of the Becquerian legend, but a man so extraordinary, novel, and unconnected with the structured, banal existence of middle- and upper-class society that he cannot be had; he is *impossible,* and none of Castro's characters ever get more than a passing glimpse of him.

## Feminine Desire and *El caballero de las botas azules*

Most nineteenth-century women writers were not struggling middle-class intellectuals for whom publishing meant putting food on the table.[5] Not all lived a life entirely free from financial cares at some stage of their careers, but most enjoyed educational privileges that alone afforded women the opportunity to pursue a literary career. Though these writers were not university-educated, all had access to private libraries, were able to travel and purchase book subscriptions and periodicals, and were, to varying degrees, relieved of the more onerous domestic duties that fell to house servants. The problem was that the notion of a career was anathema to woman's mission as perceived by the very social classes that provided women the luxury of time and opportunities for educational pursuits. In other words, if women were driven to write, they were forced, to a greater or lesser degree, to reject the life-styles of other women in their same class. Viewed in this light, their frequent exhortations to working-class women to seek more education or to bourgeois women to learn a profession as a hedge against bad times, were more than the ideological strategy of a ruling class anxious to preserve its privileged idleness by encouraging the popular classes to honor the work ethic. Similarly, their vituperative condemnation of idle upper-class women must be seen in the context of their personal struggle for recognition as writers. Pardo Bazán's proselytizing and the social criticism that Castro wove into her poetry and fiction were part of a dialogue that women writers carried on among themselves as well as with the women and men of the ruling classes who scornfully equated feminine labor with poverty.

In *El caballero de las botas azules*, this dialogue took the form of scathing social satire against aristocratic women or their bourgeois elite imitators, whose desires are channeled into conspicuous consumption, idleness, and frivolous pastimes. In fact, Castro spoke to many of the social issues that would be taken up more militantly by such authors as Emilia Pardo Bazán. But it is not enough, says her narrator, simply to reorganize women's time by instituting a "Tertulia" (gathering) dedicated to reviving the "feminine" art of weaving. Castro's novels offer the subtle suggestion that women might be ready for a different kind of *labor* with the pen substituting the loom. *El caballero* does not attempt to portray ideal family life, then, but to explore the ways feminine desire is misunderstood or misdirected.

A woman writer in the nineteenth century was an oddity, which made it all the more difficult for her to convince her reading public of the literary value of her writing. Castro was alternatively fêted or ignored by the press and almost always judged for whatever in her work best exemplified the sentiments conventionally called "feminine."[6] But instead of reevaluating in a more positive light what I imagine critics will soon be calling Castro's *écriture féminine*,[7] this section focuses on the multifaceted representations of desire in her most important prose fiction. Of particular interest here are the problematic conjunction of social and sexual desires that differ for women characters of different classes, the implicit condoning of women's desire to write and to be recognized as a writing subject, and women's desire to know and its possible relation to the death drive.

Generally, Castro's wealthy women are portraits of excess and this excess has provided a critical focus for questions concerning Castro's class ideology. Already possessing every material advantage, they either become the consumers of men's hearts, or they seek after whatever is new, wasting their lives and those of others in pursuit of anything *different* to be the first in their circle of friends to possess. Such are most of the women of *El caballero de las botas azules*, written in 1867 when Castro was thirty years old and struggling to secure her literary reputation.[8] *El caballero* documents the change brought about in the lives of a number of mostly wealthy Madrid socialites as a result of their contact with a strange, seductive man who calls himself the "duque de la Gloria" (the Duke of Glory). Although the women and men of this novel are equally obsessed with the bizarre figure of the Duke, their desire, in fact, is only the same in that it is displaced onto the same object and impossible to satisfy. The difference between women's and men's desires resides in the complexity and undecidability of the former compared to the banality and predictability of the latter, as I hope the following sections will demonstrate.

One of the Duke of Glory's principal activities is to enthrall women sexually and then to exploit this fascination in order to ridicule their social lives and their lack of serious-minded occupation. In the process, he not only shows women the folly of their highly organized social customs, but teaches them important lessons about the mechanics of desire. From the viewpoint of desire, *El caballero* is one of the most fertile texts of Spanish literature, a catalogue of all the many dissatisfactions and drives that the novel attributes to a decadent society, in which the pursuit of pleasure never translates into satisfaction or the abatement of desire, no matter what other advantages (money, beauty, or class) that a woman possesses. But beyond the admonitions regarding feminine excess and vain desires, this novel explores the dissatisfactions that define us as subjects *because* we desire, regardless of the appropriateness of the desired object.

Paraphrasing Lacan, Jean Laplanche and J.-B. Pontalis describe desire as the gap between need and demand (483), a difficult concept that is nevertheless useful for exploring the workings of desire in *El caballero*. Need, of course, is a Freudian concept that is easily grasped: biological and instinctual, our primary needs (such as milk) are—it is hoped—satisfied by a conscientious caregiver and have no specificity in our forming consciousness. Until such time as we recognize that these objects of need are withdrawable, we have no notion of either an imaginary or symbolic order. Demands, on the other hand, are always directed at an other, and while demands are tied to specific objects (a demand for a material object, or for a person's love or attention) that are either withheld or supplied, demand is never really satisfied, because "the demand is always for something else, for the next thing the other can give, for the thing that will 'prove the other's love'" (Grosz 61). Demand, then, is really for the *other*. However, to possess or be fused with the other (our desire) implies the annihilation of the self; what really is demanded is an impossible plenitude addressed to a pre-Oedipal mother who is no longer accessible.

Desire is not a demand because it does not depend on the other to whom it is addressed, only on being "absolutely recognized" (Laplanche and Pontalis 122). Always repressed, desire is never articulated; rather, it speaks through our demands. It is that which we lack and which our demands both obscure and leave traces of. Elizabeth Grosz, also paraphrasing Lacan, writes: "Desire desires the desire of an other. Desire is thus a movement, an energy that is always transpersonal, directed to others" (65). This desire engages with an *other* not as a person, but as a place, which is the "locus of Law, Language, and the Symbolic" (Grosz 67). For this reason, desire cannot be conceived separately from the symbolic order; desire and language are what defines the subject from a psychoanalytic point of view (Grosz 67). *El caballero* offers readers many instances of how desire falls between need and demand; in other words, how desire itself seeks recognition, not as a desire *for*. In fact, desire insinuates itself so forcefully and at so many levels that it eventually becomes the antagonist of Castro's novel, a fact that has been largely overlooked by *El caballero*'s critics.

In recent years, psychoanalytic criticism has been studying dissatisfaction and desire as the very propulsive forces essential to the production of all narrative forms. Glossing Laplanche and Pontalis, critic Peter Brooks describes desire as a "perpetual want for (of) a satisfaction that cannot be offered in reality" (55). In *El caballero*, this insatiable desire is what spins the narrative, *driving* all of the characters to become part of the Duke's story. But the nature of each woman's desire is much more than what meets the eye, literally the Duke's blue boots and feather tie on which women invest their libido and which have their obvious fetishistic significance. Nor are women's demands precisely what the novel makes a spectacle of, although the Duke makes it his business to expose and ridicule what women say they want. *El caballero*'s critics usually define the novel as a condemnation of materialism and idleness, evils that inspired many a bourgeois woman to take to a career in writing. However, what is more significant than the nature of women's demands is the fact that these demands are left unsatisfied, and that women do not even *know* what they want. In fact women's general, enduring dissatisfaction serves as a material demonstration of the lesson that the androgynous muse tries to teach the faltering writer in the introduction to the novel: that is, that "the objects of our desires are always substitutes for the objects of our desires" (Bersani and Dutoit, *Forms* 66).

All narratives begin with a surfeit of desire that has reached a state of such intensity that "movement must be created, action undertaken, change begun" (Brooks 38). This desire takes the form of demands or requests that are put forth by a character in an attempt to overcome an enemy, fill a lack, or resolve a problem. *El caballero* begins with a dialogue, interspersed with stage directions, between a muse and a man, in which the man's failures and shortcomings are weighed against his ambitions. The man, a would-be writer, longs to achieve literary greatness, but has been unable to devise a "nuevo estilo" (new style) to secure his immortality. While he has overcome his lowly origins and even achieved a measure of success in the world of politics as a "diputado y ministro" (a congressman and minister) he still has not risen above the legions of mediocre writers in an age so dark for literature that inspiration walks scandalously arm in arm with any drunk, doorman, or sergeant. What remains to be written in a world filled with too much literature?

> Poemas, dramas, comedias, historias universales y particulares, historias por adivinación y por intuición, por inducción y deducción; novelas civilizadoras, económicas, graves, sentimentales, caballerescas, de buenas y malas costumbres, coloradas y azules, negras y blancas . . . , de todo género, en fin, variado, fácil y difícil. (572)

> [Poems, dramas, comedies, universal and personal stories, soothsayer and intuitive, inductive and deductive stories; civilizing novels, economic, grave, sentimental, chivalrous novels, novels of good and bad customs, smutty and fanciful novels, black and white novels . . . , of every possible genre, then, easy or difficult.]

The muse who comes to the aid of the aspiring author is, appropriately, "Novelty," who has been summoned since the age of Cain to satisfy men's cravings for the new.[9] The reason men will always desire her, she explains, is that whatever she becomes for them, a steam engine in the 1880s or something called *air travel* or *perpetual motion* in the "future" (579), will never be enough to satisfy—and thus bring an end to—their curiosity. In other words, the muse personifies desire, who, she says, bore her. She was engendered by doubt, "'esa cosa' que no se explica" (that which cannot be explained) and raised "a la sombra de los pensamientos venales y de las imaginaciones ardorosas" (578) (in the shadow of venal thoughts and ardent imaginations). Thus the existence of the muse depends on the existence of a subject whose desire "no se explica" (cannot be explained) but who imagines, nevertheless, the possibility of fulfilling it.

Following this and other detailed information regarding her origins, we can interpret the muse's lesson to the man as an expression of the most primal desire, defined in Lacanian terms as demands unfulfilled, a residue of the repressed that is reinstituted as language and that forms the true subject of this discourse on desire. The muse teaches that desire cannot be fulfilled because it seeks to recuperate an infantile satisfaction (now lacking) that we do not recognize consciously but that finds expression in narrative desire (and the desire to narrate as Brooks shows). For this reason, satisfying desire is tantamount to death, and this too figures into the muse's lesson. Once the man's desire is fulfilled, once Madrid's literary elite recognizes his work as the "libro de los libros" (the book of books), the Duke disappears and the novel abruptly ends, leaving behind a roomful of women whose stories have become now suddenly obsolete, but whose misery still binds them in a chain of desire that is still in some sense *alive* in them. As Brooks aptly put it, "Narrative is hence condemned to *saying* other than what it *would mean*, spinning out its movement toward a meaning that would be the end of its movement" (56). It is not the fulfillment of the wish that each woman harbors secretly that matters, but the way all of the women are *framed* by their vain and endless desire, a desire the book explicitly wants us to recognize as insatiable and deadly, but at the same time vital and misunderstood.

We find the clues to the nature of this desire in the story's frame. The frame is an allegory of how narration is produced by desire, how it is, in fact, a displacement or metonymy for a lack that it is the frame's business to obscure and the narration's to reveal. By this I mean that we know from the frame that there would be no story to tell at all if the man did not lack something he coveted, yet what he covets is only mediated through the desires of others expressed in the form of a narrative. In this way *El caballero* allegorizes desire not just as a social ill, but as "esa cosa" (that something) that causes stories to come into being. While the frame story is in many ways what Brooks would call a classical male plot of ambition (39), it frames a number of subsidiary "female" plots that are concerned with problems of identity, knowledge, and feminine self-assertion.

Taken together, the frame and the ensuing narrative of *El caballero* have a strong affinity with the medieval exemplum. The hypothesis upon which rests the ideological telos of *El caballero* is that men insatiably want something that, being new, has no name. This narrative given is then tested on the upper-middle and ruling classes of Madrid society. The desire for literary inspiration and innovation, the theme of the frame, is subsequently displaced onto the strange objects with which the would-be writer adorns himself after his muse transforms him into the "Duke of Glory." What the novel shows, and what we have largely overlooked in our analyses, is that the libido expended on these objects are testimonials to the complexities of feminine desire.

## The Allure of the Masculine

From the beginning, gender plays a crucial role in *El caballero*'s conception of novelty and attraction. Men and women fixate on the blue boots and feather tie for different reasons as determined by class, profession, but above all, gender.[10] When, in the frame story, the muse finally appears in person before the aspiring author, her gender is indeterminate. The writer is shocked at her appearance, finding her too unusual, even for a man like himself on the verge of suicide because the desired "idea virgen" (virgin idea) eludes him. The description of the muse appears in italics, as part of the elaborate stage directions that draw readers' attention to the frame story's scenic quality. The muse's attire, sexual allure, and, at the same time, sardonic expression forecast the identity the writer will have to assume in the story proper in order to gain fame for himself among Madrid's wealthy novelty seekers who constitute the reading elite:

> El humo se disipa y aparece una figura elevada y esbelta que viste larga y ceñida túnica, calza unas grandes botas de viaje y lleva chambergo. Su rostro es largo, ovalado y de una expresión ambigua: tiene los ojos pardos, verdes y azules, y parecen igualmente dispuestos a hacer guiños pícarescamente o languidecer de amor. Un fino bozo sombrea el labio superior de su boca, algo abultada, pero semejante a una granada entreabierta,mientras dos largas trenzas de cabellos le caen sobre la mórbidaespalda medio desnuda. En una mano lleva un

látigo y en la otra un ratoncito que salta y retoza con inimitable gracia, mientras aprieta entre los dientes un cascabel. (577)

[The mist dissipates and a tall and slender figure appears, dressed in a long belted tunic and wearing travel boots and a chambourg hat. Its face is long and oval, with an ambiguous expression; large brown, green and blue eyes seem ready both to wink picaresquely or languish from love. A fine fuzz shadows the upper lip of the somewhat thick mouth, somewhat resembling a half-open pomegranate, while two long braids fall on the delicate, partially bared shoulders. In one hand is a whip and in the other a mouse that jumps and frolics with inimitable grace while clasping in its teeth a bell.]

A mixture of sensuality and gaiety, a portrait of the street entertainer with the face and body exuding a morbid sexuality: these are some of the attributes the muse will bestow on the Duke of Glory. On the other hand, the muse's sexual indeterminacy is translated into an exaggerated masculinity in the novel proper. The muse dwells in a world of fantasy and chimeras, she literally can be anything she wishes, while the Duke finds himself in a world that prizes sexual prowess and difference. As a result, his seduction resides not only in the novelty of his accoutrements but in his *masculine* sexual appeal. The muse as stage director, then, has understood that androgyny will not be conducive to the fulfillment of the Duke's seductive mission and so she creates a more fitting masculine persona for him:

> Un joven y elegante caballero, vestido de negro, que calzaba unas botas azules y deslumbradoras que le llegaban hasta las rodillas y cuyo fulgor se asemejaba al fósforo que brilla entre las sombras, se hallaba en pie a la entrada de la antecámara agitando en una mano el cordón de la campanilla, mientras con la otra daba vueltas a una varita de ébano cubierta de brillantes, y en cuya extremidad se veía un enorme cascabel.
>
> Era el singularísimo y nunca bien ponderado personaje de elevada talla y arrogante apostura, de negra, crespa y un tanto revuelta, si bien perfumada, cabellera. Tenía el semblante tan uniformemente blanco como si fuese hecho de un pedazo de mármol, y la expresión irónica de su mirada ye de su boca era tal que turbaba al primer golpe el ánimo más serena. Sobre su

negro chaleco resaltaba además una corbata, blanca, que al
mismo tiempo era y no era corbata, pues tenía la forma exaltada
de un aguilucho de feroces ojos, con las alas abiertas y garras
que parecían próximas a clavarse en su presa. A pesar de todo
esto, el conjunto de aquel ser extraño era, aunque extraordinario
en demasía, armononioso y simpático. Sus botas, maravilla no
vista jamás, parecían hechas de un pedazo del mismo cielo, y
el aquilucho que por corbata llevaba hacía un efecto admirable
y fantástico; podía, pues, decirse de aquel personaje que más
bien que hombre era una hermosa visión. (587–88)

[A young and elegant gentleman, dressed in black with dazzling blue boots to the knee—so bright that they seemed like
a match lit in the shadows—stood in the vestibule, one hand
jangling the doorbell while the other twisted an ebony wand,
studded with jewels and crowned with an enormous cascabel.
This singular and never-before-seen man was a tall and im-
posing figure with curly black hair, slightly mussed but well
perfumed. His face was as white as if sculpted from a block of
marble and the expression of his eyes and mouth was such as
to trouble even the most serene soul. His black jacket was
adorned with a white tie that was and was not really a tie
because it was in the exalted form of an eaglet with fierce eyes,
wings spread open, and talons poised to clutch its prey. Despite
all this the overall impression of this strange figure, though
extraordinary in the extreme, was harmonious and pleasing.
His boots, the likes of which had never been seen, seemed made
from a piece of sky, and the eaglet that served as his tie gave
an admirable and fantastic effect. You could say that, more than
a person, this man was a beautiful vision.]

Wherever he goes, the Duke ostentatiously displays his symbols of
fairy-tale eccentricity combined with masculine power and prowess.
The diamond-studded wand for example, a sign that so conveniently
connects sovereign, masculine attributes both visual (genital) and abstract (fantastic), appeals to the Duke's admirers both audibly with its
tinkling bell, and visibly with its flashy diamonds. The predatory pose
of the eaglet tie, instead of threatening to clasp the throat of the wearer,
turns outward in the direction of whatever prey the Duke is facing.

The black clothes serve to set off the Duke's other accoutrements and to contrast with his marble-white face, mentioned so often that we begin to imagine it as some sort of nude display, a locus of intense physical attraction even though it is repeatedly described as a mask.

Finally, the blue boots exert a strange, mesmerizing effect over everyone, so large (to the knee as is mentioned repeatedly), unseamed (connoting perhaps their smoothness to the touch and their skinlike suppleness), and strangely colored. Their glow seems to increase in proportion to the passion with which the Duke is contemplated. For example, when he visits Casimira's boudoir, "las botas del duque despedían un fulgor que turbaba la mirada y el pensamiento . . . Quizás nunca habían aparecido más hermosas" (698–99) (the Duke's boots shone so brightly that they perturbed the body and the mind . . . Perhaps they had never seemed more beautiful). One is tempted to compare the Duke with certain animal species whose extravagant male display is adapted to attract female partners. Add to all this the Duke's piercing gaze, "penetrante como la punta de un puñal" (605) (penetrating like the point of a dagger), voice, "armonioso y dominador como el de las tempestades" (650) (harmonious and dominating like that of a tempest), and thick black curls, "aquel agrupamiento de ondeadas y recias crenchas, selva virgen o enmarañado laberinto de aliagas visto en una noche oscura" (670) (that crop of wavy, curly hair, a virgin forest or twisted labyrinth of furze seen on a dark night), and it is easy to imagine his seductive power as a masculine force, even without a Freudian interpretation of the phallic significance of his boots.

The desires that first produce and then are projected onto these complex objects and attributes proceed from many quarters that interact in complex ways. For example, the writer's desire to be desired coincides with the narrator's pretext for telling a story; desire sets the stage for the exemplum. "For desire to exist," according to Michael Riffaterre, "subjects must project their libidos onto the object and the predication expressing this projection must be negated or postponed. Otherwise, fulfillment would be attained and desire would cease to exist" (87). This means that desire is composed of a subject that desires and an object that both attracts and frustrates the subject (87). To prolong desire, and consequently to prolong the story, the man must be transformed from the desiring subject into the desired object. As such the Duke repeatedly displays himself to the residents of Madrid, and then suddenly withdraws, becoming unavailable to the desiring subjects he has created through his presence. He continues this ruse until he can be satisfied that he is the object of every other's desire, in other words, until he has successfully allegorized the above definition of desire: "Desire desires the desire of the other." Like the pagan priests of old, or the kings of all ages, says one frustrated character, "se deja ver poco y en momentos dados" (630) (he shows himself rarely and only at given times).

From the viewpoint of the characters, we can distinguish two types of libido, social and sexual, that either emanate from the struggling writer or are projected onto the alluring but elusive objects associated with the Duke's presence. As described by Riffaterre, social libido is the longing to obtain a certain social prestige or community standing (96). For example, prior to his metamorphosis, the Duke longs to excel above his peers because he desires to be recognized as a literary giant like Cervantes. In order to achieve this goal he sets out on a great adventure, to "bell the cat" as he often puts it, as the outrageous duque de la Gloria. For him to succeed, he must become the desire of the other, something that all of Madrid interprets as synonymous with literary success and knowledge. In this sense, he achieves partial success even before putting the bell on all of the "pedantes y malos escritores" (649) (pedants and bad writers) and publishing his own "libro de los libros" (book of books).

All of Madrid is buzzing with wonder and curiosity during the days following the arrival of the Duke. Ironically, the desire that the Duke inspires in others has nothing to do with the words for which he longs to be revered. His prestige results from men's ignorance rather than knowledge of his achievements and origins. Men interpret the Duke as whatever they believe will enhance their own social or political standing. For example, a certain general wants to be identified with him, believing that he has come to reform the Spanish army: "Viene a devolvernos el poder que hemos ejercido en tiempo de Alejandro" (607) (he has come to restore the power we once held in the times of Alexander). The secretary of a wealthy banker imagines the Duke has come to Madrid to establish a world bank (608) while others hope his mission is to preach a new political order, "cuyos principios entrañan la colosal ambición de Napoléon Primero y el mancomunismo de los mormones" (608) (whose principles would penetrate the ambition of Napoleon I and the Mormon congregation).

With the exception of Mariquita, the middle-class characters of the novel proper are anxious to associate with the Duke chiefly in order to enhance their class standing. The narration is particularly critical of this group of social climbers. Zuma, the Duke's servant, reports to his master that the middle class:

> se agita en su estrechez, semejante a un hormiguero. Las más comodadas sueñan y discurren cómo han de hacer vestidos de princesas, y las más pobres deliran con la seda y los encajes, mientras sus padres se afanan por otro lado en reunir a toda costa tesoros que han de gastar en una noche, con tal de que puedan brillar en ella a los ojos de mi señor. (675)

> [is squirming in its paucity, like ants in an anthill. The more comfortable dream and talk about how they are going to order the gowns of a princess, the poorer ones rave about silk and laces, while their fathers work furiously to gather at any price the treasure that will be spent on a single night, all so that they can shine in the eyes of my master.]

The collective desire of the daughters of the lawyer, the doctor, the lieutenant colonel, and the treasury worker is to form part of a social circle that by virtue of their fathers' professions is denied them. They are sarcastically referred to as Madrid's "aristocracia que, semejante a ciertas tisis, pudiera llamarse 'incipiente'" (725) (aristocracy that, like a certain stage of tuberculosis, is described as "incipient"). Clothing helps to blur the boundary between the middle class and the established aristocracy, as well as to ensure that the former are not confused with "la última clase de la sociedad" (730) (the lowest class). In a scene worthy of Galdós's *La de Bringas*, an ambitious professional-class mother tries to convince her husband of the importance of providing her daughters more funds for clothing and accessories in order to attract the Duke's attention. The husband, with only one hundred "duros" to last until the end of the month, flatly refuses, complaining of the extravagant consumption of "todo el producto de los negocios de España" (731) (Spain's entire national production). The narrator's frank condemnation of this social climbing voices a response to rising bourgeois ambitions that will be echoed time and again in the novels of succeeding decades: "A costa de vergüenzas y sacrificios tales va

Fig. 6. "Lo que sueñan las muchachas."

soportando la clase media el aparente fausto que la desdora y la pone
en su último trance" (732) (at the price of such humiliations and sacrifices the middle class supports its extravagant display that is tarnishing
it and leading to its downfall). Since Madrid's finest ladies are suddenly appearing in public with sky-blue dresses, feather hats, diamonds, and bells, the daughters of the professionals rush to emulate
them by donning what they believe to be portable class equalizers.

When he sees their useless display, however, the Duke adds his voice
of condemnation to the narrator's disapproving tone. The moral of the
Duke's lesson, his belling of the "bourgeois cat," so to speak, consists
of demonstrating that bourgeois women would do better to stay at
home doing piecework to supplement dowries than parading in public
trying to pass for aristocratic ladies. If a doctor works for a living, he
reasons, why not a doctor's wife and daughters:

> ¿Pertenecerán ustedes realmente a la clase media? Pues en ese
> caso, señoras, ¿por qué no querer calcetar gorros de dormir
> cuyo par da de ganancia seis duros? ¿No trabajan sus papás?
> Pues trabajen ustedes también, señoritas, ye déjense de esas
> apariencias de riqueza que ocultan una miseria vergonzosa y
> un orgullo tan ridículo como inútil. (759)

> [Do you truly belong to the middle class? Then in that case,
> ladies, why not knit sleeping caps that earn you six duros?
> Don't your fathers work? Well then, work also, young ladies,
> and stop dressing with such ostentation that only hides a
> shameful poverty and pride as ridiculous as it is useless.]

A less affluent class of women are raised in the working-class suburb
called the Corredora del Perro. The young women who live there are
subdued and timid, taught to scorn material goods of which they
possess very few. "Todas estas fruslerías han sido hechas para hacerles
gastar dinero a los ricos" (615) (all of those trinkets are made just to
waste the money of the rich), they are told. But at night, they too
dream of the goods they have admired on the spacious avenues and
squares of the city and they imagine themselves among all the elegant
and lovely women that circulate there (616).

Ironically, for the wretched Mariquita living in the shadow of the
neighborhood cemetery, the Duke does not represent the fulfillment

of a desire to rise above her lowly surroundings. What preoccupies her are not the "fruslerías" (trinkets) she can not afford to buy but the husband, a clean-shaven "sacristán," that her father has arranged for her to marry without consulting her wishes. A neighborhood gossip puts into words what Mariquita, with her "educación demasiado insociable" (619) (overly unsociable education), has only vaguely understood:

> es el caso que se manda que la mujer ame y respete al que se le ha dado para ser 'apoyo de su debilidad' —yo siempre he pensado, niña mía, que mejor que eso fueran dinero y buena salud—, y en fin, que le obedezca ye le cuide, y mil cosas más que solo la práctica enseña. . . . ¿Entendiste, Mariquita? Pues bien: te diré todavía, porque te quiero, que si el matrimonio es cruz, vale más andar sin cruz que con ella, que el buey suelto bien se lame, y que para una boca basta una sopa. (619–20)

> [it happens that a woman is ordered to love and respect the one given her as a "support in her weakness"—I have always thought, my child, that the best solutions for this were money and good health—and also that she obey him and take care of him and a thousand other things that only experience teaches you. . . . Do you understand, Mariquita? Well then, here's more, because I like you, if marriage is a cross, better to live without it than with it, for the unharnessed donkey licks himself best, and for one mouth one bowl of soup suffices].

When she glimpses the Duke in the cemetery, Mariquita is immediately taken with his powerful physical presence that contrasts so pitifully with her sacristan, "que cuanto más le veía, menos gusto tenía que mirarle, produciéndole enojos el solo recuerdo de los lazos cabellos" (621–22) (whom the more she saw, the less she wanted to look at; just the thought of his knotted strands of hair irritated her). Mariquita, then, does not associate the Duke with social and material advantages but with romantic excitement produced by physical beauty and exoticism. If her father has to marry her off to someone, it might as well be the tall, thin, pale-faced Duke with the blue boots up to the knee, and not the homely Melchor who reminds her classmates of a lizard.

Having unwittingly inspired this impossible love, the Duke feels
honor-bound to convince Mariquita of the unsuitability of their match.
He does this by satisfying her curiosity, that is, by informing her
that behind his youthful, masculine mask is really the wrinkled and
cadaverous face of an old man. When the mystery of his identity is
revealed, his novelty wears off for Mariquita, who resigns herself to
life without a husband. In compensation, the Duke explains to her
spurned lover how to become more seductive to women: he should
establish residence in the center of the city, grow a beard, and buy
some fashionable clothes. The stage is now set for Melchor and Mariquita to fall in love. We are left with the impression that in time
Mariquita will be attracted to this more appropriate suitor, from the
*right* class.


## What (Rich) Women Want

Because the Duke has taken the time to transform the "lizard" Melchor
into a lesser version of his seductive self, Mariquita is eventually compensated for her loss. But in the case of aristocratic ladies who fall
for his charms, the sacrifices the Duke demands are greater, and the
compensations none but the knowledge of their own folly and self-
enslavement. But what their impossible demands finally reveal is that
beyond women's sexual desire lies the will to know and understand
things, that is, to be in possession of the words that would make the
unknown familiar (named), that drives all of the women characters to
the brink of madness and masochistic behavior. The bulk of the novel
is dedicated to describing the passion the Duke inspires in Madrid's
most splendid ladies: the Creole poet Marcelina la Blonda, the cruel
Marquise de Mara-Mari, the exotic Casimira, the Countess de la
Pampa, and the beautiful Vinca Rúa. The catalogue of ladies who
throw themselves at the Duke's feet is so extensive that readers begin
to understand that what these women, who already possess all the
lovers and material goods imaginable, want is precisely what the Duke
in his prior existence longed for. They all want to *know* something and
they are willing to enslave themselves in order to obtain the knowledge
they seek. Thus the Duke's *belling* of the aristocratic cat involves providing women with the knowledge of their sex; he doesn't speak of the

mysteries they long to hear about the exotic world they think that the Duke symbolizes, but of what they are or have become as women: the slaves of men. Taken collectively, the stories of the Duke's lovers embody a subtle, and I believe as of yet unexplored, testimonial regarding women's enslavement to society, to misdirected whims, and, especially, to men. Some of the episodes of this testimonial may seem especially graphic and cruel, even misogynistic. Yet, as I shall discuss below, the sarcastic laugh of the masked poet only thinly masks the pity and commiseration of another, contradictory voice that makes itself heard immediately after every exaggerated scene demonstrating women's worthlessness, immorality, or stupidity. What women want, the narration implies, is much more complex than what meets the eye.

Although all of the rich women "fall in love" with the Duke, the libido that is transfixed on the Duke's boots and other attributes by these pleasure-seeking society women is both sexual and social, and yet, at the same time, something else. For example, Casimira desires the Duke, she says candidly, because she wants to be regarded by him "como superior a las demás mujeres" (705) (as superior to other women). A desire for distinction and uniqueness drives Casimira and her friends to throw themselves at the Duke's feet. But the sensual buildup to their expressions of love leaves little doubt that their passion for the Duke is also meant to be an expression of sexual desire. In the case of Casimira, her desire is so strong that she has become enslaved by it. She even offers the ultimate sacrifice, to forgo being the Duke's lover, and resign herself to being a masochistic object, an "esclava humilde y fiel entre todas las esclavas" (704) (a humble and faithful slave among all his other slaves). She would be willing as his "friend" to sacrifice all to prove her friendship, even to the point of playing the woman's part in a certain sadistic medieval marriage rite that the Duke describes in detail to test her force of will. In medieval times, says the Duke, slaves, especially love slaves, obeyed their masters:

> Algunas veces el noble caballero, montado en soberbio corcel, deja que su amada le siga a pie y jadeante. Desgarrados los pies de la pobre niña, tiñen de roja sangre las piedras del camino, y las blancas margaritas nacidas al pie de los pantanos se coloran tristemente cuando su planta fatigada las huella. Sus sienes laten con fuerza, le parece que va a faltarle con su apoyo la tierra que en torno de ella gira y se desvanece, confundiéndose

con el cielo, y apenas le quedan fuerzas para respirar el aire suficiente que le hace conservar un resto de vida. Mas él le dice: '¡Sígueme!', y ella, amenazando a la muerte, todavía corre y corre tras él hasta que llegan al castillo, y casi moribunda da a luz, en el pesebre en donde descansan los caballos, un hijo del noble castellano. Solo entonces él consiente en hacerla su esposa. (705–6)[11]

[Sometimes the nobleman, mounted on a superb charger, has his loved one run along behind him on foot. With her bleeding feet, the poor woman stains the stones of the road, and the white daisies beside the marshes are colored sadly when her tired foot steps on them. Her lungs gasp for air, it seems as though the earth were going to slip out from beneath her, the ground turns and fades about her, confusing itself with the sky, and she is barely able to take the breaths needed to keep her alive. But he shouts, 'Follow me!' and she, at death's door, runs on and on behind him until they arrive at a castle, and in the stable where the horses are kept, she, half-dead, gives birth to the son of the nobleman. Only then does he consent to take her as his wife.]

Although Casimira agrees to submit to this cruel test to demonstrate her complete submission to the Duke, it is not to obtain sexual gratification, but to experience the pleasure of knowing and understanding the mystery of the Duke's origins:

Mas si salgo victoriosa (ya he dicho que no pretendo ser la amante ni la esposa del señor duque), lo que sí pretendo es que en tal caso me haga su confidenta, la depositaria de sus secretos . . . , que me mire, en fin, como su amiga predilecta, como la única digna de ser llamada fuerte y fiel guardadora de los misterios que nadie sino yo entienda. Sí, señor duque: quiero saber su historia; quiero saber qué significan esa corbata y esas botas. (708)

[But if I am victorious (I have already told you that I do not demand to be the lover or the wife of the Duke), what I do want is to become his confidante, the depository of his secrets . . . , I

want him to regard me as his preferred friend, the only one
worthy of being the steadfast and faithful guardian of the mysteries that only I will understand. Yes, Sir Duke, I want to
know your history; I want to know the meaning of your tie and
those boots.]

The theme of female enslavement in relation to female knowledge
and desire is also pertinent to the Duke's encounters with the Countess
Pampa, whose principal occupation is hosting balls and playing seductive games with a variety of eager suitors. Laura de la Pampa and her
friends are mockingly called "independientes" (independents) by their
male friends because they are capricious and unfaithful. For example,
Laura is admonished by her cousin Carlos because she exemplifies the
"cáncer" that is devouring modern society (637). She retorts that she
satisfies herself sexually as the only avenue of escape from "el círculo
estrecho" (636) (tight circle) that men prescribe for women of her class.
Even when women seduce men, she complains to her friend Casimira,
who is really seduced? "¿ . . . si ellos son los que triunfan y nosotras
las que nos rendimos?" (639) (if they are the ones who triumph and
we the ones who surrender?). For Laura, bored with the string of
mediocre poets and fawning cousins who nightly pay her court, the
Duke holds the promise of an exotic love. With her "imaginación am-
biciosa y sedienta de algo nuevo" (638) (ambitious imagination ever on
the look for something new) the Countess desires the Duke not for his
riches, but because he represents some yet untasted and exotic love,
perhaps her "Liermontov,"[12] who would speak to her of the mysterious Caucasus.

When the Duke reads into the heart of the Countess he understands
that her ambitions and desires are infinite, but that above all she desires
to know and understand his obscure origins. In his admonishment of
the Countess's curiosity, the Duke suggests a relationship between the
desire to know and what is conventionally called the death drive in
Freudian psychoanalysis. Lifting the veil that would dispel doubt is
tantamount to glimpsing death, the Duke warns:

—Dicen que es insoportable la duda; pero hay ocasiones en que
la incertidumbre es más insoportable todavía . . . , infinita-
mente más. ¿Por qué nos empeñamos siempre en descorrer el

velo que oculta algo a nuestros ojos? ¿Sabemos acaso si ese algo
es la muerte? (738–39)

[They say doubt is unbearable; but there are occasions when
uncertainty is even more unbearable . . . , infinitely more.
Why do we insist on drawing the veil that hides something from
our eyes? Do we perhaps know that that something is Death?]

The Countess looks for beauty in—and chooses to love—only that
which is unknown and impossible to know, and even though the Duke
warns her that to love only what is unknown is to "adorar la nada"
(adore nothingness) she insists that she will never be cured of her
passion for the unknown (739). Like Casimira and her other aristocratic
friends, the Countess longs to "ver descorrerse ante ella el velo que
oculta ciertos misterios" (741) (see the curtain drawn that hides certain
mysteries from her), but she also understands, like they, that desiring
is living, and that death and the absence of desire are synonymous.
The Duke warns that she may die after finding out what she wants
to know, but Laura counters that she will die if she does not find out,
and that anyway she is willing to face death, "¿Acaso he nacida et-
erna?" (645) (Was I perhaps born inmortal?), she asks. All of this talk
of death, desire, and knowledge sounds strangely philosophical in a
social satire about upstart authors and idle rich women. But here as
elsewhere in *El caballero*, a subtle dialogue is carried on between the
Duke's critical and authoritative position toward women's desire, and
the arguments of the women who are the brunt of his criticism. With
the narrator seemingly straddling the two positions, the argument
takes the guise of a philosophical debate that forces readers to reconsider even the lives of Madrid's most frivolous women.

Gradually, the Duke's ambition to become a renowned author fades
as the focus of the narrative shifts to a discussion of women's desire and
how to satisfy it. This subplot gives a voice to women and concurrently
repeats the frame story with interesting transmutations. All of the
men and women of the novel want their voices to be heard and their
stories told. What women want is not so different from what the
would-be poet wants, except that they lack the wherewithal to achieve
it, and the audience for *their* stories is inadequate. In short, in *El
caballero* feminine desire is shown to be not just the motor that propels
the narrative, but an effect of the male writer's desire. The man of

the frame has all of the advantages needed to foster a literary career: he is well educated and traveled, he has financial security, he is a man, and he has a muse, albeit an unorthodox one. The only thing that he lacks is the inspiration for a new literary style; he literally cannot think what to say. One is a subject, according to Lacan, only so far as he speaks. Significantly, the subject of the frame cannot find his place in the symbolic order because words fail him; he simply has nothing to say that makes him in any way different from anyone else. But, since the muse interprets the new as that which precisely has no name or is prior to the named, for the writer to gain fame, words are unnecessary. Rather, it is his withholding of words that produces the illusion that words are the thing they stand for, the desired object, that everyone is after.

In the frame, the frustrated man stands as a universal symbol of the writing subject, coming to terms with the meaning of the symbolic order. But the issue of *who* gets to represent this writing subject broadens in the novel proper. Do women who enjoy the same economic advantages as the minister also write? The novel subtly focuses on this issue by connecting female idleness with female containment. In fact, images of binding, enslavement, and suffocation are even more frequent in the sections devoted to the descriptions of Vinca Rúa, the Countess Pampa, and their cohorts than in the sections portraying the regimented, conventlike existence of Mariquita and her friends in the Corredora del Perro. When one of the men attending the Countess Pampa's ball remarks that society women appear "metidas en jaulas de acero" (643) (locked in steel cages), the Countess argues that the physical constraints of women's dresses are less onerous than their mental repression and she complains bitterly to her cousin that "la sociedad que los hombres han hecho a su gusto hasta nos prohibe pensar" (639) (the society that men have fashioned to their taste prohibits us from thinking).[13]

Later the narrator joins her [?] voice to those of the Countess and friends by pointing out that women are obliged to waste too much time covering up their imperfections "haciendo su papel de mujeres" (667) (playing their part as women) until they die. In fact, she insists, women fulfill their gender role, whether by bearing the "cruz de matrimonio" (cross of matrimony) or resigning themselves to a virtuous existence (667), better than men fulfill theirs. Perhaps women's role *(papel)* should be broadened to include writing as an acceptable feminine pastime, even if women's writing reveals a vulgar taste and impressionable nature, and even if women writers are inferior to the always beautiful and talented women represented in novels who speak "el lenguaje de las musas y escriben poco menos que Madame Sévigné" (666) (who speak the language of the muses and write like Madame Sévigné).[14] Perhaps, continues the narrator, that is why, when men see women's general lack of writing talent, they exclaim in protest:

> 'No la pluma en tus manos, mujer nacida para educar mis hijos: la aguja y la rueca son tus armas.' Y tienen razón al hablar así. Pero ¿no han previsto que sus hijos tendrían dos madres? ¿Que la rueca caería en desuso y que la aguja quedaría relegada a las costureras? ¿En qué han de ocuparse entonces la mujeres? (667)

> ["Not for your hands the pen, woman born to educate my children: the needle and the distaff are your arms." And they are right to speak so. But, do they not foresee that their children will have two mothers? That the distaff will fall out of use and the needle will be relegated to the seamstresses? Then how will women occupy their time?]

For the present, sadly, women's writing consists chiefly of billetsdoux. Examined closely, the love notes women send to the Duke reveal what he is so zealously trying to prove, that women are slaves; the only thing they have to speak of is their wish to be admired by a man. But the prophetic warning to men about what the future may bring for women when the needle and the spinning distaff fall to the hands of seamstresses should not be overlooked. In some future world, the narrator warns, women will be twice a mother: creating life and creating books.[15] True, it is a man who writes the *book of books*, but *El caballero* also clears a space for the discussion of women's place in a man's world. Although "belling the cat" in the context of *El caballero* primarily signifies revealing the mediocrity of modern literature, the Duke's other *belling* is the revelation of the crime of "devoured" female energy and talent, and of female slavery in the midst of affluence, privilege, amorality, and sexual permissiveness, themes that form part of the subtext of *El caballero* having to do with what women want. The terrible irony played over and over again in the nineteenth-century bourgeois novel is that class does not guarantee women access to better education or more intellectually stimulating occupations. In the following passage the Duke proposes (to whom is unclear) that whoever "bells the cat" about this women's issue will have to search for a remedy to this situation:

> Hablo del gato al que hay que ponerle el cascabel. Tantas criaturas devoradas por la miseria y el trabajo; tantas otras devoradas también por el fastidio y el ocio . . . Es una terrible calamidad, y en vano se hable de adelantos, de progresos; las mujeres siguen atormentadas: las unas, teniendo que hacerlo todo, que trabajar par sí y para los demás; las otras, haciéndose vestir y desnudar la mitad del día, teniendo el deber de asistir al baile, a la visita, viéndose obligadas a aprender la equitación y las lenguas extranjeras . . . ¿Cómo no sufrir? ¿Cómo no cansarse y aburrirse de todo eso? El que ha de ponerle el cascabel al gato procurará buscar un remedio eficaz para tan grandes males; pero en tanto, señora, oiga usted mi opinión sobre el particular. Dicen que las mujeres no deben ser ni literatas, no politiconas, ni bachilleras, y yo añado que lo que no deben es dejar de ser buenas mujeres. Ahora bien: ninguna que no sepa hacer más que andar en carretela, tumbarse en la butaca y decir que se fastidia, por más que sepa así mismo la equitación, las lenguas extranjeras y vestirse a la moda, nunca será para mí otra cosa que un ser inútil, una figura de cartón indigna de oír la más pequeña de mis revelaciones. (723–24)

[I am speaking of the cat that must be belled. So many creatures devoured by misery and work, so many others devoured by boredom and idleness. It's a terrible calamity. And in vain we speak of advances, of progress. Women continue to be oppressed: some, forced to do everything, to work for themselves and for others; others, spending half their day dressing and undressing, bound by duty to attend balls, pay visits, obliged to learn horseback riding and foreign languages. . . . How not to suffer? How not to tire and grow weary of all of this? The one who bells this cat will have to find an effective remedy for such great evils; but meanwhile, madame, hear my opinion concerning this. They say that women should not be writers, nor politicians, nor graduates, and I add that they should re-

Fig. 7. "A cada edad su labor."

main good women. Well then, any woman who can only parade around in a coach, collapse in an easy chair and complain how bored she is, for all her horseback riding or foreign languages or elegant dresses, she will never be for me anything but a useless being, a cardboard figure unworthy to hear the least of my revelations.]

In the end, the most powerful truth that the Duke leaves with the elite assemblage of authors, literary agents, and aristocrats before disappearing is not of the disposability of modern texts or of his easy triumph in a society of decadent vision and morality, but of the powerfulness of feminine desire despite the universality of feminine silence and subservience. When everyone is gathered at his feast, he suddenly beckons a group of veiled women, his aristocratic lovers dressed as slaves, to come forward and kiss his boots. The Duke is calling on women to act and dress the part that they symbolically play in society. By acquiescing, the women not only succumb to this symbol of mysterious masculine attraction, they demonstrate that their desire is not limited to the fathers, husbands, and sons who, outraged, rush to kill the Duke to prevent this act of submission. But the Duke has come to stand for impossible desire, and every woman in the room will pay homage to it:

—Venid ahora vosotras, esclavas mías, hermosas hijas de libre pensamiento, que lucháis por romper unas cadenas que solo desata la muerte: valientes Amazonas que no vaciláis en medir vuestras fuerzas con el gigante invisible que os vence . . . Acercaos para rendirme homenaje . . . ¡Mis botas os esperan! . . .

Las esclavas vacilaron un instante, y aun retrocedieron como si rehusasen obedecer; pero al fin una tras otra se inclinaron a los pies del poderoso duende. (822)

[Come now to me, my slaves, beautiful daughters of free thought, who struggle to break the chains that are only broken at death: valiant Amazons who do not hesitate to measure your strength against the invisible giant that conquers you . . . Come near to pay homage to me . . . My boots await you! . . .

The slaves hesitated an instant, and even drew back as if they would refuse to obey, but finally one by one they bowed to the feet of their powerful master.]

Belling the cat as far as women are concerned means showing that their freedom and independence are really just a slavery to a different master. Although these *modern*, freethinking women have adopted a moral code that grants them a great deal of sexual freedom, the Duke demonstrates before this entire assemblage of desiring subjects that to change masters is not to strike a blow for liberty: "Esas pobres hijas de la esclavitud aman la libertad como el mayor bien de la vida, pero no han comprendido todavía la manera de alcanzarla" (823) (these poor daughters of slavery love liberty as the greatest good of life, but they have not yet understood the way to achieve it). The way to obtain this freedom, which is clearly related to women imagining themselves as writing subjects, is what the Duke, as the beller of the cat, has promised but does not deliver to his group of slaves.

This is why the ending of *El caballero* may leave women readers with a sense of betrayal and frustration. The men who see their wonderful books go up in a huge bonfire feel outraged because another man has written the book of books not they, but women cannot even aspire to be writing subjects until they are able to resist their slavery:

> He aquí cómo en vez de ser fuertes como la encina os mostráis débiles como la hoja marchita a quien el viento más liviano arrebata donde quiera. ¡Todas lo mismo! Será, pues, forzado que os devuelva la libertad; mas no sin deciros que la mujer, así en Oriente como Occidente, así en la civilizada Europa como en los páises salvajes, solo podrá vencer sabiendo resistir. (823)

> [This is how instead of being strong like an oak tree you prove you are weak like a dried leaf that the wind blows in any direction whatever. All the same! I will have to restore your freedom to you; but not before saying that woman, in the East and as in the West, in civilized Europe and in savage countries, will only succeed if she knows how to resist.]

Here one last time Castro's narrator delivers the message that Pardo Bazán repeated so often in her essays: freedom and civilization have different meanings for men and women, not only for different classes.

The much-admired freedoms that the West has won for its privileged classes have not raised the European woman above the Asian woman. Woman's bondage, we are asked to conclude, is universal: "Compadez-cámoles, no obstante. Toda mujer es digna de compasión, solo por serlo" (823) (Let us pity them, however. Every woman is worthy of pity, just for being one).

*El caballero* harbors strong indictments against the idle and decadent rich, or ambitious and materialistic social climbers, of modern (nineteenth-century) society. But nature provides no antidote for social ills as it does in Castro's other novels. In fact, the Duke, who also plays to our desire by making us hope that he will turn out to be the cure for society's ills, heightens everyone's dissatisfactions, redirecting a desire that forever remains unsatisfied. As readers, we share some of the same frustrations and desires as the characters. First and foremost we want to understand the Duke's origins. We long to know where he is from, who he is, and what connection he has with the frustrated writer of the frame story. The narrator must forestall these revelations in order to prolong dissatisfaction, and therefore desire, because this is what it means to tell a story.

As a by-product of the women's dissatisfaction, we are also teased into wishing we knew what women really want, what they are willing to die or be enslaved for. Each time we think we know what it is that Woman, a woman, or a group of women want, the narration takes another turn, feeding our desire to have the veil drawn on our ignorance. Bourgeois women want a feather hat and blue clothes, but, it turns out, these demands are merely symbols for social and economic status. When status is not an issue, as in the case of the aristocratic women, it is sexual satisfaction that is demanded of the Duke: the Duke embodies the Romantic hero, a Pechorin who will rescue them from ennui. Yet, it turns out, these same women are willing to forgo sexual pleasures, what they *really* want is to think, and to write, and more than anything, to know. And if knowing means death as the Duke warns, then it must mean, we conclude, that women want to die. Or, perhaps, since their desires can never be satisfied, it is they, not the Duke, who really demonstrate what it means to be alive.

This is why what is dissatisfying for historical readers of this novel (that is, the failure of everyone's desire not just to be fulfilled but to be properly defined) may be precisely what makes *El caballero* such an exciting text for twentieth-century readers interested in the mechanics of narrative desire. *El caballero* describes the unpleasurable experiences of women who demand too much, or who want impossible things. The knowledge that the Duke imparts to women at his great feast is that even the richest women are pitiful slaves to their desire. It does not answer Freud's famous question "What do women want?" by converting women into mysterious or exotic objects of fear, lust, or adoration. Rather, it constructs a charged symbol of masculinity that women seek to possess for a variety of reasons that we can only partially understand if we remain on the level of manifest plot; that is, if we ignore desire's need to be "absolutely recognized," and imagine nineteenth-century women as merely consumers of men's goods.

## Chapter 4

# Bearing Motherhood

> *. . . a concrete woman, worthy of the feminine
> ideal embodied by the Virgin as an inaccessible
> goal, could only be a nun, a martyr, or, if she is
> married, one who leads a life that would remove
> her from that "earthly" condition and dedicate her
> to the highest sublimation alien to her body.*
>
> —Julia Kristeva, "Stabat Mater"

THE CONTINUED POPULARITY of the nineteenth-century Real-
ist novel reflects our obsession with what Peter Brooks calls representations of "authority, legitimacy, the conflict of generations and the
transmission of wisdom" (63). In our readings of the manifest content
of Realist novels we often connect these concerns with the trajectory
of male characters who, we hypothesize, restage Oedipal conflicts and
fail or succeed in their quest for an identity distinguishable from that
of their mother and analogous to that of their father. The task that
still awaits, one complicated by our fascination with Oedipality as well

as by conflicting notions of gender construction, is the deconstruction of Realist representations of the psychological trajectory of the female subject. The relationship between female development and female sexual identity, the imaginary identifications inherent in the representations of women characters, and the Realist obsession with maternity and the maternal body as figurative of the culture/nature dichotomies are some of the topics that have been until recently only of secondary concern to the Spanish literary establishment that forever seems to be talking about men even when the "subject" is women (or more precisely, woman). Without exaggeration, we could transform Brooks's statement and say that issues of maternity also dominate the Realist novel, at least in the case of the Spanish novel, a genre as fascinated with paternal authority and legitimacy (Pereda's *Gonzalo González de la Gonzalería* [1878]; Pérez Galdós's *Torquemada* series [1889–95]; and Alas's *Su único hijo* [His Only Son] [1891]), as with the transmission of maternal discourse and wisdom, and the definition of authentic motherhood (Pérez Galdós's *Fortunata y Jacinta* [1886–87]; Pereda's *La Montálvez* [1887]; and Alas's *Doña Berta* [1891]).

In this chapter I look at the mothers and fathers of *Los pazos de Ulloa* [The Ulloa manor] (1886) and other novels by Emilia Pardo Bazán to explore issues relating to the fetishistic representation of the maternal in late nineteenth-century Spanish fiction. Clearly, both maternity and paternity are central to every stage of Pardo Bazán's fiction: in *El cisne de Vilamorta* [The swan of Vilamorta] (1885) a mother learns tragic lessons about the incompatibility of sexuality and maternity, while *La Sirena Negra* [The siren of death] (1908) teaches the father the connection between life and the child as the essence of paternity. In *Los pazos de Ulloa* (1886), however, the questions *who* is the father and *what* is the mother—as well as *what* is a father and *who* is the mother—are especially acute. An understanding of the novel's intersubjective representational modes, stereotypical gender roles, familial and political ideology, and notions of biological versus foster parenthood may permit speculations about female subjectivity as it was discursively constituted in nineteenth-century women-authored texts. Specifically, I hope to show that in *Los pazos de Ulloa* maternity and paternity are highly problematic notions that countermine the conventional codes of nineteenth-century bourgeois society that were so blatantly preached in the domestic novels studied in Chapter 2. At the same time, the gender system inherent in this novel also reinforces a class conservatism shared by the author and her presumed middle- and upper-class readers. So, while the multiplicity and contradictions of the maternal representations hold out the possibility of disruptive or contestatory postures, they are predicated on political *truths* that can only reinsert gender and class back into the dichotomous relations that foster unequal power relations.

Contemporary feminist theory has helped us understand the maternal fantasy that both supports and subverts the symbolic order and the Law of the Father that we commonly understand as the generator of the stories we write about our selves. We cannot, speculates Julia Kristeva, say what woman is, only what men imagine her to be. But what of the mother?

> If it is not possible to say of a *woman* what she *is* (without running the risk of abolishing her difference), would it perhaps be different concerning the *mother*, since that is the only function of the "other sex" to which we can definitely attribute existence? And yet, there too, we are caught in a paradox. First, we live in a civilization where the *consecrated* (religious or secular) representation of femininity is absorbed by motherhood. If, however, one looks at it more closely, this motherhood is the *fantasy* that is nurtured by the adult, man or woman, of a lost territory. (Kristeva, "Stabat Mater" 234)

For Kristeva, motherhood is synonymous with the "lost territory" that both sexes inhabit and must suppress in normal development. Consequently, there is no way for a mother to speak since our entry into the symbolic order is predicated on her silence and her status as fantasy. The questions to pose are How do women writers underscore the fact that women never truly escape maternity as it is conventionally represented in our phallocentric discourses, just as they never truly embody its ideal? Is maternity ever imagined differently in the fiction of the women contemporaries of Realist authors like Galdós and Alas? Would such a difference even be possible in view of the fact that the conventional representational systems constituting gender in men's Realist fiction were the same ones available to women writers?

## Motherhood and Intersubjectivity

With its conspicuously male (Oedipal) plot, *Los pazos* inspires mainstream critics to define its plot as a Romantic odyssey, an uninitiated man's travels to adventure in search of a proper identity. Yet even this most "patriarchal" of novels shows that the "family romance," beyond its reenactment of an Oedipal trajectory that necessarily relegates the feminine[1] to the margins, can also encompass more obscure psychological relations that some feminist scholars associate more positively than previously with the presymbolic and hence maternal stages of human development.[2] As yet, it has gone unremarked that when the hero descends into Hades/Ulloa, he encounters a woman who not merely helps him to achieve his destiny as a separate self (when she is lost), but who cries out—pitifully but also compellingly—for him to share in a different notion of subjectivity, what Jessica Benjamin would call intersubjectivity. Through a shared experience of motherhood, Julián experiments with erasing the difference that isolates him from women and children, attempting to share his isolation with the isolated.

As described in Chapter 2, intersubjectivity presumes a shared recognition of more than a demand for separate but unobjectified subjects. Nucha does not demand recognition as a deserving subject from the voyager Julián as, say, Fe Neira does of Mauro Pareja in *Memorias de un solterón* [Diary of a bachelor]. Rather, she reveals that she is eminently worthy to be connected to his thoughts, held in high regard and loved, despite her insignificance, lack of passion, and the prohibitions that delegitimize the seemingly "natural" knowledge of intersubjectivity that draws them together. Although Julián and Nucha fail in their mission to rescue the *pazos* from moral and physical decay—a fact that has led critics such as Maurice Hemingway to stress their ineffectiveness (29)—their very failure reminds us that what they set out to save deserves instead to be lost, while what they find, and what the novel somewhat timidly celebrates, is a sense of connectedness that Benjamin distinguishes as one of the feminine "bonds of love." In *Los pazos* and especially *La Madre naturaleza* [Mother Nature] (1887), Pardo Bazán has juxtaposed the Oedipal narrative with its "traditional plot of upward mobility" (Massé, *In the Name* 56) with a parable of the prepatriarchal green-world (See Ordóñez, "Paradise"), in which feminine receptivity and maternalness and the search for fulfillment through love rival the transmission of father-right. The kind of love Nucha and Julián conceive and nurture in their *offspring* Manuela and Perucho threatens to eclipse in importance and complexity the theme of an illegitimate marquis recognizing and passing on the patriarchal torch to his illegitimate son.

The family plays an equally important role in *Los pazos* as in any archetypal (Freudian) family romance, but the notions of family and legitimacy are constantly called into question as *socially* binding concepts at odds with what *emotionally* binds people together. Although the novel might be best described as moral melodrama, it also highlights the relation between institutions and psychological gender conflict.[3] Just as in the typical family romance with its "imaginary construction of plots according to principles of wish fulfillment" (Hirsch 10), Pardo Bazán constructs a story that explains and elicits difference; only the difference that it imagines is *different:* it is not only Julián's separation from his mother that precludes his becoming a man. What signals his true moment of maturity is his willingness to recognize his bond with another and to sacrifice his social and religious principles to preserve that other; in other words, his willingness to be different from what a *real* man was presumed to be in terms of nineteenth-century Spanish rural society.[4] Thus he stands in marked contrast to the country landowners who hunt, drink, argue about national affairs, seduce servants, and beat their wives.

Julián is both more and less than the "man-who-would-understand," defined by Marianne Hirsch as someone who combines paternal authority and maternalness (57–58). His lack of authority in *Los pazos* surpasses even Nucha's hyperfeminine powerlessness. On the other hand, more than simply empathizing with Nucha, he slips into a radical form of self-identification with her, presenting physiological as well as psychological empathic symptoms. For example, during Nucha's lying-in, he assumes a kneeling position, which gradually provokes a trancelike state punctuated by pain in which "[s]entíase desvanecer y morir" (he felt himself swoon and die). Finally, in a fit of "doloroso vértigo" (painful vertigo) he hears the magic words "Una niña" (a girl). He tries to rise, "exhalando un gran suspiro" (breathing a deep sigh), but once on his feet, "un atroz dolor en las articulaciones, una sensación de mazazo en el cráneo, le echaron a tierra nuevamente. Desmayóse" (an acute pain in the limbs, a sensation of a blow to the skull threw him to the floor again and he fainted) (1:232). Days later Julián remains debilitated and "desmejorado" (sickly) (1:233), as any mother would.

While Julián's empathic lying-in entitles him to share symbolically in the responsibility for Manuela's mothering, it also symbolizes Julián's ritual-like gender rebirth: scorned by men for lacking authority and hunting skills and for being too effeminate, he is ceremoniously admitted into a feminine circle of holding and touching. A baby as much as the baby he is learning to tend, he receives his first lessons in touching and caressing at cribside. A high point of his emotional apprenticeship comes when Manuela urinates on his lap and he interprets the sensation as a melting of the "nieve de austeridad, cuajada sobre un corazón afeminado y virgen allá desde los tiempos del Seminario, desde que había propuesto renunciar a toda familia y todo hogar en la Tierra" (1:236) (snow of austerity frozen upon an effeminate, virginal heart back even before his days in the seminary, when he had decided to renounce a family and earthly home). Soon he abandons his task of restoring the Ulloa family archives to devote all of his energies to the nursery, familiarizing himself with the details of women's subculture, heaped together here in conspicuous excess: "gorras, ombligueros, culeros, pañales, fajas, microscópicos zapatos de *crochet*, caprillos y barberos" (1:235) (bonnets, swaddling clothes, diapers, sashes, microscopic crocheted booties, frocks, and bibs). Although unable to encounter the reality of his own nude body, Julián learns to see Manuela's body as an innocent object of his gaze. In fact, some of the most beautiful and tender descriptions of a child's body in nineteenth-century Spanish fiction are seen through Julián's loving looks (1:235–36).

Julián's decision to abandon the family's archives to enter this world of mothers and their babies is significant for what it implies about the importance of intersubjectivity in passing along family tradition. The words of family history recorded by generations of Ulloa noblemen in books now crumbling into dust in the library, cede to the sounds, rhythms, and words of family intimacy passed on by Nucha in the nursery. Pardo Bazán's interest in the mother-child relationship shows her special capacity, shared by other European women authors, to juxtapose "women's placement as the silent object in the traditional male view of language and a mother's more positive wish to reproduce the nonsymbolic language of infancy" (Homans 33). One way she does this is through what Margaret Homans calls the *literalization* of linguistic practice, shifting from the place of the signifier to the place of the object to reproduce the nonsymbolic language that women shared with their mothers and then remember and acknowledge in

their writings, even during the most patriarchal of eras like the late
nineteenth century. In the following passage Nucha lulls her daughter
to sleep through the repetition of sounds unmediated by the symbolic.
Her Galician lullaby, ending with prolonged, tender notes, removes
her to a moment of babble that allows her to partake in an identification
with her daughter, creating the sense of a hallowed, dreamlike space
that completely envelopes mother and child:

> su madre no cesaba de arrullarla con una 'nana' aprendida
> del ama, una especie de gemido cuya base era triste: ¡*lai*..., *lai!*
> la queja lenta y larga de todas las canciones populares en Gali-
> cia. El canto fue descendiendo, hasta concluir en la pronuncia-
> ción melancólica y cariñosa de una sola letra, la *e* prolongada.
> (1:242)

> [her mother would always rock her to sleep with one of the
> housekeeper's lullabys, a kind of sad and soft lament: *lai*...,
> *lai!*, the slow, drawn-out complaint of all the popular songs of
> Galicia. Her voice would deepen until it ended in the melan-
> cholic and caressing sound of one single letter, a prolonged *e*.]

A Kristevan reading of this passage would have us focus on the presymbolic rapture of the child expressed in the sounds that connect it to
the mother semiotically. But a strikingly different meaning is attached
to this "sola letra" (single letter) when Pardo Bazán uses it to describe
Amparo's labor pains in the earlier novel *La tribuna:* "durante aquella
hora de angustia suprema, la mujer moribunda retrodecía al lenguaje
inarticulado de la infancia, a la emisión prolongada, plañidera, terrible,
de una sola vocal" (2:194) (during that hour of supreme anguish, the dying woman reverted to the inarticulate language of infancy, to the prolonged emission, a terrible moan, of a single vowel). Geraldine Scanlon
interprets Amparo's "sola vocal" (single vowel) as an indication of feminine inarticulateness, especially acute during her difficult labor (148).
But in *La tribuna*, as in *Los pazos*, this unbroken sound of a single vowel
frames a moment of intense interaction between mother and child. For
Nucha the sound is an expression of melancholy and love, for Amparo
a terrible wail, but for both it evokes the "inarticulate language of infancy" that joins mother and child into a single entity.

   That this joining can express joy and pain underscores the ambivalence of the mother/subject who is never, the author reminds us, *not*

of this world. As tender and timeless as these moments of nonverbal communication seem in *Los pazos*, they are also tinged with sadness, complaint, and premonition. In other words, Pardo Bazán's maternal imaginary has its dark side, just as Kristeva's does. The maternal language that Nucha speaks and teaches to Julián and Perucho is the language of the victimized. Clearly, Pardo Bazán does not want us to imagine some original, essentially feminine, space that miraculously escapes cultural construction. In fact, *Los pazos*'s tragedy is about the break in the mother-child knot that nineteenth-century women authors saw as cruel but inevitable: to be the perfect mother always means to die.[5] Although in positive terms Pardo Bazán's novels figure childrearing as a reconstitution of the dyadic, presymbolic bond with the mother, this repetition of the baby does not bypass the phallus. The law of patriliny, ensuring the passing-on of the father's name and privileges, relegates the mother-daughter relationship to the margins of all that is recognized as authentic in *Los pazos* and *La Madre naturaleza* [Mother Nature]. The principal material necessity of the lord of the manor is to be propagated in the form of a son: "Esperaba el mundo un Moscoso, un Moscoso auténtico y legítimo. . . . Tiene que ser un chiquillo, porque si no, le retuerzo el pescuezo a lo que venga" (1:218) (The world awaited a Moscoso, an authentic and legitimate Moscoso. . . . It must be a boy, because if not, I'll wring the neck of whatever comes along). Because it serves no useful purpose in fulfilling strict patrilineal ends, Nucha's relationship with her daughter breaks a taboo that the very patriarchal nineteenth-century novel sometimes transgresses but almost always finally punishes.[6]

The breakdown of the legitimate, nuclear family gives way to a new family, composed of an overfeminine (neuroticized) woman; an overfeminized (castrated) man; one child who is the wrong sex (Manuela); and another, Perucho, who has no biological ties to his new *parents*. The striking illegitimacy of this family forces readers to entertain new notions of the family more accommodating to radical forms of intersubjectivity. Ironically, the iron rule of the lord of the manor fosters odious gender polarizations but also relegates certain men, like Julián, to the feminine pole, thus indirectly encouraging heterosexual relationships in which gender has no exclusionary category and therefore implies no hierarchical connotations. The Nucha/Julián identification prompts questions about the sex/gender system that assigns gender roles on the basis of biological sex. The resultant family is both a mockery of what Pardo Bazán's readers recognized as the sanctioned family unit, and a grotesque parody of the biblical family in which Julián fancies himself a new Joseph. Since it is this second, idealized, version of the family that lends legitimacy to the conventionally defined Spanish family, Pardo Bazán's mockery of both makes sense. But as the new family emerges it becomes clear that it too can only fail, not because Julián has overidealized his role or Nucha exaggerated hers, but because the social structures that govern *los pazos* cannot tolerate such intimacy between the world of adults and that of children, or, for that matter, between adult men and women who are not marriage partners. Even in this space that is represented as totally bound to the laws of nature, the Father's Law of separation and difference dictates nurturing relations and not the reverse. In the end, Nucha/Julián's story represents both the inevitability of separation from primary bonds, the nonreciprocity between the sexes, and the unbearable reality of motherhood (as depicted in Western culture at any rate), in which "women carry children in their bodies, give birth to them, and then relinquish them to a world in which they themselves are powerless to determine the course of their children's development" (Hirsch 36). Mother nature, despite Pardo Bazán's exaggerated depictions of its might, does not predetermine the failure of the new family; rather, the Father's Law does, which is why I argue that *nature* in *Los pazos* is the privileged domain of the father, not the mother.

*Los pazos* engages in what Roland Barthes calls the Oedipal dialectic of "tenderness and hatred" (*Pleasure* 47), but not merely by leading back to the Oedipus complex but by trying to rescue the silent (M)other and redefine motherhood in relation to stereotyped gender roles. When sexuality comes up against the intransigence of the Law, it becomes unstable, promoting sexual indeterminacy (Nucha and Julián are barely distinguishable at times) as an alternative to the ordinary polarizations of the sexual order.[7] This can be seen by comparing the gender roles of the good father, Julián, and the bad father, Pedro.[8] The descriptions of both men are tinged with irony, marking the same disdainful distance between narrator and character. But if we compare the two male characters in relation to their masculinity, our reaction is that Pedro's repression of feminine qualities is what leads to tragedy more than Julián's failure to embody the masculine principle.[9]

Notwithstanding her experimentation, Pardo Bazán rejects any utopian triumph of sexual indeterminacy or ensconcement in an exclusively maternal territory. Like a mother giving premature birth, *los pazos* ejects from its womb the best elements assembled there when Nucha dies (surviving only in the myth Julián created for her for his private needs), and Julián is banished to a remote mountain village. These *stillbirths* are the logical consequence of the text's ambiguity with regard to nature. Paradoxically, there is no mother so *uncivilized* that she can accommodate Julián's idealized family and yet the uncivilized world of *los pazos* cannot contain Nucha if it is to remain a place where the Law of Nature and the Law of the Father remain intact and unconcerned with female subjectivity. For the reestablishment of paternal authority to occur, Nucha's civilizing force must not be allowed to tame the wildness surrounding it. Like the Virgin Mary, whom Kristeva calls "the woman whose entire body is an emptiness through which the paternal word is conveyed" (*Tales* 374), Nucha succumbs to the uncivilized and passes her final days in a state of paranoia and mental suffering.

The death of Nucha symbolizes Pardo Bazán's dissatisfaction with the family, an empty signifier through which patriarchy conveys the word. The causes of family dysfunction are entirely external to her even though she is the family's principal victim: her daughter, instead of being prized as a complement to the family, is ignored by Pedro. Her spiritual confidante, instead of giving her advice and support, looks to her for love and instruction; her husband, instead of fostering his legitimate family, becomes entangled in an illegitimate affair with a servant. Given the stress placed on her in her role as wife, mother, and friend to weak individuals with widely varying behavior and needs, it is not surprising that Nucha exhibits symptoms of the neurotic when she fails to bring stability to her *family* collage. Crazily, but not unexpectedly, Nucha's body pays the price for this collapse of the family. Julián returns to Ulloa ten years after her death to a world unchanged: gender remains the primary vehicle for signaling relations of power, and the experiment with emotional cross-dressing that eschews patriarchal power is all but forgotten.

On the other hand, the gender disruption that Julián embodies, together with Nucha's dramatic helplessness, is complex enough to warrant a reexamination of the novel's popularity, usually attributed to its Naturalistic shock appeal. *Los pazos* probably appealed positively to men and women readers for different reasons. Perhaps the powerlessness of Pardo Bazán's women arose partially from an unrecognized desire to allay men's fears of the mother by giving them the texts they needed to survive this threat to their subjectivity. Reflecting back on earlier explanations for unequal gender relations, Nancy Chodorow suggests that male fears of women cannot be explained without reference to the powerful role women play as mothers (*Reproduction*, introduction). Women's novels sometimes try to deflect this fear by demonstrating how powerless mothers really are, constructing motherhood as a symbol of weakness and noninterference.[10] This may explain why there are no terrible mothers in Pardo Bazán's works, at least none to compete with Paula of Alas's *La Regenta* (1884) or Perfecta of Galdós's *Doña Perfecta* (1876), pulling sons back into dangerous presymbolic indifferentiation or frenetically trying to prevent substitution of mother love with love for another.

For women, the equation of victimhood with motherhood provides a basis for a critique of power relations that relegate the mother to a role of exaggerated (and therefore conspicuous) subservience in a patriarchal culture. On the positive side, for Pardo Bazán's women readers, as well as modern readers in search of subversion, the sacrificial mother was also a disguised celebration of women's power of relatedness, a notion currently much celebrated by North American social psychologists (Gilligan, Hartsock, Benjamin) whom I discussed in Chapter 1. Finally, Julián's attitude toward Nucha's child might reflect the ambiguity that some of Pardo Bazán's *maternalized* male readers felt toward their children in an era of paternal indifference to at least noninvolvement in primary childcare, as well as the frustration of bourgeois women who found parenting an oddly lopsided affair. While some readers may have been disappointed at Julián's bungled attempt at preserving a dynasty steeped in patriarchal privilege, others who contrasted the parenting techniques of Pedro and Julián may have reflected on the ethics of parenting and the meaning of parental versus dynastic legitimacy or illegitimacy.

## The Maternal Fantasy, Unveiled

To assess the novelty of *Los pazos*'s depiction of motherhood, it helps to recall the negative connotations of the common idealizations of mother love. The mother participates fully in the negative column of culturally determined antimonies that characterize representations of women and men in nineteenth-century literature: nature versus culture, other versus self, body versus mind, illness versus strength. Predictably, many of the Romantic and bourgeois clichés of the maternal presence that support these dichotomies abound in Pardo Bazán's fiction. For example, Telmo of *La piedra angular* [The cornerstone] (1891), describes what a mother at her best signifies for Pardo Bazán's male characters: a sweet and distant dream, a safe and secret space where all needs are attended to, a place exuding a scent of lavender and a "sensación de calor tibio, de nido de plumón que envuelve y abriga" (2:281) (sense of warmth, a feathery nest that wraps around you and keeps you warm).

Pardo Bazán's mothers frequently embody this ideal, although the more perfectly they perform this role, the more they tend to be represented as fantasies for an absent mother. This remembered presence has all the perfection that the young man needs to invest in his mother. She is the "phallic" mother, as psychoanalysts like Kristeva define her: "As the addressee of every demand, the mother occupies the place of alterity. Her replete body, the receptacle and guarantor of demands, takes the place of all narcissistic, hence imaginary, effects and gratifications; she is, in other words, the phallus" (Kristeva, *Revolution* 47).[11]

Generally, the quality of maternalness as exquisite caregiving does not depend on biological motherhood in Pardo Bazán's fiction. For example, although childless, Milagros (*Doña Milagros* [1892]) is the most maternal of characters, while the most notable primary caretaker is Gaspar de Montenegro (*La sirena negra*), who vociferously rejects the importance of biological parenting as a binding force. According to Gaspar, love binds two people together more closely than biological kinship:

> El chico es más mío, ¿lo oyes?, que si lo hubiese engendrado materialmente. Lo material es muy despreciable en todo; pero en eso de amor y de la paternidad es en lo que más ruin e insignificante se me figura. (2:880–81)

> [The child is as mine, do you hear?, as if I had engendered him myself. The material is in all things contemptible; but in matters concerning love and paternity is where I believe it is the most insignificant and base.]

Fig. 8. "¡Ya viene!"

In fact, alternatives to biological maternal figures seem to dominate Pardo Bazán's fiction. Although the author often relies on idealized stereotypes of the perfect—absent but idolized—maternal figure that Margaret Homans defines as the dominant figure of the Romantic male quest (41), her substitutes for it, like Julián, leave little doubt that she did not believe that biological mothers were best equipped to parent. In this way she challenged the sex/gender system, specifically the notion that women make the best primary caretakers for young children.[12] Motherhood is work that can be performed by anyone with a generous personality or a special inclination toward household management, including a sibling like Fe Neira or a bachelor like Gaspar. Oftentimes the idealized, lost, mother figure is an abstraction that foregrounds a certain nostalgic desire for connectedness (rather than a male fear of the repressed mother world) that is all but impossible to recapture between adults, but that sometimes is achieved through repetition in a new child-adult relationship of unusual intensity, such as that between Julián and Manuela.

*Los pazos* also challenges the idealized mother, the serene virgin so idolized in Spanish religious rite, art, and Romantic literature, by juxtaposing to it a physical reality of a cruder kind. Julián's framing of Nucha as the Virgin Mary parodies the usual way that nineteenth-century writing accommodates the ideology of motherhood by linking biblical or hagiographic figures to women's ideal roles. While Julián exalts motherhood as women's perfect vocation, the novel makes amply clear how dangerous this sublimation is for women's physical well-being. The very sacredness of Nucha's mission keeps Julián from taking the necessary steps to keep her out of harm's way. In this way the repeated allusions to the Virgin could be said to subvert the femininity they seem to promote. The idealization of Nucha as mother does not block out the physiological deterioration and abuse to which she is subjected, nor the fact that she clearly has no avocation for bearing children, only for mothering children born to others such as her brother or Perucho.

As propagator of the Madonna cult, Julián must constantly evaluate his ideal against the reality of what is occurring to Nucha's body and the circumstances of her daily life that emphasize her neglect by men. He may admire her slender pregnant body for its resemblance to paintings of the Visitation (1:224), but then he must witness the painful fact that Nucha's virginal slenderness makes her ill-equipped to bear and nurse children. Between placing her in the company of the Virgins of Visitation (1:224), September, August (1:225), and finally Soledad (1:234),[13] Julián also imagines the profanity of her doctor and husband treating her "como se trata a los cadáveres en la mesa de anatomía; como materia inerte, donde no se cobija ya un alma" (1:225) (like one treats cadavers on the anatomy table; like inert material in which a soul no longer resides).

These two extreme fantasies, woman as all soul or all body (in this instance virginal apotheosis or medical corpse), epitomize the way the men of Ulloa misrepresent the mother's body either as all spirit or all matter.[14] Such glaring patriarchal misprisions of motherhood are blind to the reality of physical pain as well as pleasure that constitute Nucha's unique experience as a mother. But besides representing men's fantasies of the perfect (sublimated) mother, Nucha may also be an expression of bourgeois women's unconscious fear that birthing threatens a woman's individuality (Homans 89). The building tension surrounding Nucha's lying-in also plays to a fear bound to a historical reality: that in the nineteenth century childbirth was the most dangerous moment in a woman's life, an event usually depicted as an illness in all types of literature.[15] The negative reading of childbirth in *Los pazos* is largely the result of a hostile narrative attitude toward the efficacy of men during this critical moment of a woman's life. The fact that Pedro, Julián, and the doctor Juncal are equally inept at a time when they should be just the opposite adds to our impression of the novel as a Gothic horror story that shatters the wonderful religious tableau of the "Holy Family" that composes Julián's dream.[16]

In tandem with the cult to the Virgin Mary is the myth of mother nature, which also comes under scrutiny in *Los pazos*. In the prevailing psychological narrative of Western cultures, the quest for object substitutes for the mother often leads to an identification of nature and woman, in essence, the most literal (unspeaking) of living things with a special affinity to animals, the earth, and the dark forces of the universe. As mother nature, she is everywhere and thus always available as a substitute for what was lost or a reminder of the consequences for male subjectivity of rejoining her. Perhaps this explains why a period of great popularity of the cult of mother nature does not mark an equally heightened interest in the subjectivity of historical mothers. In fact, women who identify with the myth run the risk of promoting their own objectification. One way that Pardo Bazán subverts the myth

is by juxtaposing the myth of mother nature to an account of motherhood as a lived experience. In this way, mother nature and maternal
experiences become part of a social and political reality. The myth of
male progress versus female backwardness, which underpins the myth
of mother nature, is belied by Nucha who is a bad mother (in a
physical sense), but the least backward and most *maternal* of all the
residents of Ulloa.

Nucha's virginal body also stands in marked contrast to the eroticized body of her antithesis, Sabel, and the healthy "vaca" (cow) her
husband hires to be Manuela's wet nurse. This produces a terrible
irony in that the rotund, healthy Sabel, who gave birth to Perucho in
the time it took the bread she was baking to rise (1:227), is an unfit
mother. The country doctor and country squire agree that women's
primary role is the propagation of the species: "[l]o contrario le parecía
un crimen" (1:227) (the contrary would be a crime), says Pedro, but
the model "gran vaca" (great cow), as the doctor calls Sabel, turns out
to be an incompetent mother despite the ease with which she bears
and nurses a baby.

It is important to emphasize however, that although weak and un-
blessed by *mother nature* as far as her physical suitability for childbearing is concerned, Nucha does not die from postpartum ailments as
her doctor Juncal claims in *Madre naturaleza* (1:324), but from the
physical and emotional abuse heaped on her by her husband. To repeat, it is not the law of mother nature that destroys city women,
although they are subject to its mighty influences, but the brutality of
husbands, fathers, and systems that disempower women in specific
ways.[17] In this regard *Los pazos* closely resembles the typical domestic
novel in which men are usually responsible for women's miserable lives
(Modleski 23). All the men in Nucha's life—Máximo, her doctor, Julián, her spiritual adviser, Manuel, her father, Pedro, her husband,
and Gabriel, her brother—not only fail to protect her but contribute
directly or indirectly to her death or her child's neglect. Given the
power of the myth of mother nature as life-giver, Nucha's death represents an escape from an identification with objects, not just a release
from worldly trials as Julián interprets it, but a refusal to succumb to
the material world of *los pazos* in which women are revered predomi-
nately as sacred cows. Of course, death is not a triumph over nature;
*los pazos* quickly obliterates its memory of Nucha and her daughter is
given up to nature to be raised in communion with butterflies, bird-

nests, and wild animals. We could summarize the allegory of gender in *Los pazos* like this: the natural world is dangerous for women, and the woman who dares to tame it, or confront it, risks death. When the feminine forces (Nucha and Julián) wed the primitive forces representing nature (Primitivo, Pedro), there ensues a battle in which nature crushes the feminine. The victory, however, does not exalt the masculine since *los pazos* is all the worse for the disappearance of its civilizing, female element.

Women protagonists in Pardo Bazán's fiction have no special affinity with nature.[18] In fact, natural phenomena often overwhelm them, overburden their senses, or leave them indifferent, confirming the nineteenth-century cliché—"El hombre ha sido hecho en el campo como los demás animales. La mujer fué hecha en el paraíso" (man was made in the field with the rest of the animals; woman was made in paradise) (Sinués de Marco, *La abuela* 7)—that was a common justification for promoting women's roles as domesticators and civilizers in a decadent era. In *Los pazos*, the narrator fluctuates between sympathy and antagonism for the natural world but women characters are mostly housebound and therefore excluded from an appreciation of it, meaning that nature is read through the eyes of the male residents of Ulloa. Gradually, Nucha's discomfiture with the natural leads her to reduce in eversmaller range the space she inhabits until she only feels comfortable in her bedroom and adjoining nursery. When she and Julián stare at the view from the window of the manor they are silenced by its vast and dark immensity:

> Eran las montañas negras, duras, macizas en aparencia, bajo la oscurísima techumbre del cielo tormentoso; era el valle alumbrado por las claridades pálidas de un angustiado sol; era el grupo de castaños inmóvil unas veces, otras visiblemente sacudido por la racha del ventarrón furioso y desencadenado. (1:243)

> [The mountains were dark, solid, massive in appearance, beneath the dark ceiling of a stormy sky; the valley was lit by the pale streaks of a dying sun; the chestnut trees were now still, now visibly shaken by gusts of a powerful, furious wind.]

Like Jane Austen and Maria Edgeworth (Gilbert and Gubar, *Madwoman* 136), Pardo Bazán locates the villains of her Gothic romance *at home:* the kitchen, the basement, even the bedroom become sites of horror for Nucha. But the outside world is also inhabited by villainous types like Primitivo, and this leaves Nucha with literally no place to go but the nursery, where she belongs in a sense, but also where her authority is challenged and undermined.

The men of *los pazos*, on the other hand, connect with the rhythms and chance happenings of the natural world. They gather around the fire to speak lovingly of their hounds and hunts, to tell their stories of serpents sucking cow udders and other strange sightings provided them by the spectacle of mother nature with whom the text imagines them in complete balance. They are entirely at home in it (one could say suckled by it), while Nucha and Julián, the ordering, civilizing figures of *los pazos*, often cringe before its dark forces.[19]

The graphic representation of this identification of nature and the masculine is the spider episode that reveals how closely this novel resembles the classic Gothic romance. At a determined point in the Gothic narrative, the heroine's disappointment at her unhappy married life leads her to imagine that she or those dear to her are being persecuted (Modleski 56), usually by a male whose sexuality is a threat to her. The heroine is the "passive center of the novel" (Massé, "Gothic Repetition" 680) barraged by traumatic horrors that leave her paralyzed. Nucha's screaming at the sight of a large spider in her bedroom rouses her husband to her side. When Julián appears moments later, he mistakes Nucha's panic for a fear of her husband who is lunging in her direction to kill the spider. Nucha's fear of the spider displaces her fear of her husband who, like the spider, represents the most concentrated form of evil that the natural world can summon up against a woman. Thus the spider is a metaphor for a violent husband who (as the text intimates) abuses and forces his will on his wife in the middle of the night, while Pedro, in turn, is a metaphor for the untamed, natural world that women fear because they can not control it.

Nucha and Julián's distrust of the natural acknowledges the dangers of allowing too close an identification between women and nature. The *natural* woman, as exemplified by Sabel, is an object valued for purely material reasons, such as the size of her hips and breasts, but whose animal instincts place her somewhere in the category of favored hunting dog in *los pazos*. This veiled protest against the Romantic identification of woman with nature leads Pardo Bazán to a sometimes ambiguous narrative stance: loving surrender to nature when speaking from the point of view of the men of *los pazos*, and apprehension or even dread as in the above passage, when taking the outsider's (a woman's) point of view.[20] From her constant allusions to "mother nature" and "the siren of death," one would imagine that Pardo Bazán accepted cultural stereotypes of femininity as that which lies without and threatens the collapse of civilization. But Nucha's timid response to nature, her civilizing aptitude, and her very hysteria undermine the Romantic myths obsessed with male subjectivity and female objectification. While her contemporary Ralph Waldo Emerson spoke of nature as "my beautiful mother," Pardo Bazán saw in this essentializing myth the signifying role for the Law of the Father. Nature is feminine only to the degree that it exists to explore male subjectivity. While nature and women are collapsed into man's "dark continent" in some of Pardo Bazán's representations, women are imagined in many other less objectifying ways as well. In fact, we are never quite sure what the term nature refers to in any given context until we analyze and compare male and female subject constructions.

## The Ideology of Gender Representation

Politically, *Los pazos* is a radical feminist challenge to the progressiveness of Galdós's *Doña Perfecta* (written in 1876 shortly after the period of the Restoration began), in which women are collectively the enforcers of an illegitimate (Carlist) and retrogressive political system that tolerates violence and keeps men in a primitive and ignorant state. In *Los pazos*, conversely, it is Nucha and her sisters who, as women, are collectively designated and valorized as society's civilizing agents. If Nucha's father is physically debilitated and made "soft" as a result of his long residency in Compostela, he is still far more civilized than his nephew Pedro and "moralmente bastantes años más adelante" (1:214) (morally quite a few years ahead). Women, as much as the city, brags the narrator, are the catalyst for this progress: "cinco hembras respetadas y queridas civilizan al hombre más agreste" (1:214) (five respected and loved women can civilize the most uncultivated man). In both novels political struggles invade and contaminate the private sphere; only in *Los pazos*, *civilization* is a female prerogative and in

*Doña Perfecta* it rests notably in the hands of men.[21] Such intertextual political wrangling and gender bias is also implicated in the particular version of the narrative of patriarchy and matriarchy written into these two novels. *Doña Perfecta* is the matriarchy failed: the mother (symbolic of Spain) drives her child mad rather than see her fall into the hands of progress, personified by the liberal-minded engineer Pepe Rey. *Los pazos* reverses the gender in the story of failed parenthood: Don Pedro, the bad father, neglects his legitimate child by Nucha in favor of his illegitimate child by Sabel. We could say that the father (Spain) fails to uphold the legitimacy of its privileged classes by favoring the maid's son over the aristocrat's.

In addition to a similar interaction of public and private spheres, there is in both novels a pessimism about any prospectus for positive change in either sphere. Pepe Rey is killed and his reluctant ally Rosario driven mad. In *Los pazos*, Nucha dies and her pusillanimous defender is exiled. A few good men are just as incapable of reforming a corrupt country/family as a few good "women." However, the conclusion we reach from a reading of *Los pazos* regarding men and their history is the same one Pardo Bazán repeatedly argued in her essays: revolutions and progress may profoundly change the power relations between men, but until relations between men and women change in the private sphere, it will simply be a question of more of the same for women, regardless of the political regime. If anything, *Los pazos* argues that the situation of bourgeois women would worsen under a progressive regime with their only allies, priests and clerics, under siege. The underlying message with respect to gender is that women's gift for fomenting progress by raising humanity to a more moral and civilized plane falters in the face of male violence. The Virgin Queen of *Los pazos* is no more capable of stemming male violence than Queen Isabel had been in the political sphere. While women's existence is directly affected by political upheavals, their well-being is not strictly guaranteed by progress in a political sense. This theme is a constant in Pardo Bazán's fiction as well as her essays. Even her most politically progressive characters, such as Gaspar de Montenegro, are not above acts of brutal violence against women. In an untitled article written during Isabel's reign and reprinted in *La mujer española y otros artículos femenistas* [The Spanish woman and other feminist essays], Pardo Bazán sums up her position on political progress and women in the following negative terms:

Suponed a dos personas en un mismo punto; haced que la una
avance y que la otra permanezca inmóvil: todo lo que avance la
primera se queda atrás la segunda. Cada nueva conquista del
hombre en el terreno de las libertades políticas, ahonda el ab-
ismo moral que le separa de la mujer, y hace el papel de ésta
más pasivo y enigmático. Libertad de enseñanza, libertad de
cultos, derecho de reunión, sufragio, parlamentarismo, sirven
para que media sociedad (la masculina) gane fuerzas y activi-
dades a expensas de la otra media femenina. Hoy ninguna mujer
de España—empezando por la que ocupa el trono—goza de
verdadera influencia política; y en otras cuestiones no menos
graves, el pensamiento feminil tiende a ajustarse fielmente a las
ideas sugeridas por el viril, el único fuerte. (33)[22]

[Imagine two people in the same place, then have one advance
and the other remain stationary: for every advance the first one
makes, the other remains behind. Each new conquest man
makes in the area of political freedom widens the moral abyss
that separates him from woman, making the latter's role more
passive and enigmatic. Freedom of education, freedom of religion, assembly, suffrage, parliamentarianism, means that one-
half of society (the masculine) is gaining strength and winning
rights at the expense of the other, feminine, half. Today no
woman in Spain—beginning with the one who occupies the
throne—enjoys true political influence; and in other questions
no less important, the feminine mind tends to accommodate
itself faithfully to the suggestions of the virile mind, uniquely
identified with strength.]

The intertext of gender, reform, and civilization that these two novels incorporate into the family romance makes it abundantly clear that
the Oedipal struggle on which both texts rely is irresolvable in regards
to the question of progress and the struggle to overcome decadence, a
fact that to some degree nullifies the political importance of the gender
debate the two novels carry on.[23] However, I believe that the difference
lies in Pardo Bazán's unusual exploration of the bridge figure between
the sexes: Julián, the man who, though not a father nor a mother nor
a politico like his colleagues, champions a new kind of family politics
based on trust, sentiment, and acute awareness of the feelings and

needs of others. While Galdós places his faith in the builder of bridges, Pardo Bazán imagines a way to bridge the gender gap that so frustrated bourgeois women.[24] Even though she does not challenge basic gender categorizations that Freud passed down to modern times (feminine passivity versus male activity) to the degree Balzac does in *Sarrasine*, for example (Schor, "Dreaming" 49), she does at least make clear that current gender ideology runs contrary to women's needs and desires.

## Two Classes of Mothers

The other political issue that is implicated in the sex/gender system is that of class. The bourgeois cultural mythology of motherhood sponsored in the writing of the writers studied in Chapters 1 and 2— Sinués de Marco, Grassi, Gimeno de Flaquer, Böhl de Faber, and others—regarded middle-class motherhood as a loftier aspiration than being an author. This made for an interesting working-through of the notions of public and private gender roles as well as for odd justifications for the restrictions on women's activities and movement. Whereas cultural dogma held that children belonged to their fathers and that mothers simply provided the environment, nourishment, and early religious training, women authors, most of whom were also mothers, problematized this Rousseauian notion in a variety of ways. Most, like Pardo Bazán, did so not by challenging male supremacy in the family or diminishing women's material importance, but by exaggerating women's spiritual role or splitting women into two groups, roughly though not invariably according to class:[25] those who bore and gave physical nourishment to children (Sabel, María Pepa in *La Quimera* [The chimera], etc.) and those for whom maternity means complicated and contradictory aspirations, traumas, spiritual and physical dangers, usually upper-middle-class and aristocratic women who stood in sharp contrast to their healthier but less-educated counterparts. Exceptions like Amparo of *La tribuna* or Antonia of *La piedra angular* aside, the strong peasant or working-class women—like the Galician women who toiled in the fields the same day they gave birth whom Pardo Bazán so often celebrated in her feminist essays[26]—were not the mothers she chose to write about, or at least to celebrate, in her novels. As a result, the ideal of the nurturing, tender, conserving mother figure depends

Fig. 9. Engraving from *Las buenas y las malas mujeres*.

more on class than on sex.[27] Women with leisure time, a stable living environment, and steady male companionship have the luxury to be good mothers even though tragedy may strike and break the mother-child bond, but poor mothers, like Leocadia of *El cisne de Vilamorta*, have to make hard choices that turn them into bad mothers if they are not already *naturally* inclined to be so.

This double vision of motherhood in *Los pazos* and in Pardo Bazán's other novels serves to remind us how ethnocentric the educated woman can be when portraying herself as a victim. This is why it is so important, as Gayatri Spivak puts it, to "wrench oneself away from the mesmerizing focus of the 'subject constitution'" (177) of women characters in order to understand what else, or what "other" is at stake in their representations.[28] Our understanding of Nucha as an *outsider* who erroneously stumbles in on a cultural wasteland only gains contour by contrast with the *native* version of the mother who is, despite her power over Pedro, the most conspicuous outsider in this fiction of the saintly mother. For modern feminist readers such as Spivak, Sabel would represent the excluded other woman more than Nucha because her function is to allow the *good* female subject to emerge as the one to admire and pity. Although Sabel is one of Nucha's victimizers, the text pointedly marginalizes her to the border where animal and human species are barely distinguishable. As a subcaste woman she helps to privilege the correct (upper-class) victim that Pardo Bazán's classism envelopes in an aura of sanctity. By sacrificing Sabel's subjectivity to the other maternal figure of the novel Pardo Bazán does more than unmask the category of the natural by revealing the brutality of uncivilized country life. She locates the maid in the correct, dim, field of vision within which members of one class could justify their feelings of superiority over another class. Nucha's maternal refinement and her noble stoicism highlight the maid's interior maternal instincts. Elevating Sabel to a position of power in the Ulloa household does not make us hope for a rise in her fortunes. As the *bad* mother, we can only hope that somehow she will be confined to the kitchen with the other maids and the village witch.

The contrast between the two women also reflects an argument about animal and human nature in relation to sexuality that was being debated in the decades subsequent to the publication of John Stuart Mill's *The Subjection of Women* (1869), a book that Pardo Bazán greatly admired for its position on the education of women (*La mujer* 113–34).

Mill describes the sexual instinct as essentially debasing. He urges the suppression of the sexual impulse according to Susan Mendus, as a bourgeois form of population control (179), but also as a way to privilege spiritual perfection over the brute forces of nature. This repudiation of man's sexual nature was a commonplace in Romantic Spanish fiction long before the influence of John Stuart Mill came to be felt on novelists like Pardo Bazán. For example, love in Catherine Mac-Pherson's *El hilo del destino* [The thread of destiny] is a special power that women possess to raise men from the mud, instilling in them virtuous and spiritual sentiments "cual fluido eléctrico en el alma" (86) (like an electric current in the soul).[29] Despite the fact that in many of Pardo Bazán's novels wanting to become a mother whatever a woman's status is described as the noblest of aspirations, birthing, and by implication the sexual act, are portrayed as they were likely to be experienced by many nineteenth-century women: a time of anguish and health risks and a game of possession and power. If for Mill the curtailment of sexuality signifies the possibility of human progress, Pardo Bazán less optimistically dwells on the negative consequences of heterosexual relations: for the mother, physical debilitation (Carmen of *La prueba*), illnesses related to maternity (Nucha), loss of individuality and poverty (Leocadia of *El cisne de Vilamorta*); and abuse and neglect for the child. Most of the children in Pardo Bazán's fiction would have been better off had they never been born (such as Rafael of *La sirena negra* [The siren of death], or Domingo of *El cisne de Vilamorta*).[30] Their short, sad lives bear testimony to the animal passions that debase the soul and reveal the author's basic mistrust of human sexuality and reproduction as well as her distaste for male aggression. As for her mothers, if we try to determine who should have babies, the frail, refined lady or the country "vaca," we have to conclude that neither woman suffices to cope with both the trauma and then the responsibility of motherhood and that it takes one of each (not necessarily both of them women) to do the job of mother adequately.

In the branch of psychoanalytic criticism often identified with Kristeva's work, motherhood is associated with the primitive semiotic, the underside of culture that precedes our entry into the symbolic. This description is from the point of view of the developing child whose unconscious memory of the maternal bond is the "source and fading point of all subjectivity and language" (Rose, "Kristeva" 27), always threatening the male subject with collapse. Pardo Bazán's representations of motherhood at times connect with this psychological narrative, especially during the first, most materialistic stage of her fiction. But even in her early works, such as *Los pazos*, we can distinguish two divergent conceptions of mother, one taken from the child's perspective and the other from a mother's point of view. For the former, mother nature represents the primitive maternal, a remembered maternal presence threatening presymbolic nondifferentiation and, by extension, the collapse of the civilized. She belongs to the realm of the masculine imaginary rather than representing motherhood as a lived experience. The woman who embodies this fear in Pardo Bazán's fiction is a woman of inferior caring instincts and often inferior class to which Pardo Bazán feels comfortable assigning the negative category of the mind/body and nature/culture dichotomies. But the second and prevalent representation of motherhood, taken from the perspective of those adults who give themselves over to mothering, represents society's "civilizing" feminine element that fosters a sense of community and intersubjectivity and checks sexual appetites. This is the maternal *ideal*, or we could say *imaginary*, that Pardo Bazán wove into her fictions of motherhood. Women who do not readily accept the responsibility of this type of motherhood—usually poorer or uneducated women in Pardo Bazán's classist view of things—bring death to their children and chaos to their households; they are not, in other words, *true* mothers.

Galdós's *Doña Perfecta*, like the nineteenth-century novel in general according to Brooks (307), is a question of fathers and sons, of doing things right and becoming a man a father can be proud of (of becoming the father). *Los pazos* is also a novel about fathers, but not about fathers in relation to sons. Rather, it offers a vision of a good (maternal) versus a bad father, of what makes for a good father. If motherhood is unbearable in Pardo Bazán's fiction it is because fatherhood has not yet evolved a notion of caretaking that is proper to it.[31] In her essays, Pardo Bazán expressed this notion when she praised Concepción Arenal's work:

> aún sería más ejemplidero preparar al hombre, toda vez que a la mujer la enseñan la maternidad, el sentimiento y el instinto, mientras al hombre propenso a descuidar el deber paternal, conviene disponerle a cumplirlo por medio de una preparación reflexiva. (*La mujer* 193)

[it would be even more appropriate to train a man, if a woman
has to be taught maternalness, sentiment, and instinct; it would
be useful to provide a man, more apt to neglect his paternal
duty, with a thorough preparation for his duties.]

As long as paternal legitimacy is tied to the notion of biological paternity, a notion of ideal fatherhood will remain paralyzed. Julián illustrates this critique of patriarchy by showing that the route to
fatherhood is through becoming more like the mother. That this hope-
ful journey ends in tragedy shows that Pardo Bazán understood the
social unacceptability of this parental cross-dressing. No one, laments
Julián, can usurp the place of the head of the family; his intention of
establishing the ideal Christian family has failed. "Recta había sido la
intención y amargo el fruto" (1:263) (Honorable had been his intention
and bitter the fruit).

*Chapter 5*

# New Women

Todas las noches, a solas, encerrada en mis
habitaciones, me doy una fiesta a mí misma.

*[Every night I lock myself in my room and throw
myself a party.]*

—Emilia Pardo Bazán, *Dulce Dueño*

IN THIS CHAPTER I explore a number of beyond-the-norm female
characterizations in the late works of Emilia Pardo Bazán and several
of her contemporaries writing at the turn of the century. While Emilia
Pardo Bazán is widely known outside of Spain for her Naturalist novels
and essays, her Catalonian countrywomen Dolors Monserdà i Vidal
(1845–1919) and Catalina Albert i Paradís (1869–1966) are less well
known even to Peninsularists familiar with the nineteenth-century
novel. Monserdà i Vidal (also known as Dolores Moncerdá de Maciá),
wrote novels she called "novelas de costums" (novels of customs) in
both Spanish and Catalán. Her zeal in defending working women and

her support for the unionization of women textile workers are evident in her essays, conferences, and novels. In 1909 she published an important collection of essays entitled *Estudi feminista* [Feminist studies], in which she discussed the relation between women and politics, education, and religion. Another collection of essays, *El feminisme a Catalunya* [Feminism in Catalonia] (1907) explored the issue of women's syndicates, "bajo un feminismo de inspiración cristiana" (under the guise of a Christian inspiration) (Simón Palmer, *Escritoras* 442). Unfortunately, most of her novels have not been reedited and are not available in the United States. The novel discussed here is one of her more well known works, *La fabricanta* [The industrialist], published in 1904 shortly before Pardo Bazán began publishing her series of what have been called "spiritual" novels starting with *La Quimera* in 1905.

Catalina Albert i Paradís published her entire life under the penname Víctor Català. Her realist stories and novels continued to be read in Catalán into the 1980s when the twenty-second edition of *Solitut* was published in Barcelona by Editorial Selecta. Although all of her works were published after the turn of the century, her novel *Solitut* (1905) strikes me as a fitting conclusion to this study about the ways women cope with neglect and solitude. Albert i Paradís's characters are, like Ana Ozores, unable to adapt to their environment, and the end of most of her stories is tragic.

My object in reading several turn-of-the-century novels is to test out Chodorow and other critics' assumptions of the female subject as it constitutes itself both as mirrored from the position of another's perceptions, and as a rebuttal or revision of that mirrored perception. The characters examined in this chapter inherit the negative attitude toward female idleness that Rosalía de Castro's Countess Pampa expresses in *El caballero de las botas azules*, only instead of just complaining about feminine idleness, dependency, or educational disadvantage, they take matters into their own hands. They are not *liberated* in any modern sense of the word, but neither do they imagine themselves as victims of social and familial conventions in the way that their predecessors of a few decades earlier did.

To see this difference in late nineteenth- and early twentieth-century novels requires first an exploration of "what women wanted," both in terms of their expressed desires and what those desires may reflect about female development and maturity. The assumption underlying both of these issues is that women's wants and needs are determined as much by the privileges society denies them by virtue of their being female as by the biological fact that they are born without a male organ. In other words, I focus on female development as a product rather than a producer of culture. But in doing so, I recognize that our norms for development are distorted by the fact that female sexuality is still seen by many in terms of ideal male psychology and that it is, strictly speaking, impossible to talk about uniquely *feminine* ideals outside of a specific historical context. Women cannot be analyzed separately from cultural representations of women that are largely determined by male aesthetic, psychological, and sexual constructions. Finally, I will comment on the creation of male characters, relating their representation to the way Spanish women in general write about men and what fictional men might symbolize in terms of female psychological constructs.

When we think in terms of the *new* woman in late nineteenth- and early twentieth-century literature, we may at first imagine that what women wanted was not to be *women* anymore; that is, not to personify the Christian virtues of charity, humility, self-sacrifice, but to manipulate traditional exploitative roles in order to resist regression, embrace progress, separate from family tutelage, and go out into the world. In other words, we may be tempted to assume that women wanted to be *men*, since our notion of normative psychological development is derived from a male model based on the Oedipal trajectory of separation and succession to the throne. In the emerging psychoanalytical forums of the turn of the century, female development is always imagined as a derivative, albeit problematic and incomplete, reflection of the normative male model. "Directing his gaze at the penis, whose primacy in the order of gender he never questioned, Freud concluded that castration was the pivotal threat in the development of both sexes" (Garner et al. 19). Much debate has subsequently centered on the vital question of whether or to what degree the female psyche pines endlessly for the missing organ, barred from it and from many other things as a consequence of this lack. Even revisionist readers of Freudian psychology, notably Lacan, interpret gender difference as a function of the phallus, a signifier of desire that is supposedly nonrepresentational (not related to genitality), but that nonetheless defines us according to the Law of the Father as men or women.

Among Lacan's most important contributions to gender psychology are his persistent explorations of the concept of subjectivity and the relation he established between speaking and the human subject, a subject that is not a fixable entity with *an* identity, but a mirage, according to Lacan, "created in the fissure of a radical split" (5). Paradoxically, we would not be able to address the issue of female subjectivity (a notion Lacan disputes) if it were not for his ground-breaking work on male subjectivity. But one problem with the post-Freudian description of female development is that it does not account for the effects of certain preexisting gendering systems that historically valorize one or the other gender and thus determine difference long before a woman is born and long after the Oedipal stage, those systems for which a woman finds herself "signed up without having begun to play" (Irigaray 22). As Annis Pratt explains, "when we seek an identity based on human personhood rather than on gender, we stumble about in a landscape whose signposts indicate retreats from, rather than ways to, adulthood" (6). Thus psychoanalytic paradigms often fail to distinguish the relationship between language and female as opposed to male sexuality (Gallop, *The Daughter* 23), and critics looking for a *new woman* are often disappointed by what they find.

Had he focused more closely on the female subject instead of *barring* it as a hopelessly undefinable "not all" (144), Lacan might have been better able to account for what Nancy Chodorow calls the more fluid ego boundaries of women, and the "female tendency to perceive reality in relational terms" (Garner et al. 20); in other words, the importance of women's relation to familial, social, and cultural experience as a shared experience. He might also have been more perceptive about the meaning of women's great skill of psychological survival in a man's world. These notions, touched on in Chapter 1, will be explored here in relation to such female characterizations as Pardo Bazán's Fe Neira *(Memorias de un solterón)* and other female subjects who are to a greater or lesser degree consciously (not vaguely, as in the domestic novel) uncomfortable in a patriarchal society.

In the latter decades of the nineteenth century and proceeding into the twentieth, women novelists began to experiment with characters who, unlike the heroines of the earlier domestic novel, want something more than to be wanted by men. We can group these descendants of Böhl de Faber's María *(La Gaviota)* and Castro's Countess de Pampa *(El caballero)* into two categories. The first is the "new woman" in the British style, that is, the woman who longs for increased educational and professional opportunities and who challenges patriarchy for rights that she has been unjustly denied: to vote, to dispose of property, to change her legal status and so forth, and to make decisions regarding her body. The second is the woman who, refusing to play the role of social leech and primping doll, insists upon being a working, contributing member of society. Examples of the first type of "new" woman, some are disappointed to find, are exceedingly rare in nineteenth-century Spanish fiction, although they are frequently represented pejoratively in periodical literature and iconographic art. The second type is much more common. Bourgeois women writers, weary of the Romantic horror of physical labor,[1] often championed the middle-class woman's right to enter the workplace even as they documented the sometimes dire consequences of doing so or, on the contrary, idealized the working woman's noble character. While these two types of new women have in common the refusal to accept idleness and regression as a mode of adult femininity, they are often represented as being at odds with one another in Spanish literature, and there seems to be a clear preference for the second woman who defines fulfillment in terms of her work to benefit a family or society at large.

This can be seen clearly by comparing the two heroines of Dolors Monserdà i Vidal's novel *La fabricanta* (1904). Florentina, one of the two heroines of the novel, enjoys every imaginable material advantage yet she feels incomplete because she has failed to find the masculine ideal that she has learned to expect from reading too many novels by her favorite Romantic authors, among them, Manuel Fernández y González, George Sand, Alexandre Dumas, Eugène Sué, and Victor Hugo.[2] Like Laura Pampa, she awaits a Werther who will be attuned to her every emotional need. Having read and seen too many Romantic books and plays, Florentine begins to think her life is a dreary affair and her marriage a "dogal asfixiador" (asphyxiating knife). Because in her marriage there is no compatibility of character or sentiment and no esteem or sense of shared suffering, she concludes that her husband is a vulgar despot. Refusing the role of the long-suffering heroine of the domestic novel she announces that she will do anything possible to divorce him or at least separate from him. In the following passage the narrator outlines Florentina's predicament from a not-too-sympathetic point of view toward women's literary adventures.

> I la pobre Florentina, la febrosa somniadora assedegada de quimérics ideals en el paroxisme del sentiment, plorant amb el

Toda la correspon-
dencia al Administrador
G. Osler, Espíritu San-
, 15.—Madrid.

# El Mundo Femenino

Se publica todos los
domingos.
Número atrasado 25
céntimos.

Suscripciones: Por 6 meses 3'50 pesetas.—Por un año 6.—A los corresponsales, 2'50 la mano.

Fig. 10. "La mujer del día."

desconsol de *Hero* per la mort de *Leandro*, la de les seves illusions ofegades en corrent de l'amarga realitat de la vida, després d'aquells sis dies en els que apenes havia menjat ni dormit, posseïda d'una forta agitació nerviosa, prengué la teatral resolució d'abandonar el marit, anantse'n amb els seus fills, després de deixar-li escrita una llarga carta, a on, en el sentit que havem exposat, li formulava un gros capítol de càrrecs; assegurant-li que ella també l'avorria tant com l'havia estimat; que la seva resolució era irrevocable; i que, una volta arreglada la qüestió d'interessos, se n'aniria a viure a l'estranger, per a no tornar-lo a veure mai més... (161)

[And the poor Florentina, the feverish dreamer besieged with chimeric ideals in a paroxysm of sentiment, weeping disconsolately like *Hero* for the death of *Leandro*, with illusions drowned in the bitter current of the realities of life, after six days in which she barely ate or slept, while she was possessed by a strong nervous agitation, took the theatrical resolution to abandon her husband, escaping with her children, after leaving him a long letter in which, as mentioned before, she gave him a large list of things to do, assuring him that she now abhorred him as much as she had once esteemed him; that her resolution was irrevocable; and that, once their finances were straightened out, she would go abroad to live, never to see him again.]

Antonieta, the novel's second heroine, is a more mature, if less educated, version of her vain cousin Florentina. She does not pine away for the perfect soul-mate because she has never been contaminated by such an impossible ideal through the vice of novel reading. Instead she longs for the sanity of work and the feeling of being a team with her husband as well as a useful member of society. On her wedding day she convinces her radiant bridegroom to cancel their planned wedding celebrations and invest their money in a small workshop that they will run together. Instead of three days of celebration with their friends, they will spend their time moving the workshop into their home and setting up their machinery to begin weaving. With the money from this enterprise, they will soon be able to buy their own factory: "Jo t'ajudaré com ho feia la mare i buscaré la manera de vendre a les botigues els mocadors que to teixiràs i que, amb l'ajuda de Déu, seran els fonaments de la fàbrica de can Grau" (109) (I will help you like my mother helped my father, I will find ways to sell the handkerchiefs that you make to the stores and, with the help of God, this will be the foundation of the House of Grau).

Antonieta is given books but, with the exception of Saint Theresa, she neglects to read them. She inherits a dowry from her father, but refuses out of pride to claim it. Still decades away (the novel appears to be set in the 1880s) are the anarchists' bombs and "autoritaris decrets de la *Internacional*" (the authoritarian degrees of the *International*), so she is not required to concern herself with politics and labor unions. The only right she claims are the freedom to work on the factory floor (eventually supervising a home workshop), and the free use of the profits from her enterprise to help raise her family and invest in their future. In a modern twist to the domestic novel, she even saves her brother from bankruptcy when the market collapses. In short, Antonieta is the woman who goes to the factory without losing any of the cherished qualities of the domestic angel.[3]

Although the portrait of Florentina is wholly unsympathetic, as in Castro's *El caballero de las botas azules*, Monserdà's condemnation of the idle upper-class woman is not without contradiction. Specifically, Antonieta rallies in Florentina's defense by criticizing men's reluctance to embellish their fine deeds with fine words: "I a vegades les dones serien felices amb tan poca cosa!... I tu, Pep, com el meu mateix home, ets un bon tros exut, sec, esquerp... i si bé les obres proven les estimacions, les bones paraules són el foc que les embelleix i les alimenta" (182) (And sometimes women would be happy with just a word!... And you, Pep, like my own husband, are so dry and rough,... and if it is true that deeds are what prove a man's esteem, good words are the fire that embellish and feed it). On the other hand, the practical-minded Antonieta is proud that she manages without men's tender words to gain a sense of self-worth, and that she has achieved great success with only vague notions of what can be learnt from books:

> Educada de franc per les monges de l'ensenyança, quan aquestes tenien encara el seu convent en el centre de la ciutat antiga, dels poquíssims llibres que es cursaven en aquella época en els collegis de noies, en el cervell de l'Antonieta, sols hi havien quedat impresos amb completa claredat, els preceptes

de la doctrina cristiana i les bones màximes de la *Urbanidad* i
de *El libro de las niñas.* (60)

[Educated for free by the teaching nuns, when they still had
their convent in the center of the old city, of the very few books
that at that time were taught in the schools for novices, in the
brain of Antonieta there had only remained with complete clar-
ity the precepts of Christian doctrine, and the sane maxims of
*Urbanity* and *The Guide for Girls.*]

Everything else Antonieta had been taught is a jumble of useless
names: she confuses biblical figures Abraham, David, and Moses, with
all the Pelayos, Alfonsos, and Ramiros of Spanish history. Her only
knowledge of history, sacred or profane, is that God produced Adam
and Eve, and that after a long line of conquerors and kings, Spain
now has a queen whose name is Isabel II. The object here is to demonstrate how little a woman needs to learn from books in order to be a
success. Antonieta and her husband become rich by dint of their hard
work and determination, not through their education, while too much
literature contaminates her cousin Florentine and puts her fortune and
family at risk.

Monserdà i Vidal's countrywoman Catalina Albert i Paradís also
creates women heroines who move painfully and erratically toward
independence (rather than feminine interdependence) *despite* not *because
of* social pressures. Her most famous character, La Mila of *Solitut*
(1905), is an embattled and neglected wife who retreats into solitude
and silence when the pressures of married life in a backward mountain
community become unbearable. In *Solitut*, as in Castro's *La hija del
mar* [Daughter of the sea], family life is so stifling and perverse that a
solution must at all costs be found, even at the risk of death. In a
rigidly moralistic rural society, La Mila cannot simply change her fate
by changing partners. In fact her great achievement in the solitude of
her daily existence is to subsist, spiritually and economically, despite
her poverty and debts caused by her husband's gambling and her
longing for social interaction and companionship.

La Mila's first accomplishment is a self-taught indifference to the
misdeeds and neglect of her husband. In time she comes to accept the
fact that she cannot rely on Matias either for emotional or economic
support. Instead of censuring him, she learns to regard him with

"benèvola indiferència" (benevolent indifference), letting him go his own way:

> Es sentia lliure i mestressa de si mateixa, i amb la secreta llibertat, regnava en tots sos actes, ben cert que era una harmonia apagada, sense nervi ni empenta, mes per això mateix grata a son estat, puix no li reclamava cap esforç cansador.
> La Mila revivia amb lentitud, com un soldat dessagnat en el camp de batalla i que ha de recobrar la seva sang de gota en gota. (198–99)

> [She felt free and the mistress of herself, with this secret liberty, reigning in all of her actions; true, there was a quiet harmony about her, without nervousness or impulse, and yet this was good for her state, since nothing required a difficult effort.
> La Mila revived slowly, like a soldier injured on the battlefield who must recover his blood drop by drop.]

What Albert i Paradís describes in this passage is a kind of noninstitutionalized divorce that was not unusual in the domestic novel of the nineteenth century. In this case, however, it does not mark the ending of the story. The narrative goes beyond the domestic novel's discovery of female fortitude, showing how La Mila's *solitut* is constantly marred by masculine violence and social castration even after she has learned to cancel her emotional ties with her husband. What differentiates her from Sinués de Marco's characters, for example, is that self-sacrifice is not the solution, only an effect of abuse. Any second chance for her could only come through her own initiative, not from the sudden appearance of a savior Pygmalion.

La Mila is treated as a moral outcast by her neighbors even though she dutifully rejects the advances of her neighbor L'Arnau and suppresses her love for the shepherd who is her only friend and companion. Finally, on a feast night when her husband has abandoned her for the gambling tables, she is attacked in her home by a man who thinks she will sell herself to him since she is the village outcast. It is then that La Mila decides that the word *home* has no meaning for her, since it offers her none of the protection or comfort that the domestic novel assures women exists there:

> —Ara, ja t'ho deus pensar... Jo, allà dins, mai més! . . .

—Tampoc amb tu. Mai més... No provis pas de seguirme...
Te... mataria.

I resolta, se'l mirà de fit a fit, como volent fer-li penetrar fins
a l'ànima la terrible amenaça.

Després baixà lentament del regatell i sense afegir altre mot,
sense tombar la cara, sense res més que la roba de l'esquena,
la dona, èrtica i greu, amb el cap dret i els ulls obrívols, empren-
gué sola la davallada.

Les filtracions de la solitud havien cristallitzat amargament
en son destí. (305)

[Now, you must already know... I will never go back inside,
never again!

Not even with you. Never again. . . . Don't try to follow
me... I... would kill you.

And, resolute, she looked at him face to face, as if to make
her terrible menace penetrate to the depths of his soul.

Then she slowly walked down the stairs and without saying
another word, without lowering her face, with nothing else but
the clothes on her back, the woman, erect and grave, with her
eyes straight before her and wide open, started to descend the
mountain by herself.

The filtrations of solitude had bitterly crystallized her fate.]

La Mila's bitter solitude is destined to follow her everywhere she
tries to go, but at least she has bravely resolved to escape an abusive
home atmosphere. Readers may not believe that La Mila will ever be
able to escape the haunting circumstances of her young married life,
yet the physical distance that she puts between herself and her "home"
certainly could be interpreted as a critique of the norms governing
married life in Catalonian society.

## Female Identity in *Memorias de un solterón*

Monserdà and Albert i Paradís imagine the path to feminine perfection
through a populist work ethic that can manage without great books
or family and social support systems. On the contrary, Emilia Pardo
Bazán is less belligerent toward education, and in fact, defines it as

promotional of, not detrimental to, women's productiveness. More than any other author, perhaps, Pardo Bazán recognized that the gulf between middle-class women and men was so great, primarily because of the fact that women were so poorly educated (Lobato Villena 275). To see this, we have to look beyond Pardo Bazán's canonical works like *Los pazos de Ulloa*, in which women are largely incapacitated victims, and consider some of her minor, much less well received, novels.

Pardo Bazán has often been cited for her *masculine* prose. To some this is an indictment because impersonating male authors, especially those whose prose tends toward the starker realities of the Naturalist school, was unseemly. To many others, on the contrary, it is only the most virile of her novels that have, then as now, *something to say*. In other words, what was good about her was her capacity to write manly prose. Fortunately, Maryellen Bieder, Ruth El Saffar, Diane Urey, Elizabeth Ordóñez and other critics are beginning to see the *other* side of Pardo Bazán's *masculine* novels like *Los pazos de Ulloa* and *La Madre Naturaleza*. But very little has captured the critics' attention in Pardo Bazán's allegedly *frivolous* novels such as *Memorias de un solterón* [Diary of a bachelor] (1896) and *Insolación* [Sunstroke] (1889).

Perhaps the lack of tension and conflict in these last works precludes their *canonization*, but it is also possible that their tension has been misunderstood or devalued because their heroines do not become anything in the end except wives. In other words, their only heroism consists of coming to terms with what was possible for a woman to be in nineteenth-century Spanish society. The silence of critics regarding *Memorias de un solterón* and other works mentioned in this chapter also speaks eloquently of the fate of minor works of famous women in general. They simply are not part of the cherished canon because they don't fit established norms of literary taste and judgment. I realize that many of my readers will not have read these novels and yet may be very familiar with, for example, Galdós's *Tristana* (1892), an earlier version of a woman-who-would-be-free story, about which everyone, including Pardo Bazán, rushed to comment.[4] Perhaps this lack of critical focus will be an advantage for those who wish to negotiate the text without creating a counterreading of previous critics. I hope to show why it is relevant to reevaluate *Memorias* by studying its quirky bachelor as an identity-fulfilling fantasy especially destined to validate the female subject instead of the reverse. In other words, Mauro does not grow in our eyes, enlarged by a female muse; rather, he is willed into becoming what the female subject, Fe Neira, requires in order to be substantiated and validated as a subject.

*Memorias de un solterón*, together with a handful of other works—including *El tesoro de Gastón* [Gastón's treasure] (1897) and the short novel *Insolación*, the stories "La dama joven" [The young woman] and "Naúfragas" [The shipwrecked women] among others—correspond to that historical category of writing Elaine Showalter classifies the "feminist phase" of women's writing roughly from 1880 to 1920 (138). The feminist story dramatizes the "ordeals of wronged womanhood" or looks longingly toward perfected societies that find a place for the "New Woman." In Chapter 1 I speculated, via Nancy Armstrong, that the "ángel de hogar" (domestic angel) was more a productive than reflective representation. Similarly, the new woman, and especially the new man (Mauro), were representations destined to produce the desire for the appearance of historically liberated men and women. In "Revising Realism," Elizabeth Ordóñez interprets Mauro as an indication of one of the "divergent male attributes in a changing Spanish society" (152). But according to Giuliana Di Febo, there is very little evidence that men as enlightened as Mauro actually existed outside of fiction. In her desire to establish the plausibility of *Memorias* (and perhaps to castigate Pérez Galdós for his cynicism about the novel), Ordóñez paints a much more optimistic picture of Spanish society than do sociologists like Di Febo, who conclude that female participation in the public workplace was limited to a tiny minority. Pardo Bazán uses her art to imagine a potential social change, as Ordóñez herself notes in her conclusion where she suggests that Mauro's function is to "increase the ranks in Spain of men like the British philosopher Mill" (163). Pardo Bazán puts it best in a letter to Galdós quoted by Ordóñez: "let us construct, with the freedom of art, the situation that society could have provided us" (*Cartas a Galdós* [Letters to Galdós] 91; quoted in Ordóñez 160).

In *Memorias*, as in some of the works of Pardo Bazán's Catalonian, American, and British contemporaries, there is an explicit rejection of male government, laws, and social institutions. Yet implicit in its accommodationist ending is also an earlier model of feminist writings typified by the novels of George Sand, such as *La petite Fadette*. Characteristic of nearly all of Sand's prose works, is her pragmatic retreat from whatever perfected society could be imagined to embrace the new woman. Fe's renunciation of the "free life" in Madrid typifies Pardo Bazán's tactical retreat from what she knew readers would consider either an impossible utopia or an undesirable one. Taking the more common ground, she opts, as Monserdà does in *La fabricanta*, for the romance of the exceptionally perfect *pareja* (couple). Like Sand, it is as if Pardo Bazán were unable "to conceive that a woman's voice, alone or in consonance with other women's, might be capable of generating harmony and resolving conflict" (Deutelbaum and Huff 277). In fact, in the case of *Memorias*, the ideal married life, though *arranged* and *agreed upon* before the wedding, does not form part of Mauro's diary. Mauro suggests that perhaps he ought to write a *Memorias de un casado* [Diary of a married man] to describe his life "con mujer tan singular como la que [le] tocó en suerte" (2:527) (as unusual as the one fate had dealt him), but no such narrative exists in Pardo Bazán's fiction. Simply suggesting the possibility of a companionate relationship was perhaps a sufficiently radical strategy for an increasingly restive woman reader, writing the story of one was simply *unimaginable.*[5]

On the surface, *Memorias de un solterón* is, despite its title, a *female* bildungsroman that predictably reduces the alternatives a woman faces as a young, unwed adult to what kind of victim she allows herself to become as she is gradually integrated into patriarchal society. Fe's choice is complicated by the fact that, psychologically, she is both the daughter seeking among the minefields of an unsympathetic social climate for an accommodation with the Law of the Father (like Laura Pampa seeking words, knowledge, and a world beyond perpetual feminine infancy and silence), and at the same time the embodiment of the *eternal* (as society interpreted it) female nature seeking the validation of her nurturing, maternal tendencies. If she agrees to replace the missing mother—her mother—to her erring sisters who are all bent on self-destruction in the absence of parental guidance, it may appear that her own life, in terms of growth potential, will come to an end. Lacan might say that by showing in exaggerated fashion how a woman's growth is arrested at the most critical juncture of her development, Pardo Bazán reenacts the story of the girl-child's stormy refusal to enter the symbolic order, with romance's palliative solution thrown in to mitigate or disguise this tragedy.

Unless we apprise carefully the relationship between male and female subjects, Fe's choice will indeed seem a tragic negation of her life goals, or their subsumption to the goals society expects women to embrace. The androgynous hoyden cancels her masculine side and, becoming all woman, chooses marriage in order to facilitate her role as mother to her siblings. As Freud would have it, she accepts womanhood as a negation of her delusion of wholeness. She washes her hair, cleans her fingernails (we're never told if she loses the telltale moustache on her upper lip) and puts aside her general desire to be (free) like a man. As a woman, she comes to accept a role as the teacher and regulator of morals of her dysfunctional family, compensating for the missing mother and ineffectual father whom she also replaces. At last she allows the desire of others who need her, whether to affirm themselves or merely to survive, to override her own desire to stand free of others. One is tempted to perceive her purely in terms of the self-sacrificing woman who facilitates the growth of others. And yet, we should also recognize that Fe freely makes the choice to be defined in relation to others only after she, like Böhl de Faber's Clemencia, assesses realistically what it means to choose, and her choice can be seen in a positive light if our model for female development is not phallocentric.

To determine if Pardo Bazán betrays Fe by having her set aside her desires in order to marry the *solterón*, we also have to appreciate to what extent female desire transforms Mauro Pareja from the misogynist bachelor into a suitable alternative to the life of freedom the young woman ostensibly seeks. If we take Mauro at his word that finally he is the only one in Marineda "que tasaba a Feíta en su justo valor" (2:494) (able to measure Feíta's true value), then Fe's choices may not seem so diametrically opposed, so observing of the gender dichotomies that expressed nineteenth-century fears of disappearing gender boundaries. To do this requires the knowledge of what Fe stands to gain by entering into what Paula Marantz Cohen calls a "companionate marriage" (90). The advantages of marrying in these circumstances, perhaps more obvious for contemporary readers of Pardo Bazán, compensate for the freedoms Fe will be forced by convention to relinquish, freedoms modern readers may overestimate.

The first step in elucidating Fe's decision is to trace Mauro's transformation from Fe's antagonist to her perfect complement. Instead of trying to change anything about her character, Mauro allows himself to be molded into her ideal mate. Fe looks so intently upon his face— when first they meet in his library (2:468), when she appears to him in his dreams as a snake (2:477), even through the library walls (2:484)—that Mauro finds himself mesmerized into a register of her integrity and her subjecthood. In this sense *Memorias* is also a male bildungsroman because Mauro's formation clearly hinges upon his ability to undergo transformation; his mission is to understand a woman as something other than a narcissistic projection of his needs and ideals. Like in a medieval *espejo para príncipes* (mirror for princes), Mauro learns through trial and error, that is, through challenges to his gender ideology, how to conduct himself in the light of uncommon social and moral practices. But, unlike the prince of old, he himself becomes the specular agent, allowing us to see Fe as a subject.

The transformation process is slow but not painful, resisted but not destructive. Mauro loses nothing by becoming Fe's ideal mate because he was nothing to begin with. Rather, he is a somewhat worn reflection of society's collective view of women, a catalogue of generalizations, misconceptions, and perceptions crying out for contradiction. Happily, society's spokesman for the patriarchal order agrees not only to be a defector but to become a champion of a new gender order. After his transformation, Mauro abandons his collective specularity as he begins to reflect back to this one remarkable woman what it is that sets her aside from all others. While the business of Leopoldo Alas's narrator in *La Regenta* is to show that his most famous character Ana Ozores is "tan mujer como tantas otras" (2:528) (just a woman like any other), Pardo Bazán answers with a woman who is uncommon even when measured by reductive male standards. Hence the text does not need to destroy her (as Galdós does Tristana or George Sand does Fadette, for example) because Pardo Bazán was able to imagine a male subject capable of surviving *in the face* of a self-aware female subject.

Fe's father calls his daughter a monster, "un fenómeno aflictivo y ridículo" (2:473) (an afflictive and ridiculous phenomenon) but it never occurs to him to lock her up in a house, convent, or asylum. The town gossip, Primo Cova, clicks in disapproval over Fe's escapades, but zealously defends her secrets and honor on every occasion. Mauro vociferously condemns Fe's outlandish conduct and statements while privately agreeing with her deep in his "yo esencial" (essential being). Unlike the men Pardo Bazán complained of in her articles (*La mujer* 53), Mauro does not perceive intimacy and affiliation as a threat to his masculinity. This is the important difference between novels written toward the end of the century and the novels described in Chapters 1 and 2 on domestic fiction. The issue is not the transference of women between two families, although *Memorias* certainly is about courtship and marriage; rather, it concerns the definition of a woman both in relation to her immediate family, and her new position in the husband-wife relationship. It does not entail merely a solidification of previous arrangements or a genealogical transference of father right, but a more complex and satisfying (for a woman at any rate) alternative to patri-lineage. Mauro is not taking the place of Fe's father. Mauro and Fe together are assuming that role, with Fe poised to play the more active part. In the unique role Fe has determined to play, she will take charge of her siblings. Her motive is not only to save herself from the embar-rassment of being attached to a worthless family, but to rehabilitate other members of her family to a fuller and more productive existence. In this new family, a woman will not just care for children, but will empower herself to reach out to an extended family, making decisions formerly reserved for the male head of the household.[6] The result is a return to bourgeois family stability, but not in its most repressive forms that were promoted in the earlier domestic novel.

Pardo Bazán clearly did not set about to argue that this freedom-loving, studious woman or curiously cooperative man whose only re-sponsibility is to himself, were any kind of visible historical reality that Spanish society should awaken to. She believed in the existence of such men and women in France, England, and the United States, but her pessimism regarding Spain's new woman is well established both in her fiction and essays. Spanish women were what Spanish men made of them, she complained, "The defects of the Spanish woman, given her social state, can largely be placed at the feet of man, who is, so to speak, the one who molds and sculpts the feminine soul. . . . In Spanish contemporary society, of any ten daily acts a woman performs, at least nine obey the dictates of the man who sug-gests them" (La mujer 26).[7]

This pessimism, however, did not prevent Pardo Bazán from imagin-ing what a woman possessed of her own ideas would be like,[8] and to this end she had to create men capable of seeing this woman as some-thing other than a monster or freak. Thus she did what writing women have done throughout the centuries in their most romantic representa-tions, she created in Mauro Pareja a man capable of sanctioning a woman's most extravagant desires, an exceptional man who could rec-ognize, live with, and, most important, report to others his approval of the exception. My contention is that Pardo Bazán's political notions about collectivity and individuals[9] are not reactionary when interpreted as a replaying of this lesson in the realities of Spanish female adulthood. When Mauro exultantly argues that even in collective *partidos* (political parties) only an individual man can affect for the good the course of history, he not only voices the bourgeois panic at the prospect of disappearing class boundaries, he reflects the author's oft-repeated argument that the exceptional woman will only find justice in the eyes of an individual man, never society at large. Pardo Bazán could only imagine sexual complementariness, the utopian ideal on which this notion is based, at the level of the individual family unit. Society and laws will not rescue Fe, argues Mauro:

> La sociedad actual no le reconocerá a usted esos derechos que usted cree tener. Solo puede usted esperar justicia..., ¿de quién? Nunca de la sociedad; de un individuo, sí. Ese individuo justo y superior será el hombre que la quiera a usted y la estime lo bastante para proclamar que es usted su igual en condición y en derecho. (2:510)

> [Today's society will not recognize the rights you believe are yours. You can only hope for justice..., from whom? Society, never; from an individual, yes. That fair-minded and superior individual will be the man who loves and esteems you enough to proclaim that you are his equal in condition and right.]

In her creation of the ideal mate, Pardo Bazán expresses the notion that developmental psychologists like Carol Gilligan argue is one of the most enduring tenets of female maturity: that relations take primacy over social orders and laws (24–32). Problems are best mediated on the interpersonal level; while society's laws and restrictions can affect her life negatively, only a unique, loving individual can have a positive influence on a woman's life. Clearly, like many modern feminists, Pardo Bazán was skeptical about finding solutions to the problems of gender relations in both repressive and progressive institutions. Thus, instead of recognizing the relation between women and other classes brutally marginalized in bourgeois society, she opted instead to portray all ideologies as oppressive to women.[10] The more rights men gain, she felt, the greater the gulf marking the difference between the sexes (see above quotation, 133).[11]


## What Young Girls Dream About

In an 1885 full-spread sketch in *Madrid Cómico* entitled "Lo que sueñan las muchachas" [What young women dream about] (see Fig. 6), a woman's dreams are dramatized in tiny sketches above her sleeping head: money, carriage-rides, and romantic strolls in the park, trays of jewels, a proliferation of obsequious male figures all bowing to her. To the side the weights and pendulum of a heart-shaped clock are labeled "vanidad, coquetería, interés" (vanity, coquetry, self-interest) in case distracted readers missed the point. This conception of Spanish women was, as we know from Alicia Andreu's *Galdós y la literatura popular* [Galdós and popular literature], a popular one that censored the bourgeois woman's crass materialism while at the same time feeding it to new heights of consumption. In the backwaters of Marineda, Pardo Bazán is able to counter with a different vision of what a woman can want, and the contrast is stark. Fe dreams of freedom that she equates with exploring Marineda alone, on foot—a privilege every Spanish man considered a birthright:

> ¡A salir, a andar sola, a no depender de nadie! ¿Lo oye usted? ¡De nadie! . . . Libertad, libertad sacrosanta, nuestro numen tú siempre serás. . . . ¡Qué sano es andar! Me siento otra. Andar a prisa, andar sola, sin apéndices, sin rodrigones. (2:479)

> [To go out, to walk about alone, to not depend on anyone! Do you hear me? Not anyone! . . . Freedom, holy freedom, you will forever be our deity. . . . How healthy it is to walk! I feel like another person. To walk fast or slowly, without accompaniment, without escorts.]

Days after her self-decreed emancipation Fe feels healthier because she is experiencing herself as alive and separate from others for the first time. She acknowledges that she is becoming a subject by dint of the

actions she initiates at caprice, instead of as a reaction (emphasis
added):

> Ahora *salgo* temprano, sin acompañamiento; *cruzo* las calles, *dejo
> atrás* la ciudad, *me meto* por los sembrados, los huertos, los
> caminatos vecinales; tengo sed o tengo hambre: saco mi vaso,
> ¿lo ve usted?, aquí en el bolsillo va, *bebo* en el primer arroyo o
> en la fuente de la carretera..., *cojo* un mendrugo de pan y le
> *hinco* el diente... Si se me ha olvidado echarme en la faltriquera
> el mendrugo, *compro* un cuarterón de *brona* y me sabe a gloria
> divina... *Ando* una legua, dos leguas, tres..., y *vuelvo* a Marineda
> en estado de beatitud. Dígame usted, *Abad*, pero con la concien-
> cia en la mano: ¿hay algún mal en esto? (2:486)

> [Now I go out early, alone; I cross streets, leaving behind the
> city, I enter the fields, gardens and country paths; if I am thirsty
> or hungry: I take out my cup, do you see it? here in my purse
> is where I keep it, and I drink from the first stream or fountain
> by the road..., I take a crust of bread and sink my teeth into
> it... If I have forgotten to put one in my pocket, I buy a quarter
> loaf of brona and it tastes like heaven to me... I walk a league,
> two leagues, three..., and I return to Marineda in a beatific
> state. Tell me, my abbot, but in all sincerity: is there anything
> wrong in this?]

A celebration of the mundane; no doubt a banal catalogue of activities
for the palate of male readers, but then, as Jane Miller reminds us, a
novel about the small things that make a woman's life interesting "is
bound to conflict with conventions deriving from the ways men have
devised to make their lives sound interesting" (191).

To propose alternative ways for women to *picture* their lives usually
involves confronting the problem of economic independence from
men, a thorny subject in a country where only male children could
inherit wealth and where the worker, much less the female worker,
was often despised or misunderstood by the reading public. In the
cartoon "What Young Women Dream About" (Fig. 6), a shower of
coins pours from the mouth of a corpulent gentleman onto the head
of the sleeping beauty. That it comes from his mouth graphically
demonstrates the link between gender and material well-being, a link

that Fe's modest accomplishment belies. When she earns her first month's salary for tutoring the children of wealthy families, she exults over the handful of coins, raising them with "infantile" gesture to her lips to kiss them. The pleasure, she insists, is not in the power to purchase that the coins symbolize, but the power they grant her to be exempt from male mediums of exchange:

> ¡Qué bien me sabes! ¡Qué embelesada estoy contigo! Te he ganado yo, yo misma; no te he recibido de manos de ningún hombrón; no eres señal de mi esclavitud, ¡eres prenda de mi emancipación total y absoluta! (2:487)

> [How good you taste to me! How thrilled I am with you! I earned you, myself; I didn't receive you from the hands of some fat man; you are not a symbol of my slavery, you are the pledge of my total and absolute emancipation!]

Nineteenth-century culture reenacted over and over the metamorphosis of the poor girl, usually an orphan of uncertain class origin, dressed in tattered dress and preposterous boots, suddenly transformed into an elegant courtesan. She embodied both the myth of the "alluring vacuum of the uncultured woman, waiting for the artist-male to fill her" (Auerbach, "Magi" 116) as well as bourgeois anxieties about class identity and institutions (Cora Kaplan 168). Countless novels and stories retell her adventure; the pages of the popular arts magazine *Madrid Cómico* are filled with her image. It was presumed that the sexual function of the transfigured woman was to dress to attract men and she stood, in popular culture, for the proneness of the female to consume the goods (and seed) of men. Fe is the transformed waif, but with an important twist. After about a month of roaming the city streets and country lanes, the ugly duckling suddenly appears before Mauro with clean hair and fingernails, whiter collars, and more feminine apparel. The fastidious bachelor is so gratified at what he mistakenly interprets as the classic female metamorphosis that he remarks about the appropriateness of women dressing for men's pleasure. Fe reacts swiftly and with spirit against the notion that female beauty is for the recreation of men: "¿Qué obligación tenemos de recrearles a ustedes la vista? ¿Somos odaliscas, somos muebles decorativos, somos claveles en tiesto?" (2:488) (What obligation do we have to please you?

Are we odalisques? are we pieces of decorative furniture? are we carna-
tions in a flower pot?). Women should dress as a sign that they have
evaded savagery, for their own hygiene, out of respect for their own
bodies, "por coquetería, niquis" (2:488) (for coquetry, no way).[12] It is
knowledge, then, that inspires Fe to set aside her hoyden image, not,
as most male novelists would have it, a man's love or need that awakens
her to femininity. On the contrary, she steadfastly refuses to acquiesce
to the "masculine" system of representation whose "self-reflexiveness
and specularity disappropriate women of their relation to themselves"
(Jacobus 38).

The most paradoxical result of Fe's emancipation is not her sudden
interest in her physical appearance, but the fact that liberty has made
her more responsive to her family's needs. Unless we accept this seeming contradiction, her marriage to Mauro will appear incongruous.
Being free to roam outside the confines of her home, claims Fe, has
instilled in her a growing desire to be of use to her family. "¡Sí, señor!
Desde que he roto las cadenas, he visto que aquel modo de sentir mío
era perverso. A mí debe importarme la familia. Y me importa. ¡Cui-
dado si me importa!" (2:487) (Yes sir! Since I broke my chains, I can
see how my way of thinking was perverse. I should care about my
family, and I do. Truly I do!) Being on the outside has permitted Fe
to open new windows inward, onto the area of her intelligence that
allows her to picture herself as the solution instead of an effect of her
family's economic and moral predicament. "No crea usted, esto de la
libertad tiene de bueno que ensancha el meollo y le abre a uno a no
sé qué ventanas allá en el entendimiento" (2:487–88) (No mistaking,
what is good about freedom is that it enlarges your brain and opens I
don't know what windows there in your intelligence). The development of the female subject, Pardo Bazán intuitively understood, depends on the establishment of relations, including kinship relations.

In a way, Fe does not really give up the ideal of the self-supporting
woman when she marries the well-to-do Mauro. Rather, she transfers
that ideal to her now-destitute family members. She sends her sister
Argos to Barcelona to be trained as a singer and musician, realizing
that "[e]mpeñarse en hacer de Argos una mujer casera y metódica, es
errarla" (2:526) (insisting on making Argos into a domestic and me-
thodical woman is mistaken). Her youngest sisters are put to work as
seamstresses assisting Rosa in the dress shop that Fe equips for her:
"—Ya hemos dejado de ser señoritas—repetía la independiente—. A

arrimar el hombro todas" (2:526) ("We are no longer ladies," repeated
the independent Fe. "Everyone must put her shoulder to the task").
No doubt Fe's self-defined mission expresses a celebration of the bourgeois work ethic, but it is also a recognition that women's talents should
be exploited in the public as well as the private sphere.


## The Ideal Pareja

Mauro Pareja metamorphoses into the other half of this ideal *pareja*
who will help Fe fulfill her redemptress mission. His most positive
attribute then is his malleable character. This makes him flexible, in
deed if not in word, with regard to stereotypical sex roles. In the end
there is also a certain unmanliness about his willingness to be defined
solely in relation to another that makes him appear less threatening to
Fe. Miraculously, his solicitations and passion are in tandem with Fe's
needs. For example, when she wants to consult him she raises her
hand to knock at the library door leading to his apartments at the very
moment Mauro is poised to knock on the other side of the door. In
fact, from the day he first gives Fe the key to the library, Mauro seems
to have no other occupation in life except to anticipate what Fe wants,
needs, or should have. Mauro also possesses wealth, that essential ingredient that lies at the center of the poor woman's predicament. In
most works about an unmarried woman the relationship between
money, male dominance, and female independence or self-determination is resolved for better or worse. It is usually evident that a poor
woman who turns herself over to a man's keeping has either much to
gain or lose in exchange for her hand or her body. Whatever the result,
it is also clear that men are always the bestower of what is gained or
the engineer of the loss, and this fact will color any future accomplishment. In *Memorias*, Mauro astutely recognizes that from a male point
of view, Fe stands to lose as much or more than she would gain by
marrying him. Implicit in their relationship is this unusual admission
that while his wealth translates into respectability, freedom from poverty, perhaps an education for her children, and a restitution of her
family's name, Fe will be giving up all that she most cherished during
her few unfettered months as a tutor. From the viewpoint of feminine
psychology, on the other hand, Fe cannot be of *use* to anyone but

herself, she cannot *replace* her mother, without Mauro's money and
social position. The relationship between money and the harmony and
restitution of family respectability is clearly the axis on which Fe's
choice hinges.

Two years prior to the publication of *Memorias*, Pardo Bazán partici-
pated in the much-debated "Congreso Pedagógico Hispano-Luso-
Americano" (The Hispanic-Luso-American Pedagogical Congress)
dedicated in part to the problem of female education. Pardo Bazán
argued that it was only through improved public education, including
higher education at that time denied to them, that women would be
able to break lose from their "perpetual tutelage" to men.[13] The reaction of her peers was swift. Although he did not attend the congress,
Leopoldo Alas later read the public discussion portions and reacted
violently against Pardo Bazán's proposals. A woman's education, he
argued in one of his *paliques*, should take place in the home. He shivers
at the thought of having to explain to a group of coeds the meaning
of *spadones* (eunuchs) (197). Educated women clearly posed a threat to
even the most educated of Spanish men. The much-maligned Pardo
Bazán pursued the debate two years later in *Memorias*. In the beginning
Mauro echoes Clarín's concerns by arguing against women being permitted to read indiscriminately. Ignorance and innocence are so becoming in a woman, he whines, "Son esos fatales libros, son ciertos
estudios... impropios... los que destruyeron en usted el mayor
hechizo de su edad y de su sexo..." (505) (it is those fatal books, and
certain improper studies that have destroyed in you the greatest charm
of your age and sex). Mauro's lament would be expressed over and
over in turn-of-the-century men-authored stories in which, as Gilbert
and Gubar attest, "men perceive the smallest female steps toward autonomy as threatening strides that will strip them of all authority"
("Tradition" 204). But Fe's response is a reminder to those who fear
for the morality of an overeducated woman that the home could also
be a book: "¿Dónde habrá libro más inmoral que mi casa? . . . Por
eso no quiero leerlo. Lo cierro. Si pudiese, lo quemaría" (2:505) (Where
is there a book more immoral than my home? . . . That is why I
refuse to read it. I will close it. If I could, I would burn it). Fe
challenges the cherished notion that the home is woman's haven and
that danger lurks outside of woman's traditional sphere. At the same
time she champions a less hypocritical, more worldly definition of
female morality that recognizes both the magnitude of what women

learned in the untutored domestic sphere, as well as its paucity and limitations. Unlike Monserdà's Antonieta, Fe recognizes the importance of knowledge learned in books and worldly experience. Again, it is only because she has claimed the right to read in other books that her final decision to read the book of her family can be seen as a choice and not an inevitability. Fe freely relinquishes a life of personal freedom outside the home only when she understands that her role in the writing of her family's book will no longer be passive.

Here too Mauro plays an important role as facilitator. Despite his dim view of her book reading, his key to a private library allows Fe to indulge in her favorite pastime whenever she chooses. So, while women facilitate Fe's introduction to learning (her mother by dying, the Duchess de La Piedad by collecting the books before she died, and Doña Consolación by convincing Mauro that Fe should be granted access to them), the books cannot be read without Mauro's key, which he turns over to Fe with only the most cursory of objections. As such, Mauro's key symbolizes the crucial role men played in decisions regarding the education of women, a role that Pardo Bazán constantly assailed in both her fiction and articles. Turning over the key to his library also preludes Mauro's surrender of bachelorhood. In terms of male development, Mauro is, by all indications, entering a midlife crisis. His youthful illusions are beginning to calcify like his bones. His arguments against marriage are the stock of trade clichés of the nineteenth-century misogynist: intimate contact with the female is a dangerous path leading to a precipice that he hopes to permanently avoid. He is given to multiple, short-lived relations with women and pleased with the fact that his affairs do not involve any level of commitment beyond a signature on a dance card or a bouquet of flowers. All the pond-lily types he is attracted to easily meld into the category of Woman, *Mujer* with a capital *M*, a fruit whose sweetness derives from the fact that no matter how many bites he takes from it/her, the fruit never disappears. Once married, the freshest fruit would no longer be his for the picking and the erotic pleasure and power he feels picking the most beautiful dance partner would end. Worse, his wife would probably cheat on him, he predicts (2:459).

The problem is that something of Mauro disappears each time he wakes up from his latest dream/fantasy, "se rompe algo de mí mismo, alguna fibrita de un rincón delicado" (457) (something of myself is broken, some fiber in a delicate corner), leaving him with the uneasy

conviction that his years are slipping away. We learn all this before Fe
bursts into Mauro's life and the moment she does we know that their
meeting will spell a special bond between them if not the end of
bachelorhood. Bachelor- and maidenhood and the way these roles
carry over into adult relations and affiliations, then, are the pivotal
questions for both main characters. How and why Mauro will fall in
love with the scruffy, androgynous Feíta, and how Fe will inexplicably
give up her brave dreams of freedom to attach herself to this stuffy,
middle-aged dandy absorbs us with the usual narrative feints of the
Romantic novel: delusions, evasions, stylized scenes of auto-revelation,
incantations against the inevitable union followed by tender scenes of
rendition when both characters at last broach the question of marriage.
It sounds as trivial as any bedroom romance, especially if we feel that
the romance of the bedroom is trivial (it clearly was not for nineteenth-
century female readers), and if we fail to take into account certain
explorations of gender-linked behavior that inform the subplot of
Fe's predicament.

   Differentiating between male and female fantasies, Freud describes
the latter as generally erotic, and the former as egoistic and ambitious
(44; quoted in Nancy Miller, "Emphasis Added" 346). Resisting these
popular stereotypes, Pardo Bazán crafts a female character whose fantasies of ambition are vastly incompatible with the realities of family
life in Spain. By contrast, Mauro spends his creative energies arranging
his toilette, keeping abreast of Marineda's love affairs, or reminiscing
about his own and trying (unsuccessfully he assures us) to imagine
what the headstrong, "ufana, intrépida, desgreñada, empecatada"
(haughty, intrepid, disheveled, incorrigible) Fe might look like in the
act of loving, "la expresión de su rostro cuando mirase rendida" (2:495)
(the expression on her face when she surrendered herself). In short,
Mauro exhibits what Freud would call a female imaginary. Conversely,
in her recognition that she is also an individual to whom she must
act responsibly, Fe carves out a small subjective space that appeared
scandalous and egotistical to some of the novel's readers: "La cosa que
más me interesa a mí es Feíta Neira, . . . Después, lo que sigue. Pero
antes, el número uno" (2:487) (The thing that most interests me is
Feíta Neira, . . . And after that, everything else. But before anything,
number one). Her adamant and guiltless rejection of total selflessness
marks an unusual acknowledgment of self-importance. Mauro's maturity, on the contrary, will be marked by the basic acceptance that self

and other are co-dependent, that he does not stand alone in the world, so his maturity resembles what feminist social psychologists argue should be the norm for both sexes.

In many novels written by women, marriage is the happy *ending*, not the *beginning* of a woman's life adventure (Jane Miller, *Women Writing* 3). When the prize is someone as unexceptional as Mauro it makes us wonder, as we do when we read *Clemencia* or some of the British novels in Miller's survey, whether or not *happy* is the precise term to use. But if we examine Mauro alongside some of the other ideal consorts that people Pardo Bazán's minor works, the attraction is easier to fathom. For example, what do Mauro and Pacheco of *Insolación* share that make them desirable candidates for the more exceptional Fe and Asís de Taboada? Is their attraction primarily sexual (Pacheco) and financial (Mauro) as the heroines' actions and admissions seem to indicate, or are there other reasons that make these two men suitable mates for women so obviously superior to them?

The wild and frizzy-haired tomboy selects the cultivated, conservative, aging bachelor; the cultured, well-bred Asís settles for an egotistical, jealous idler for a mate. One could advance the old truism about the attraction of opposites that at least adds spice to otherwise colorless affairs. Or perhaps their choice has more to do with social convention and the play of power and submission between the sexes. Fe's poverty grants her a good deal more personal freedom than does Asís's gentility, but both women resent the stifling social taboos and rituals that hamper their activities and their spirit. In Mauro, Fe finds someone who adopts, despite his highly developed sense of decorum, a conspicuous laissez-faire attitude during their courtship rituals. It strikes him as odd, but not *that* odd, that a woman should be as bright, well-read, and streetwise as Fe, and her family finances and social status seem to have no bearing on their plans. On the other hand, the reckless Pacheco tempts the very proper Asís away from her staid and boring widow's existence, offering her the pleasurable sensation of breaking social taboos. Both men, therefore, are facilitators, a mixture of what women want to have as mates and what they wish they themselves could become. Most important, both men invite women to resist control over their personal lives by a restrictive social order and both are permissive with regard to social convention. Finally, like many a romantic hero, both men are willing to make radical concessions in their life-style in order to marry the women they love and they both do so definitively, extending their love and sense of duty to the ready-made families that exist as a symbol of their willingness to commit themselves fully. For both men, just as for the mature women that Gilligan studies (20–35), developing a relationship comes to bind all their energy and care: Pacheco vows to dedicate all the time necessary to winning over Asís's daughter. Usurping the role of father, Mauro comes to the rescue of Fe's erring sisters.

To appreciate the endings of these novels, however, it is important not only to understand what characteristics might inure Mauro and Pacheco to women, but also what historical realities color literary convention. In the very abruptness of the "happy ending," suggestive of, if not depicting, wedding bells, is a silent but relentless historical reality that governed Spanish women's lives of all classes. The consequences of not marrying and still having pleasure (freedom, education, passion, etc.) were nearly inconceivable. A wealthy, unmarried, or widowed woman would be bound either to self-enforced seclusion or to an endless routine of bourgeois social practices, flitting from parlor to parlor, making small talk and gossiping, conforming, at least in appearances, to a rigid moral code that applied ironically only to women and not to men. For the poor woman, as Miller puts it speaking of Austen's creations, real life did not offer many alternatives outside of marriage; thus Austen concentrates on the only true feminine adventure, "those brief months of a woman's life during which everything seems possible and which will end in failure or a wedding" (*Women Writing* 61).[14] Only men can afford to be indifferent on the subject of marriage since they enjoy, as Fe puts it, "las ventajes del matrimonio sin arrostrar sus inconvenientes" (2:471) (the advantages of matrimony with none of its inconveniences).

These two very different men are facilitators for both the women they marry and for readers invited to imagine at least the possibility of new masculine modes of conduct. They also allow us to see the very real perils of women's lives in both upper and lower strata of the bourgeois life. A man of exceptional powers of observation, Mauro is able to uncover for female readers—to whom he almost seems to be lecturing at times—the hypocrisy of other men. The perils and conflicts of *Memorias* and *Insolación* may only be apparent to those who are able to understand how historical women readers might have negotiated this text. Far from trivial, the conflicts are life-threatening, especially if we consider the relationship between boredom, that

Antes de Jesucristo
pasa la escena.
Así robó... ¡tunante!
Paris á Elena.

Costumbres *puras* del siglo quince.
Trapa el alféizar el trovador,
salta la dama, cógela en brazos
y escapan luego, locos de amor.

Siglo presente: Un simón,
una intención del demonio,
y en seguida ¡a la estación!
Los pescan, y... ¡matrimonio,
per saecula *seculón*!

Y como progresamos
rápidamente
así serán los raptos
del siglo veinte.

Fig. 11. "Raptos."

nineteenth-century female plague that nearly all the women of *El caba-llero de las botas azules* suffer from, and a meaningful existence; social castration, that other *othering* of the other sex; the various forms of female prostitution that were the price of conduct outside the norms of male-dominated society; and, in general, the destructive nature of male power and female vulnerability.[15] Exploring the moment a woman submits to the bonds of marriage, and the binding of her will that this symbolizes, is just as illuminating as describing what happens in the wake of her subordination to the wrong man, such as Pardo Bazán does in *Viaje de novios* [The honeymoon] or *Los pazos de Ulloa*. *Memorias* possibly satisfied two sides of what Jean Wyatt calls the "split reader: the part of the reader that wants to be a good girl, and also the re-pressed drives for independence, power, and autonomy that linger alongside her compliant gender identity" (10).

## Feíta and Tristana

Comparisons between Galdós's *Tristana* (1892) and Pardo Bazán's *Me-morias* (1896) are inevitable; there is a clear sense of shared readers in Pardo Bazán's and Galdós's divergent formulations of the ambitious woman's predicament. Pardo Bazán thought that her friend Galdós had missed a great opportunity by turning his back on his protagonist's "slavery" reinforcing the notion that women should not venture out-side the protection of the home. And yet feminist readers often react with similar disappointment at Fe's sudden decision to marry Mauro and give up her dreams of independence in Madrid. I shall end this section by comparing the retreat into domesticity that marks the end of each woman's worldly aspirations. Just at the moment it seems Tristana might break loose from her sordid family life, *mother nature* plays a very dirty trick on her. A bout with cancer leaves her with only one leg. As a result, she loses her spirit of independence, her ambition, her talent, and even her memory of the kind of woman she was or wanted to be. After all of the best of Tristana is slowly hacked away, she simply fades out as a thinking, acting subject. If she was intended as a lesson to Galdós's overzealous lover, Concha-Ruth Mo-rell, it could certainly be said that she "brought the lesson home." Tristana is punished for her ambitions both physically and psychologically and women readers are likely to be relieved to close the book on her life as soon as this happens.

Pardo Bazán's freedom-loving Fe learns much the same lesson as Tristana, but, significantly, she learns it from a man interpreting wisely what society offers or does not offer a self-liberated woman. It is not the violence of nature or a man's passion that changes her mind, but the rational arguments of Mauro, interpreting society from a miraculously feminine perspective. It is not that Fe has little to offer society, he explains, it is that society has little to offer someone of Fe's talents. A liberated Fe will have to wait until 1980, he predicts:

> ...aqui me tiene usted, Feíta, diciendo que le sobra a usted la razón..., pero que le falta la oportunidad, el sentido práctico, el saber de qué lado sopla el aire... Todas las novedades que le bullen a usted en esa cabecita revolucionaria serán muy buenas en otros países de Europa o del Nuevo mundo. Lo serán tal vez aquí en mil novecientos ochenta; lo que es ahora..., ¡desdichada de usted si se obstina en ir contra la corriente. (2:510)

> [...here you have me, Feíta, telling you that you are certainly right..., but what you lack is opportunity, practical sense, the knowledge of which way the wind is blowing... All of those ideas boiling inside that little revolutionary head of yours are good in other European countries or in the New World. Maybe they will be good here in the year 1980; but for now..., Woe be to you if you insist upon going against the current.]

The fact that it is her future husband who says this could mean that Fe's surrender to family life would not be so loathsome as she feared. Although she abandons her unrealistic dreams of exploring the world on her own and earning her own living, she will not play a powerless role as Mauro's wife. In fact, Mauro insists that she will still have her freedom within certain unspecified bounds. Mauro is portrayed as a prisoner of his love for Fe, not vice versa. The love, power, and educational opportunities awarded to Fe within the bounds of this relationship are, then, compensatory for her physical and economic dependence. *Memorias* is not, like *Tristana*, just another story of female energy converted into quiescence. True, Fe's decision echoes the common story that Naomi Schor studies in Sand's works, in which the young girl is enjoined "to abandon the active mode of the phallic phase and accept the passive stance that will ensure her smooth development into femininity" ("Reading Double" 255). But Fe will not be locked up alone in her apartment at night because, seated beside her "en asociación constante del hogar" (2:510) (the constant company of the home) will be that ideal husband, working hand in hand to solve her family's problems. Mauro is willing to suspend all claims to superiority, to "proclamar que es [Feíta] su igual en condición y derecho" (2:510) (proclaim that she is his equal in condition and right).[16] Feíta is not gaining a dueño, but a "hermano, compañero, . . . amante" (2:510) (brother, companion, . . . lover).

*Memorias de un solterón* permits us to see how the ideal mate imagined in women's literature becomes both something more and something less by the end of the nineteenth century. We can see this by comparing Mauro with his predecessor Pablo in Böhl de Faber's *Clemencia*, written approximately forty years earlier. Pablo performs heroic deeds for Clemencia, like saving her from a charging bull (which Noël Valis has interpreted as rescuing her from unbridled sexual passion ["Eden" 256]). Mauro seems unlikely to *save* Fe from life's trials, although he will certainly help her to face them. In fact he holds the keys (money and books) that make Fe's options seem less pathetic. What is similar about both men—and I believe, extremely significant for understanding the masculine *ideal* in women's fictions—is their likeness not to each other, but to their chosen brides. Summing up Pablo, Valis concludes: "Clemencia chooses Pablo not because she loves him passionately, but because he symbolizes all those virtues a good Christian possesses: because, in short, he is good. No hint of evil or forbidden temptation is associated with Pablo for, despite his maleness, he is nearly like Clemencia as the author could make him without falling into the trap of incest" ("Eden" 258).

Being a man in *Memorias* does not signify a special relation of power and dominance; rather, it amounts to a void, a hole only filled when in *asociación* with the other sex. Instead of settling the question of the relation between man and woman in terms of active and passive oppositions, Pardo Bazán salvages her character from a life of disillusion by granting her the grand consolation prize of a *brother* spirit. Seen thus, the imagined mutuality between Mauro and Fe could be interpreted as a subversive reaction against the noncommunication of the real Spanish couple that Pardo Bazán argued was eroding Spanish family life (*La mujer española* 53).[17] As a strategy for confronting the choices of adulthood, the *asociación* together with the burden of caring and responsibility it implies is what, finally, marks the difference in Pardo Bazán's prose.

At best, we could say that it prepares the way for a Spanish version of the "undomestication of women" (Griffin Crowder 122) in the twentieth century. Pardo Bazán's explorations of female psychological identity and its relation to social boundaries are perhaps clumsy, sometimes angry, but always different, always speaking from an *other* perspective. That she envisions what Annis Pratt calls the equal-marriage relationship (41) indicates Pardo Bazán's ability to transcend the realities of Spanish life. On the other hand, that she refrains from portraying how this dream association functioned, beyond the few vague sentences quoted here, reveals her refusal to indulge in utopian fiction, as I indicated above. Fe's decision to accept partnership stands out in contrast to the "esclavitud moral" (moral enslavement) (Saínz de Robles 5:549) to which Galdós abandoned the hopeless, one-legged Tristana. Her choice obviously involves self-sacrifice, but it could also be exploited to afford her a degree of power commensurate with the freedoms she will be renouncing. This type of power through dependency, according to Patricia Meyer Spacks, was the unlikely possibility women learned of in nineteenth-century fiction:

> Nineteenth-century women, if women novelists are to be believed, share a dream of dependency. Gratified, it may give them the opportunity of control, or it may lead to the recognition that it involves some fundamental denial of the self. . . . [T]hese novels reflect woman's difficulty in accepting her condition—but also the ways in which she can exploit to her own purposes the consequences of social oppression, finding freedom and power in the most unlikely situations. (95)

Whether we believe dependency will bring mastery or misery to Fe depends on our faith in Mauro's ability to measure Fe's true value, but it also depends on whether Fe can accept the fact that caring for others is the only rewarding feminine vocation open to her. Her ability to accept this rests not upon any innate craving for dependency but on her growing awareness of what social realities are open to her outside the family, her evolving maturity that permits her to take advantage of the limited resources available to her within it, and her knowledge that the choice to remain bound to others is an informed choice.

During the later decades of the nineteenth century, there is a timid but growing exhortation addressed to women to embrace a work ethic that goes beyond the domestic chores and family care that is usually associated with the ideal of the *ángel del hogar*. Pardo Bazán chided Galdós for not imagining that there could be more than the three careers that the maid Saturna in *Tristana* says are open to women: wife, actress or showgirl, or prostitute (*La mujer española* 139). However, this was also a time when competition for jobs was keen and women were not particularly welcome in the factory and workshop if it meant competing for scarce jobs.[18] Certain public sector jobs were more open to women (the tobacco industry, and the textile trades), but most women working outside the home were servants, wet nurses, or prostitutes.[19] Perhaps as a response to this reluctance to accept women in its secondary sector, Spain's new woman usually devises a career that allows her to stay at home and that does not cross traditional gender barriers. In the 16 May 1882 issue of the magazine *Instrucción para la mujer* [Instruction for women], G. Vicuña urges, for *moral* reasons, that poor women who must work dedicate themselves to professions that can be practiced at home. Factory work is not only unsuitable morally, it is dangerous to the stability of the family:

> obliga a la mujer a desatender el cuidado de su casa, distrae al niño del cultivo de su inteligencia, separa al hombre de los goces del hogar, contribuye a relajar los lazos del parentesco, es incentivo constante para la desmoralización y materia dispuesta para las revoluciones. (81)

> [it obliges woman to neglect the care of her home, distracts the child from the cultivation of his intelligence, separates man from the pleasures of his home, contributes to the loosening of parental ties, is a constant incentive for moral laxity and material for revolutions.]

Domestic work, on the contrary, has great moral and physical advantages since women can do this work at any hour of the night and day, not according to a rigid schedule like in the factory. Pardo Bazán and several other women authors writing in the last decade of the nineteenth century created characters who work in factories, such as Amparo of *La Tribuna*, but these women usually harbor aspirations to a life of middle- or upper-class ease that in Amparo's case comes about in *Memorias* when she appears "recostada muellemente, luciendo una manteleta negra con flecos de azabache" (2:517) (reclining comfortably, sporting a black shawl trimmed with jet beads) in the opulent coach of Baltasar Sobrado. Even though she continues to work for many years after her marriage, "La fabricanta" (the woman industrialist) eventually sets up her factory at home, so that she can attend both to family and to business. Similarly, Fe arranges for her sisters to embrace careers that can either be practiced at home or that do not compete for men's jobs. Pardo Bazán may have railed against the "gross materialism" that relegates women to the domestic sphere because of the "apparatuses and organs destined to the reproduction and conservation of the species" (*La mujer española* 158–59), but in her fiction, she did not portray many women who, like herself, chose a career that takes them out of the domestic sphere.

## A Sweet Master

By the end of Pardo Bazán's illustrious career, the independent-minded women who had made their tentative appearance in her work in the closing decade of the nineteenth century disappeared from her fiction, or they were victimized and marginalized into pathetic and ineffectual creatures, such as Annie in *La sirena negra* [The siren of death] (1908), whose arrogance is punished with rape. It is not that Pardo Bazán relinquished her ideal of a superior woman, only that she found it increasingly more difficult to find a comfortable place for such a woman in the social milieux that had been her focus in the 1890s. In the first decade of the new century, she expressed her disappointment at the period of political and moral decadence that Spain was experiencing. But rather than grounding her narratives in the sociopolitical struggles that were raging around her, she instead promoted a narrative of exquisite individualism, whose characters would rise above the banal and corrupt realities of everyday Spanish life. Of *La Quimera* she explains: "I am convinced that in a person's life the only important thing is what individuality discovers" (quoted in Clèmessy 1:203). For the

totally exceptional women characters that Pardo Bazán imagined in
her last novels there was no Mauro Pareja, no earthly man capable of
the spiritual depth and total commitment to love of Clara Ayamonte
(*La Quimera*) or Catalina Mascareñas (*Dulce Dueño*). Especially in this
last novel, Pardo Bazán gave herself over completely to the notion
of a mystical love that she had so much admired in Pérez Galdós's
*Angel Guerra*.

*Dulce Dueño*, published in 1911, was Pardo Bazán's last novel-length
fiction. If, as Marantz Cohen argues, what distinguishes protomodern-
ist or modernist fiction is a central character who is "generally defined
through his complete alienation from family ties, or through an intense
and encompassing subjectivity that obscures or radically distracts these
ties" (179–80), we can clearly call *Dulce Dueño* a modernist novel. Unlike the nineteenth-century novels studied in the previous chapters,
*Dulce Dueño* shows signs of a growing malaise with prevailing gender
arrangements and a recognition of feminine superiority and intellectual aptitude vis-à-vis masculine affective and interrelational inferiority. On the other hand, it is also the ideal terminus for this exploration
into nineteenth-century fiction because of its betrayal of feminine subjectivity, its condemnation of feminine idleness and male treachery,
and its exaltation of otherworldly love.

Like the conduct books and hundreds of occasional pieces in
women's periodicals, *Dulce Dueño* provides a ready-made model, in this
case Saint Catherine of Alexandria, with which to explore a unique
woman's spiritual and emotional traumas. A lengthy account of Saint
Catherine's conversion to Christianity precedes the novel and serves
as the absolute point of reference for judging and predicting its out-
come. This version of Saint Catherine's life, retold in the subsequent
story of her modern-day equivalent, Lina Macareñas, tells of a superior
woman's seduction by an ideal lover, who then becomes her *sweet
master*, followed by a cruel martyrdom as a result of her socially inap-
propriate choice of love object. In other words, both stories tell of a
woman superior to her opportunities and environment who is punished for refusing to be satisfied with what conventional society expects
will make women happy. An old story, no doubt, but one that was
also very familiar to many Spanish women.

In most of Pardo Bazán's works, feminine perfection is defined by
the interrelational maturity that women foster usually in a domestic
context. To contemplate this attribute fully as the touchstone of femi-

nine superiority, Pardo Bazán removes her heroines, Catherine of Alexandria and Lina Macareñas, from family responsibilities altogether, much as Fe is removed from the Neira family in order to foster her maturity. No family member depends emotionally on either Catherine or Lina; both have the time and money to pursue whatever activities appeal to them. Although surrounded by beauty and access to knowledge, both women feel incomplete because, like Castro's heroines, they long to be devoured by an absolute, all-encompassing love. Catherine squirms on her lion-shaped throne made of gold and marble, draped in long linen veils embroidered with silver. What good is a library to her? Her soul longs to be lit afire with a great love, but for whom? "¿Dónde encontrar esa suprema belleza de la forma que según Plotino transciende a la esencia?" (57–58) (Where would she find that supreme beauty of form that according to Plotinus transcends essence?).

Combining her admiration for the myth of the magnificent Catherine of Alexander, various Greek and Roman philosophers, and the mystic adventures of Teresa de Jesús, Pardo Bazán imagines this encounter between the superb woman and the perfect lover as a mixture of the sensual and the sublime. For example, Catherine is given a potion—symbolizing her wounding by love—made from the venom that a furious scorpion has just "ejaculated":

> Un horrible bicharraco se destacó del grupo y avanzó. Catalina le miró fascinada, con grima que hacía retorcerse sus nervios. La forma de la bestezuela era repulsiva, y la Princesa pensaba en la muerte que su picadura produce, con fiebre, delirio y demencia. Veía al insecto replegar sus palpos y erguir, furioso, su cauda emponzoñada, a cuyo remate empezaba la eyaculación del veneno, una clara gotezuela. Ya creía sentir la mordedura, cuando de súbito el escorpión, amansado, acudió a la mano raigambrosa que Trifón le tendía, y el asceta, estrujándolo sin ruido, lo mezcló y amasó con el óleo. (71)

> [A horrible insect separated from the group and started to advance. Catalina looked at it in fascination, with a disgust that made her nerves jump. The form of the insect was repulsive, and the Princess imagined the kind of death its bite would produce, with fever, delirium and dementia. She saw the insect retract its feelers and stiffen, furiously, its venomous tail, after

which followed an ejaculation, a clear stream of venom. She believed she could feel its bite, when suddenly the scorpion went passively to the gnarled hand that Trifon extended to it and the hermit silently crushed it and mixed and mashed it with oil.]

Repulsed by the Egyptian and Greek gods who seem lacking in love for mere mortals, Catherine is seduced by the Christian *son* of God, to whom she calls out tenderly "—Ven, ven, amado, que no sé resistir. . . . Herida estoy, y no sé cómo. Se sale de mí el alma para irse a ti" (73) (Come, come, my love, I cannot resist. . . . I am wounded, I know not how. My soul leaves me to come to you). The first time she sees him, Catherine's lover is more beautiful and seductive than she could have imagined a man to be, but when she is led to the altar to marry him, the man who puts the ring on her finger turns out to be a young male child. Catherine suddenly stands out, a dazzling maternal icon, married in a perfect love bond to the perfect son/lover. Her subsequent martyrdom can be construed as a victory over mediocrity and shortsightedness because it allows her to be united in a perfect, everlasting love with both the son and the man. However, we must also read this scene as an exaggerated representation of women's total submission to the masculine will. On the one hand it exhibits what Kristeva would call a worship of sublimation, "a process that neutralizes the body, passions, and everything that recalls, more or less closely, the family/cradle of desires" (*Tales* 325–26). On the other hand, it marks the death of the self and the subjection of feminine subjectivity to the *holy* family.

In her solitude, Saint Catherine's successor Lina Macareñas has evolved a similar craving for the perfect love. Lina longs to taste the honey and nectar that are the beauty of love (126); "el Dueño extraordinario, superior a la turba que va a asediarme" (131) (the extraordinary Master, superior to the rabble that is going to besiege me). Like the love that Castro's Laura Pampa seeks, the strength of this love will consist in its power and its mystery: "El también poseerá su fuerza propia. Será fuerte en algún sentido. Algo le distinguirá de la turba; al presentarse él, una virtud se revelará, virtud de dominio, de grandeza, de misterio" (131) (He also will have his own strength. He will be strong in some sense. Something will distinguish him from the rabble; When I meet him, some virtue will be revealed to me, the

virtue of authority, greatness, mystery). When at last she finds this
otherworldly love, Lina is prepared to abandon the world of material
being altogether. Possessed, fused and burnt up with love, she is re-
maindered to the nearest mental institution where she plans to lead a
wholly contemplative life.

How is it that in 1911 Pardo Bazán imagines the solution to this
love quest in much the same way that María de Zayas did for her
character in "La esclava de su amante" [Her lover's slave] or Teresa de
Jesús did in her descriptions of the path of the mystic? Was it simply,
as some critics suggest, that *Dulce Dueño* was written during her spiritual period beginning in the early 1900s? The answer to this question
lies not only in Pardo Bazán's explorations of spirituality which, after
all, are a constant in her prose fiction, but in the types of male characters she devises to pay court to her unusual feminine characterizations.
The idealized figure or *dulce dueño* that Lina creates for herself when
earthly men fail her is a figure of excess and delirium, so impossible
that it even fails as a narrative solution, making feminists edgy about
it (Mayoral 39) and all but guaranteeing the novel's obscurity. What is
important to understand, however, is the full narrative weight granted
this woman's love: she feels it and speaks it and challenges patriarchy
for the right to understand it as something real to her.

According to Kristeva, a collapsed idealization reveals the persecution that produced it in the first place (*Tales* 28). *Dulce Dueño* is steeped
in persecution that justifies the excess of its odd conclusion and is
therefore, like many women-authored texts, a back window onto
women's disillusion with patriarchy. Lina, a wealthy heiress who can
afford to be choosy when selecting a companion from among her many
"procos," or suitors, describes their defects and hypocrisy in telling
detail. Her first interest, an opera tenor named Cristalli, is quickly
dismissed for his imagined vulgarity. His heavenly voice takes her
breath away, "hasta tal punto me avasalla. Anhelo morir, disolverme;
tiendo los brazos como si llamase a mi destino... apremiándole" (153)
(he literally enslaves me. I long to die, to dissolve myself; I
stretch out my arms as if my destiny called to me... compelling
me). But this imagined Lohengrin is really just a "muñeco" (doll) on
which Lina has momentarily draped "la tela de un devaneo psíquico"
(154) (the cloth of a psychic delirium). After hearing him perform,
she pauses to imagine his postconcert revelry, basking in the success

of his recital by gorging himself on food, champagne, and the women who form part of the divo's entourage (154).

Lina's first serious suitor, Hilario Aparicio (clearly a play on the words *hilarious apparition*), is a corrupted version of Amparo's son in *La Tribuna:* an impassioned anarchist who praises her intelligence but, when all is said and done, covets her money more than he admires her talents. Hilario is the most exaggerated statement of Pardo Bazán's dissatisfaction with political *progress* that has been mentioned repeatedly in this monograph. If Lina chooses Hilario, her former tutor assures her, she will feel doubly fulfilled as a woman because she will be expressing her love not just for one man, but for all of humanity (158). But when she broaches the subject of love with Hilario, she finds his ideas not so dissimilar from those of her conservative tutor, who believes that women's "sagrada tarea maternal" (sacred maternal duty) prevents them from being more than the disciples of men. Lina has no desire to follow her tutor's recommendations regarding ideal gender arrangements. She mockingly leads Hilario to believe that he is up to the task of taking the raw material that constitutes her desire and infusing it with a masculine *soul*. As a test, she proposes that they join together in a perfect union, renouncing her entire fortune and living only for their revolutionary work, the "triunfo de los ideales" (triumph of ideals). Hilario then exposes the hypocrisy of his political ideals by suggesting that for decorum's sake he be placed in charge of administering their fortune, provoking a gleeful response from Lina: "No pude contenerme. Solté una risa jovial, victoriosa. . . . Un marido como otro cualquiera, ante la iglesia y la ley. Porque así, yo le pertenecéa, y mis bienes lo mismo, o al menos su disfrute (171) (I could not contain myself. I let out a jovial, victorious laugh. A husband like any other, before law and church. Because I would belong to him, and my fortune as well, or at least he could use them).

As a love partner, Hilario leaves much to be desired, both physically and spiritually. Not only are his ideas about love bankrupt, nothing attracts Lina to him physically. He smells of cheap perfume and shoe polish and has overdressed for their meeting. His new boots and gloves creak unpleasantly, his nearsighted eyes look timidly out of his thick glasses that have left a rim on either side of his nose. Short and shallow-chested, he simply has nothing to recommend him to an exceptional woman in search of a beautiful ideal.

Lina's next suitor is proposed by her father (who is disguised for

the moment as her steward), but she is far from convinced that marriage will be the solution to her feeling of dissatisfaction. Looking back
on the Spanish literary tradition, she wonders why all the lords and
ladies rush off to be married (178); marriage is repugnant to her because she cannot believe in the existence of a man who can make a
woman forget that, as a wife, she is legally nothing. Although she
longs for love, that beautiful island full of grottos, streams, and verdant
landscapes, she feels certain she will never be washed up on its shore
(179). If she marries, she would lose both her physical and her spiritual freedom:

> Casarse será tener Dueño... ¿Dulce Dueño?... El día en que
> no me ame, mi Dueño podrá exigirme que haga los gestos
> amorosos... El día en que mi pulmón reclame aire bravo, me
> querrá mansa y solícita... La libertad material no es lo que más
> sentiría perder. Dentro está nuestra libertad; en el espíritu.
> (178)

> [To marry would be to have a master... A Sweet Master?... The
> day that he no longer loves me, my Master could demand my
> amorous gestures... The day that my lungs are filled with anger,
> he could demand that I be gentle and solicitous... Physical
> freedom is not what I would miss the most. Our freedom is
> within, in the spirit.]

Despite her resolve, Lina finds herself drawn to her cousin, the "Moor"
proposed by her father, because he evokes the phantasmagoric love
that, for example, Audalla felt for Daraja or Saide for Saida. With
José María as her guide, she is drawn to Granada and, especially, the
Alhambra. With its mysterious silence, heady perfume, fountains, and
white marble, the Alhambra proves the existence of the kind of extravagant, all-encompassing love that her senses tell her exists. José María's
"sentido de lo femenil" (feminine sense) makes him mimic the roles
best suited to Lina's love text:

> Mientras la noche desciende, clara y cálida, forjo mi novela
> alpujarreña. José María empieza a producirme el mismo efecto
> que la Alhambra; disuelve, embarga mi voluntad. Hay en él
> una atracción obscura, que poco a poco va dominándome. (194)

[When night descends, clear and warm, I forge my Andalusian
novel. José María is beginning to have the same effect on me as
the Alhambra; he dissolves, overcomes my will. There is in him
a kind of dark attraction, that little by little is overpowering me.]

Just as Lina starts to experience the dizziness of surrender to the
"dominio arcano" (mysterious dominion) that José is beginning to exercise over her, she catches him stealing away from her maid's bedroom,
affording her yet another deception about men's motives and desire.

The next step in Lina's love quest is to evaluate the attraction she
felt for José María and then to divorce physical contact between man
and woman from her conceptualization of the ideal union. The *feminine*
repulsion to sex, a staple in nearly all of the novels studied in the
previous chapters, finds its most exaggerated expression in Lina's sexual anatomy lesson. To understand why people are ashamed even to
speak of sex she seeks the help of a physician who can explain to her,
a virgin, the sexual act in full detail, using books and illustrations to
*show* her what she needs to know in order to determine if sex and love
are compatible. An hour in the doctor's office suffices to convince Lina
that there is every reason for the human species to feel ashamed of the
sexual act: "[p]or algo pesa sobre ello la reprobación religiosa; por algo
la sociedad lo cubre con tantos paños y emplea para referirse a ello
tantos eufemismos... No se coge con tenacillas lo que no mancha"
(208) (with reason religions condemn it; with reason society covers it
over and uses euphemisms to refer to it... You don't pick up with tongs
what does not stain). Going a step further, Lina insists upon knowing
about the various types of sexual perversion that humans are capable
of, so the doctor tells her of all the "corrupt" activities that humans
are capable of:

> las anomalías de museo secreto, las teratologías primitivas, hoy
> reflorecientes en la podredumbre y el moho de las civilizaciones
> viejas; los delirios infandos, las iniquidades malditas en todas
> las lenguas, las rituales infamias de los cultos demoníacos. (210)

> [the anomalies of the secret museum, primitive teratologies,
> flourishing again today in the rot and stagnation of ancient
> civilizations; unspeakable deliriums, cursed iniquities in every
> language, infamous rituals of demonic cults.]

"Never! Never!" she vows in horror at the abject sexual act (211), and yet Lina decides to give love another chance when she meets the ambitious lawyer Agustín Almonte. Unlike Hilario and José María, Agustín doesn't need Lina's fortune and he is not interested either in satisfying sexual desire or propagating the species. Rather, he is searching for a friend, an "amazona" or social queen (225) to help him achieve his political ambitions. "Nuestra fuerza"—he convinces her—"nos la dan las mujeres. Si no me auxilia usted por amor, hágalo por compañerismo. Subamos de la mano" (240) (Our strength comes from women. If you choose not to help me for love, do it for companionship). To emphasize fully the colonization of the female that Agustín's proposal implies, Pardo Bazán provides a couple that exemplifies Agustín's imaginary *compañerismo*. Did not Hernán Cortés have his faithful companion Marina? In Agustín's eyes they formed the perfect pair since Cortés "necesitaba a doña Marina, su conocimiento del ambiente, su lealtad para prevenir emboscadas y traiciones" (241) (needed doña Marina, her knowledge of the ambience, her loyalty to prevent traps and treachery).

When this relationship based on *compañerismo* no longer satisfies him, Agustín asks Lina to marry him, and the heroine once again finds herself the object of a love that purports to be uncompromising. So vast is his love that Agustín is even prepared to sacrifice his life to it. "¡Qué dicha, arrostrar peligros por ti! ¡Salvarte, a costa de mi existencia!" (248) (What joy to suffer danger for you! To save you, at the price of my life!). However, when the boat they are in capsizes and Lina tries to cling to her lover's neck, he brutally pushes her away to save his own life. In the end he drowns and Lina is saved, but any illusion about the existence of an absolute love on a human scale ends in this catastrophe.

In the twists and turns of Lina's love quests, *Dulce Dueño* comes to the conclusion that love is impossible because men's words fail to match up to their deeds. In the last chapter of *Dulce Dueño* Lina has been cured of her search for a man to love and turns her eyes instead to heaven. Since no mere man is good enough for her, there is no advantage to being wealthy, so she abandons her house and fortune. And since beauty is a merely a physical, not a spiritual attribute, she pays a prostitute to smash her face with the heel of her boot in order to sacrifice her physical beauty to God and thus demonstrate her belief in a higher form of beauty: "La Belleza que busco . . . ni se rompe,

ni se desgarra. La Belleza ha empezado a venir a mí. El primer sacrificio, hecho está" (269) (The beauty I seek . . . can neither be broken
nor ripped apart. Beauty has begun to come to me. I have performed
my first sacrifice). All the men she has known have only wanted her
to fulfill *their* economic or physical needs; their love is reduced to a
mere physical craving for power over her and the goods she possesses.
Her solution, admittedly repulsive to modern readers, is really just an
exaggerated version of the bound-for-the-convent ending of so many
women's novels.

On the other hand, just as in narratives of female self-obliteration
(studied in Chapter 2 on social masochism), those who stand to gain
most from Lina's incarceration are the men closest to her: her uncle,
who has her committed to the mental institution in order to claim her
wealth for himself and his son, and her spiritual adviser and patron,
who can use her as a model to show how bad the world has become
now that women have begun thinking for themselves:

> Yo veo descollar entre sus pecados una gran soberbia y un gran
> personalismo. Es el mal de este siglo, es el veneno activo que
> nos inficiona. Usted se ha creído superior a todos, o, mejor
> dicho, desligada, independiente de todos. Además ha refinado
> con exceso sus pensamientos. De ahí se originó la corrupción.
> Sea usted sencilla, natural, humilde. Téngase por la última, la
> más vulgar de las mujeres. No veo otro camino para usted, y
> tampoco habrá penitencia más rigurosa. (275)

> [I detect among your sins a great egotism. This is the evil of the
> century, the active poison that infects us all. You have believed
> yourself superior to everyone, or, rather, unattached, independ-
> ent from everyone. In addition, you have refined your thoughts
> excessively. This is the origin of your corruption. Be simple,
> natural, humble. Regard yourself as the last, the most common
> of women. I see no other path for you, and no greater peni-
> tence.]

It is dangerous for a woman to be a proud, strong individual, to be
independent and to refine her intellectual aptitude. Be "simple, natural, humble," Lina's confessor advises. Obviously what is wrong with

"este siglo" is the same thing that was wrong with the nineteenth century, which delivered an identical message to the wayward woman. *Dulce Dueño* is a distillate of all the novels looked at in this study. Like its predecessors, it is a story about the "fantasmagorías de amor" (210) (phantasmagorias of love) that are essential to feminine subjectivity as deployed in women-authored texts. This love is a disorderly concept that owes more to the extravagant mysticism of Teresa de Jesús than to the philosophies of Plato and Plotinus that Pardo Bazán cites, or even to Kant, Hegel, and Freud who, Kristeva says, have "pruned" love of its "blessed loving madness" (*Tales* 8). Given the novel's origins in nineteenth-century social and sexual convention, it perhaps cannot but be a very complex, contradictory tale of sublimation but also of sacrifice. In her idealization of the other (her creation of a perfect God to love), Catalina follows the same path to sublimation as many of the heroines who preceded her. Like they, she defines self-punishment and purification as peculiarly beneficial and therefore desirable to women. The difference between this work and the domestic fictions studied in previous chapters is one of degree more than of kind. Perfect love is available in *Clemencia* only to the woman who controls her desires and practices self-denial as a virtue, while in *Dulce Dueño*, it is only granted to the woman who has literally mutilated her body. In *Elia* a heroine finds the space to construct an ideal self-image only by retreating to a convent, leaving her confounded relatives to wonder at her decision. In *Dulce Dueño*, the woman is locked up in a mental institution by those who fear and hate her for what she has done to men. The "new woman" of the turn of the century is simply an exaggerated version of the "old woman" of the domestic novel. At the same time she makes a path for the repressive tales of a new century, such as Carmen Laforet's *La mujer nueva* [The new woman] (1955).

# Conclusion

IN HER EXCELLENT ARTICLE on *Clemencia*, Noël Valis notes how Javier Herrero's study of the novel looks mainly at its possible autobiographical indices, ignoring its aesthetic and literary dimensions. In her own close reading of *Clemencia*, Valis relates its governing metaphor of the tree of knowledge and the protagonist's life, concluding that the novel "possesses a unity of structure and content which is due to a controlling image, that of Eden and the tree of knowledge" ("Eden" 251). The implied premise behind this conclusion is that unity of structure and content determine a work's literary worthiness, and that, until now, critics have largely failed to discern this unity in Böhl de Faber's works. I read analyses such as this with a certain feeling of exhilaration and hope for a future institutional canon more in tune with my personal canon. I also agree that it is possible and even desirable to undertake close readings of many of the texts studied above to uncover similar unifying patterns and structures, making a case for their formal or ideological *integrity* as we have done for decades with the minor works of nineteenth-century men novelists that we judge to have been unaccountably dismissed. But I no longer feel shackled by the need to equate this kind of formal, *objective* value with a goal to promote the study of women's novels. Rather, I find it more meaningful, both for myself and my students, to trace the mechanism of cultural transmission of gender systems using the fictions of both men and women writers, whether or not they are *canonized*.

Naturally, if one is not careful, this tracing can lead to a kind of no-exit essentialism and functionalism that forecloses the possibility of change. The story goes like this: if, when we look at the cultural transmission of sexuality, we find that sexuality is always transmitted through dominant masculinist forms, then our description fails either to allow for change or to make sense of the exceptions to the Law (the resistance to and failures of the systems of gender transmission). On the other hand, if we go beyond description and describe only those sites where gender indoctrination is somehow subverted, we are telling the story from a utopian point of view as if we were witnessing the dawning of a revolutionary stage in the relation of sexes in which we were the final felicitous results. The critical task for the feminist critic today, as Jacqueline Rose summarizes it, is to "understand subjectivity, sexual difference and fantasy, in a way that neither entrenches the terms nor denies them" (*Sexuality* 23). This explains why Chapter 1, in which I looked at some of the more positive effects of domestic fiction in relation to female subjectivity, was offset by Chapter 2, in which I argued for a fuller understanding of the detrimental social and political ramifications of domestic fiction. Similarly, Chapters 3 and 4 identified rather than attempting to smooth out the sexual and social contradictions of culturally constructed feminine desire and roles.

There seems to be little advantage to substantiating unified, coherent women's texts when contradiction itself is what characterizes the nineteenth-century woman-authored novel. When Marcelino Menéndez Pelayo criticized Pardo Bazán for her *receptive* temperament, which led her to contradict herself "cincuenta veces" (fifty times) (*Dulce Dueño*, Introduction 17), he failed to realize that the contradiction of women's fiction was an effect of an alienation in the literary world as well as the wildly antagonistic roles that women were asked to *play* in bourgeois society. In fact, this contradiction continues well into the twentieth century when "gender trouble" becomes even more acute in women's novels. The source of this contradiction—which I hope by now is clear especially from the previous discussion of *Dulce Dueño*— has to do with the stress that the female subject experiences because of her personal goals and desires clashing or competing with a patriarchal society's needs and expectations. The result is a female character whose self-renouncing trajectory ends in stasis.

This trajectory marks a conversion of the woman into another (more perfect) version of herself who, like the Virgin Mary, can stand above all pain and misfortune. Such a woman was a standard fixture in nineteenth-century Spanish culture. Periodical literature, especially, appealed dramatically to women to seek models of conduct not only in contemporary, historical figures but in the lives of saints, holy women, and queens of eras gone by. As they proliferated in conduct books, weekly women's magazines, newspapers, and novels, these ex-

alted models competed for adherents among urban middle- and upper-
class sectors of the population by representing in very specific detail
a moral guidepost and course of conduct to follow in times of need,
trouble, neglect, or temptation.[1] Collectively, however, they exhorted
women to suppress their individuality and to strive for the larger good
of a community composed first of the immediate family, then the extended family, and finally any sick, poor, or underprivileged members
of the community at large.

The result was, as I argued in Chapter 2, to make womanhood take
the guise of a totally private experience, disguising the consequences
of women's gender indoctrination and restrictive body practices on the
larger political body. In contrast to the move of Spanish men into the
market economies that characterized other European countries in the
latter half of the century, Spanish women were being asked to preserve
a sense of communality and service that emanated from, and regen-
erated itself in, the domestic sphere. A glance at the illustrations I
have included in this study perhaps gives an idea how pervasive this
feminine ideal was in popular culture. Not surprisingly, then, most
women writers embraced this ideal. If Spanish bourgeois society
longed for women to be a rose, like the lovely maiden in Figure 1,
then writers of domestic fiction would show women the way to become
that rose despite the thorny path that must be taken to achieve this
objectification. Not surprisingly, some authors, notably Emilia Pardo
Bazán, occasionally emphasized the destructive aspects of the sexual
disparity it fostered. *Los pazos de Ulloa*, especially, chronicles the de-
structiveness and untenability of sexual polarizations, as noted in
Chapter 3.

Ironically, the phenomenon of fictional women fading into selfcon-
tained stasis contrasts sharply with their authors' selfish wish to be
recognized as writing subjects in a public sphere. Although occasionally—for example, in Rosalía de Castro's *El caballero de las botas azules*—
this desire for recognition finds expression in fiction, the norm in
domestic fiction was to repress feminine desire and exalt feminine
duty. In this sense Spanish women writers used their fiction as a way
of mitigating their guilt for being more than what society allowed women to become, for not embracing one of the three careers Saturna
claims are open to women. This produced texts like *El caballero de las
botas azules*, in which repression was rampant, but in which contradiction constantly challenged conventionalism and the man/culture–

Fig. 12. "Madrileños en Jueves Santo."

woman/nature dichotomy. This is why in my concluding chapter I focused on one of the most contradictory and least understood of Pardo Bazán's novels that I believe exaggerates to the fullest many of the *stories* told by previous novelists, as well as the author's earlier versions of feminine repression. My goal throughout this study has been, as Rose challenged feminists, to look at female subjectivity, sexual difference, and fantasy, not to see them as inevitably constructed but to understand, in their contradictions, where challenges (or acquiescence) to an existing order lay.

When discussing women's fiction, scholars have tended until very recently to contrast the womanly virtues practiced or preached in it with the excluded world of politics and extrafamilial relations and occupations. To a certain degree this contrastive analysis flows logically from the radically dichotomous gender ideology that pervades this fiction. The challenge, which I have tried to keep before me but which has also constantly eluded me because of its vastness and complexity, is to account for this sexual polarization without either reinscribing it or celebrating women's accommodation to it. Adopting the arguments of Edward Said and Raymond Williams, Nancy Armstrong speaks of the connection between middle-class hegemony and the tendency to construct "separate historical narratives for self and society, family and factory, literature and history" ("Some Call It" 60). If we maintain these divisions when we study culture, we are in effect seeking to preserve a "sanitized" area or safe house, where we imagine that history was somehow excluded; in other words, we allow ourselves to be seduced by the imaginary division that the domestic novel sought to establish.

Even though women novelists often defined the home as a safe haven for feminine virtue, as the century drew to a close, the home was increasingly recognized as a site of danger, deception, and repression that inevitably participates in whatever political and social realities it sought to evade. The domestic novel's own exclusionary practices should not disguise the fact that, as an enterprise, domesticity was as productive as it was reactive. In other words, domestic fiction was both a document and an agent of cultural history, as Armstrong contends ("Some Call It" 79). The most popular novels were those in which political discourses and consumerism in general were imagined as evils subject to exclusion from a feminine safe sphere. But the very tensions within this imaginary space were also testimony to the impossibility of such a division and thus to the constitutive discourses at work in both public and private spheres.

Today's readers must recognize that there is no safe house from history and little advantage in celebrating women's adaptability to its exclusionary practices. Explaining how women coped with unequal power relations, which was my goal in Chapter 1, is not the same as accepting the inevitability or desirability of sexual differences as they were commonly conceived by bourgeois society. It is also not sufficient to *narrate* the stories of feminine sexuality by eliminating their contradictions and taking a stand *for* or *against* the kinds of novels we wish to promote. It is important to understand that domestic ideology relied on women believing that a gulf separates them from the sphere of politics and Culture with a capital *C*, but we should not limit ourselves by accepting the noncommunication of these spheres as anything other than an abstract belief that was bred in a climate of unprecedented social and sexual revolution. Unless we begin exploring the historical contexts of the domestic culture that gave rise to the novel in the nineteenth century, our conception of gender ideology and gender indoctrination will fail to take into account the complex, converging relation between domestic culture and political culture, writing and subjectivity, power relations that impose themselves from above, and those that are constituted in the local discourses emanating from the domestic sphere. Clearly this is a Foucaultian project that requires the investigation of the productive (not just the repressive) interplay of multiple power sites at even the most private level of individual experiences that were the focus of the domestic novel.[2] But, as I have tried to make clear throughout this study, we should not engage in such an enterprise without taking into account gender differences and the peculiar form of "feminine" consciousness that is inherent in our discourses about desire, power, politics, and domesticity.

# *Notes*

## INTRODUCTION

1. For a discussion of the role of this last factor, see Barbara Herrnstein Smith's "Contingencies of Value," especially part 2, "The Economics of Literary Aesthetic Value"; part 3, "The Multiple Forms, Functions, and Contexts of Evaluative Behavior"; and part 4, "The Cultural Reproduction of Value."

2. Perhaps this is why *Webster's Ninth New Collegiate Dictionary* defines the word "canon" as "an authoritative list of books accepted as Holy Scripture."

3. See Herrnstein Smith for a description of the privileged subjects who are the policemen of aesthetic taste (18–19).

4. For example, unknown to me, the Spanish novels and plays I read in college and even graduate school grew out of Marcelino Menéndez y Pelayo's xenophobia, his emphasis on an "uninterrupted continuum of Catholicism, national tradition and *latinidad*" (Gold 184).

5. Several nineteenth-century women writers have been published in this series: Emilia Pardo Bazán, *Dulce Dueño* [Sweet master], edited and with an introduction by Marina Mayoral, 1989; Gertrudis Gómez de Avellaneda, *Poesía y epistolario de amor y de amistad* [Poetry and epistolary of love and friendship], edited and with an introduction by Elena Catena, 1989; Carolina Coronado, *Poesías* [Poems], edited and with an introduction by Noël Valis. Madrid: Editorial Castalia, 1991.

6. See Herrnstein Smith (12) for a discussion of how our personal economy ("constituted by the subjects' needs, interests, and resources—biological, psychological, material, and experiential") intersects with our *environment* or market economy.

7. One of the defects most often attributed to women's novels involves structural disequilibrium. In analyzing Catalina Albert i Paradís's novel *Solitut*, for example, an otherwise adulatory editor Manuel Montoliu regretfully notes the novel's structural flaws (Introduction 35). I have found that, while the structural inconsistency of male-authored texts is sometimes regarded as evidence of complexity and innovation, such inconsistency is often used to explain the mediocrity of women's fiction.

8. Carey Kaplan and Ellen Cronan Rose point out that the period (at the end of the eighteenth century) when Samuel Johnson wrote his canon-making *Lives of the Poets* was another such critical historical moment in "biblical canon formation" (27), when the "old courtly literary order was falling apart in a flood of printed books and an increasing rational skepticism about the value of letters" (17). I share their skepticism about the suitability of present-day literary canons. Today, according to these authors, the reading public is "multicultural, multilingual, not at all sure that value inheres in the humanities curriculum in place in universities for the past century and promulgated to the general public as a list of Great Books" (23–24).

9. According to Herrnstein Smith, institutionalized evaluative procedures bolster authority: "[I]nstitutions of evaluative authority will be called upon repeatedly to devise arguments and procedures that validate the community's established tastes and preferences, thereby warding off barbarism and the constant apparition of an imminent collapse of standards and also justifying the exercise of their own normative authority" (18).

10. The "value" of a literary work has much to do with its availability. Since many of the works read for this study have either never been reedited or have been out of print for many decades, it is difficult to speak of their value. As Herrnstein Smith points out, all forms of evaluation and selection "whether performed by the common reader, professional reviewer, big-time bookseller, or small-town library, have functions and effects that are significant in the production and maintenance or destruction of literary value" (25).

11. For a useful exploration of Lacan's work in relation to feminist theories of the subject, see Elizabeth Grosz's *Jacques Lacan: A Feminist Introduction*, especially chapter 6, "Lacan and Feminism." Jana Sawicki explores the relation between feminism and Foucaultian Discourse in *Disciplining Foucault: Feminism, Power, and the Body*.

12. Giuliana Di Febo reports that the rate of consumption was lower relative to men than the rate of production in which women were somewhat better represented (53).

13. Some of the sources where data about literacy and women readers can be found are: Giuliana Di Febo, "Orígenes del debate feminista en España. La escuela krausista y la Institución Libre de Enseñanza (1870–1890)" [Origins of the feminist debate in Spain. The Krausist school and the Institución Libre de Enseñanza]; Concepción Sáiz, *La revolución del 68 y la cultura femenina* [The Revolution of '68 and feminine culture]; Miguel Martínez Cuadrado, *La Burguesía conservadora 1874–1931* [The conservative bourgeoisie, 1874–1931]; Geraldine Scanlon, *La polémica feminista en la España contemporánea (1864–1974)* [The feminist polemic in contemporary Spain]; and Cristina Enríquez Salamanca, "¿Quién era la escritora del siglo XIX?" [Who was the nineteenth-century woman writer?]. According to Enríquez de Salamanca, who uses Martínez Cuadrado as her source, the illiteracy rate in 1887 was 81 percent for Spanish women and 62 percent for men. Di Febo, using Sáiz as her source, says that in 1870 only 716,000 out of a total of 7,900,000 Spanish women were able to read and write, or, approximately 9 percent.

14. Fernán Caballero [Cecilia Böhl de Faber] is the most common, others are: Jorge Lacos [Pastora Echegaray Eizaguirre], Martín Avila [Isabel Cheix Martínez], Tirso de Tebas [Josefa Codina Umbert], Felipe Escalada [Gertrudis Gómez de Avellaneda], and Ibo Maza Beata de Jaruco [Agar Eva Infanzón Canel]. According to Simón Palmer, the use of masculine pseudonyms is not extensive, but women writers often used feminine pseudonyms, or they modified their name:

> The very fact of participating in a literary endeavor, something considered a masculine activity in the nineteenth century, hindered feminine initiative and forced women to justify continually their conduct. In principle, a woman "literata" inspired serious suspicions that were most effectively allayed by adding "of" [de] after her first surname, to join her to her husband, in order to lend her book a certain credibility. Sometimes women reduced their first name to an initial and other times they eliminated it altogether as in the case of Sofía Casanova or Eva Canel. There were even those who used both paternal family names in order to gain an advantage from an inherited reputation. (*Escritoras* xv)

15. This epithet is commonly applied to Pardo Bazán's work, even by modern critics.

16. I will repeat here Hélène Cixous's caveat about the ambiguous term *feminine*: "We always get confused because of those words [like *feminine* and *masculine*], but we have to deal with them, we have to struggle with them. . . . Every time I say 'masculine' or 'feminine'

or 'man' or 'woman,' please use as many quotation marks as you need to avoid taking these terms too literally" ("Reaching the Point" 1). In the context of recent feminist criticism it is no longer possible to take for granted what words like *feminine, woman, women,* and even *feminist,* mean even when used with quotation marks to indicate the author's awareness of their ambiguity. Briefly, the terms *woman* as well as *women,* as used here, will always refer either to a specific person(s) or character(s), or to a category into which all women are placed, blindly and erroneously, by a specific phallocentric discourse; it will in no case mean women in general. *Feminine* will not refer to any innate characteristics attributable only to women, but to a behavior or mode of being that has come to be culturally identified with women but that is not biologically determined, and which therefore may be exhibited by men. Finally, *feminist* and *feminism,* like *woman* and *women* will refer to a specific set of ideas that do not speak for all women who call themselves feminists nor to feminist thought in general. For a further discussion of the stages and types of feminism, see "Variations on Some Common Themes" by the editors of *Questions féministes.* For a problematizing of the terms *gender, woman,* and *women,* see Judith Butler's recent study *Gender Trouble.*

17. For a discussion of the subject of feminist criticism from this perspective, see Ellen Messer-Davidow's influential "The Philosophical Bases of Feminist Literary Criticism." Grouping together feminists from all disciplines, she writes:

> Our subject matters can be: (1) ideas about sex/gender in themselves, analyzed formally, comparatively, and historically; (2) people who conceive, articulate, use, or otherwise embody these ideas, as well as their inventive and expressive processes; (3) the effects these ideas have on people individually and collectively; (4) the media of language, literature, and criticism where these ideas are expressed, as well as the associated processes; and (5) our self-reflexive feminist study of subjects, subject matters, methods, and epistemologies. (79–80)

The subject of this book will encompass several of these points, especially points 2, 3, and 4.

18. In her argument for gender as a "useful category of historical analysis," Joan W. Scott defines the term as having two parts based on interrelated propositions: "gender is a constitutive element of social relationships based on perceived differences between the sexes, and gender is a primary way of signifying relationships of power" (*Gender and the Politics of History* 42). The same argument underlies my study: late nineteenth-century culture wallowed, crisislike, in its determinations about sexual difference. Because difference is always about power, as Foucault has shown, the notion of gender cannot be separated from the notion of power.

19. I am not making the case that these books are somehow *more* indoctrinating than, say, Leopoldo Alas's *La Regenta* or Benito Pérez Galdós's *Fortunata y Jacinta,* for ideas can be just as persuasive when not immediately detected, as James Winders maintains (27).

20. This moral tendentiousness no doubt contributed to the neglect into which these authors have fallen in the twentieth century, as Maryellen Bieder asserts ("Feminine Discourse" 459). For example, several women writers, such as Pilar Sinués de Marco, were tremendously popular during their lifetime but are barely remembered today. Only a few of the novels, notably Pardo Bazán's *Los pazos de Ulloa* [The Ulloa manor] and *La madre naturaleza* [Mother Nature] can be considered part of the high Spanish canon. Several others, like Böhl de Faber's *La familia de Alvareda* [The Alvareda family] or *La gaviota* [The seagull] were for brief decades considered important for their role in the emerging Realist mode, but are hardly ever studied today for aesthetic reasons. Most nineteenth-century Peninsularists do not know who Spain's most prolific woman novelist was (by my count María del Pilar Sinués de Marco) or which women writers devoted their novels almost exclusively to

exposing the problems of the urban proletariat (Ana García de la Torre and Dolors Monserdà i Vidal) or the rural poor (Catalina Albert i Paradís).

21. In this context it is useful to read Joan W. Scott, whose discussions of gender have influenced this book. See her "Gender: A Useful Category of Historical Analysis."

22. By "sort out" I do not mean categorize into neat masculine or feminine traits, but rather to sort out the positive and negative values ascribed to certain behavior and traits and question whether and why these differ for men and women writers.

23. Bridget Aldaraca argues similarly that the vociferous defense of domesticity in the conduct literature of the second half of the century acts as a barometer to "measure the gap between the projected male ideal of the perfect wife and mother, and the inevitable failure of women to realize it" ("El ángel" 66).

## CHAPTER 1

1. Nancy Armstrong argues that too little attention has been paid the historical role of domestic fiction and, in general, the relationship between sexual and political determinants. In *Desire and Domestic Fiction*, she shows how the channeling of sexual desires into the cult of domesticity not only conformed to the norms of monogamous society (97), but served diverse functions in class struggles and systems. If space permitted, I would frame psychological underpinnings of Spain's domestic ideology in relation to the political and cultural events from which they are inseparable.

2. See Noël Valis's valuable article "Eden and the Tree of Knowledge in Fernán Caballero's *Clemencia*" for a study of the dichotomy between "reason as opposed to the savagely destructive force of passion" (252).

3. As Maryellen Bieder notes, motherless women often go astray in women's novels: "In women's fiction the absence of the mother produces a defective moral character in the daughter" ("Feminine Discourse" 469).

4. The one notable exception is *Elia*, whose maternal relationships have been studied recently by Susan Kirkpatrick in *Las románticas*. Elia's decision to enter a convent, according to Kirkpatrick, is a way of bypassing "the dialectics of gendered sexuality, aiming at a beyond or a before of undifferentiated symbiosis with the maternal" (263).

5. Valis also comments on the importance of Clemencia's brief relation to her first husband: "the event provides the motivation for the protagonist's later repudiation of any serious relationships with men while at the same time its brief duration and the author's refusal to develop it any further imply a contrary-to-fact condition, a wished for state of innocence in Clemencia which no longer holds true. Her subsequent behavior confirms this contradictory and ambiguous dream of chaste ignorance" ("Eden" 254).

6. Women's project of transcending adversity is essentially a moral enterprise. By morality, I understand here Michel Foucault's definition, "a set of values and rules of action that are recommended to individuals through the intermediary of various prescriptive agencies" (*Use of Pleasure* 25). While it may seem that women make their decisions in communion only with themselves, these decisions always harmonize perfectly with well-defined moral standards.

7. In her description of the symbolic significance of Clemencia's country retreat, Valis interprets the garden as a space where the masculine is rejected. The tree of knowledge gives way to the feminized pomegranate tree, in a space where Adam (and thus passion) are denied: "Woman is very much a creature superior to man in *Clemencia;* like the pomegranate tree, she stands, beautiful and aloof, in the middle of the garden, but she can only maintain her position by expelling Adam" ("Eden" 256).

8. Valis makes the important observation that Clemencia comes only reluctantly to this

conclusion. In the calmness of her country retreat, Clemencia "feels anguished and repulsed by the mere thought of matrimony" ("Eden" 257).

9. The works of María de Zayas come to mind. See Electa Arenal's article for a comprehensive look at the positive aspects of convent life. Also see Pilar González Martínez (107–8) about the "sacrificial love" that Clara, the protagonist of *La quimera* [The chimera] (1905), chooses when her suitor does not measure up to her expectations (107).

10. Hélène Cixous and other proponents of the much-debated "écriture féminine" have recently discovered [!] these values in the texts of modern women writers such as Clarice Lispecter. In her reading of *The Passion According to G. H.*, Cixous concludes that a woman can "drop the heavy self" (18) and open herself up to another. While it is easy to fall under the spell of this modern version of woman's *mission*, my reading of nineteenth-century conduct and domestic novels, and knowledge of their social masochism (see Chapter 2), make me skeptical of this exaltation of feminine "depersonalization." Of course, when Cixous says that one has to "overrule the ego", that "[b]eing a woman . . . is being a woman continuing, extending, being a selfless woman, a woman *and*" (20), she does not mean the same thing as the thousands of exhortations nineteenth-century women heard and read to be self-less, to think of others first, and to always curb personal desires.

11. In *La senda de la gloria*, Julia sacrifices her artistic career for a jealous drifter who gambles away their money, abuses her mentally and physically, and finally abandons her. And yet Julia's paintings and talent, the author insinuates, are best appreciated *at home*. She is rewarded for her sacrifice when her blind and penniless husband repents and comes home to her at last. Imagine his amazement (and gratitude) when he discovers that his wife has been signing her paintings with his name!

## CHAPTER 2

1. Sandra Lee Bartky's definition of psychological oppression as the self's internalization of a notion of inferiority (22) is a suitable description of the field of interest this chapter addresses.

2. Krafft-Ebing insisted that the phenomenon of sexual bondage, the feminine counterpart to men's sexual masochism, was not a perversion. Although he allowed that adaptation to social conditions explained women's inclination toward subordination, he argued that instinct played the larger part: "In women voluntary subjection to the opposite sex is a physiological phenomenon. Owing to her passive role in procreation and long-existent social conditions, ideas of subjection are, in women, normally connected with the idea of sexual relations. They form, so to speak, the harmonies which determine the tone-quality of feminine feeling" (130; quoted in Louise Kaplan 210).

3. This view is shared by Susan Brownmiller who argues that "when women do fantasize about sex, the fantasies are usually the product of male conditioning and cannot be otherwise" (360), and Clara Thompson, who describes female masochism as a "form of adaptation to an unsatisfactory and circumscribed life" (133; quoted in Modleski 38).

4. The most important of these is Karen Horney, who, in *Feminine Psychology* and *Neurosis and Human Growth*, argued that masochism was a socially conditioned defense against fear. Horney believed that the cultural fact of male supremacy made it more difficult for women to escape some degree of masochism. Others who furthered this adaptational theory are Wilhelm Reich, Clara Thompson, and Irving Bieber. Bieber's analysis of female passivity summarizes the adaptational theories that have informed this chapter on social masochism: "Passivity is not a feminine characteristic: it is the manifestation of a chronic inhibition of protective resources and it is pathological for females as for males. Submission is one of the basic social responses of the species to a threat. In Western culture, however, passivity,

submissiveness, dependency are more acceptable for females; but such culture themes do not establish these attitudes and behaviors as non-pathological. Rather, they indicate that women are not yet fully emancipated" (Bieber 3:267; quoted in Belote 329).

5. Commenting on (and agreeing with) Monique Wittig's critique of the unconscious, Griffin Crowder writes: "Women's oppression results not from repression of the personal unconscious, but from very conscious political mechanisms which have alienated women from themselves and from each other, and which have silenced women's discourse" (125). While I agree that such political mechanisms have alienated women from each other, I would go further and say that they have also contributed to women's psychological makeup, contributing to their repression and regressive tendencies.

6. See Clayton for a comparison of the narrative theories put forth by these and other modern narratologists.

7. See Winnett's discussion of gender bias in current narratology in "Coming Unstrung."

8. It is well to recall that, despite the domestic novel's crude morality, texts are never read exactly as intended by authors, and their effects are unpredictable. For example, discussing British melodramatic fiction of the interwar years, Bridget Fowler argues that the ubiquitous melodramatic narrations that stocked women's magazines helped readers to imagine (in contrast to modernism), a "stable, unambiguous and comprehensible universe. Through these devices, alien eruptions of the monstrous 'other' were ultimately excluded, desire was harmonized with order and reality was apprehended without angst" (52). In other words, melodramatic fiction helped women cope with the monstrosity of an incomprehensible world. The same might be said of nineteenth-century domestic fiction. We have simply not delved deeply enough into the sociohistorical implications of reading practices to be able to speak about the influence of popular Spanish culture on its readership.

9. Andreu discovered in her survey of serialized novels that in only one of them, *María, la hija del jornalero* (by Manuel Fernando y González, 1859), was a virtuous woman allowed to express erotic emotions and notes that by the end of *María*, these emotions "se han atenuado" (620) (have been attenuated). Among the virtues ascribed by Andreu to the Virtuous Woman of popular literature are those that foster the social masochism studied here: "The Virtuous Woman expresses her love by means of her suffering and obedience. According to writers, her capacity to bear her life with resignation and to suffer with patience has been granted her by a divine power thanks to her sentimental capacity" (87). The heroine of popular fiction, she writes, is defined precisely by the opposite qualities of those of the romantic hero: "obedience, passivity and happiness in resignation" (48).

10. In *Loving with a Vengeance*, Tania Modleski claims that most women heroines of popular narratives are either "disfigured, dead, or at the very least, domesticated. And her downfall is seen as anything but tragic" (12).

11. Leopoldo Alas was one of the most vocal opponents of a more public role for women, arguing that he thought a woman could be "sabia" (wise) and "literata" without going to the university. If she wanted to study science, he recommended she should do it at home. His reason was that the presence of women in the classroom was sure to have an unhealthy effect on male students and to restrict the kind of topics that professors could broach (*Palique* 197).

12. I am using the term as originally described by Freud as a repetition compulsion that repeats trauma, but through the agency of game (here literature) enabling the subject to gain some measure of control over pain. Lacan's interpretation of the fort/da scenario, on the other hand, celebrates the experience of fragmentation. See Winders's chapter "Gender and Temporality in *Beyond the Pleasure Principle*" for a comparison of the two interpretations. Winders offers a third interpretation, based on the feminist psychoanalyst Eugénie Lemoine-Luccioni, in which a girl child associates the tossing of the spool of thread "with *herself*, her

own body whose disappearance and erasure she thus mimes" (110). At times the losses and setbacks of the domestic novel remind me of repetition compulsion as described by Freud and possibly Lemoine-Luccioni.

13. It was very popular to portray women who sacrificed themselves for a brother, such as Juana of Angela Grassi's *El copo de nieve* or María of *El hilo del destino*.

14. It should be noted, however, that while the adage "charity begins at home" was certainly in force in late nineteenth-century Spanish society, there was an increasing presence in the public sphere of women working in charitable societies. Adrian Shubert even goes so far as to suggest that the role of Spanish women in charitable organizations allowed them an even broader public role than that of American or British women (55).

15. The list is so lengthy that a separate study would be necessary to develop all of the issues they raise, which is why I have given only a few representative titles here.

16. See Andreu's chapter 3, "Manual de conducta" [The conduct manual], for a discussion of the ambiguous messages of the Spanish chapbooks on feminine conduct. See also her excellent bibliography of primary sources (197–219).

17. In the wake of protracted Carlist Wars and the tumultuous Republican experiment, it is not surprising that conservative and progressive politicians alike appealed to what Di Febo calls "the pacifying capacity of women and their political asepsis" (60). Women could preserve and renovate without ever speaking out except through her example or sacrifice: "A perfect wife, woman contributes to the harmonious renovation of society in that she stimulates but does not intervene, learns but does not criticize. Disposed to the total sacrifice of her own identity, she must incarnate the ideal of the 'strong woman' proposed by fray Luis de León" (60).

Speaking of the spiritualization of the Puritan household in England, Bridget Fowler argues in a similar vein that women's companionship and role as educator of children was called for in the rising capitalist institutions of the mid-nineteenth century: "As capitalist social relations came to dominate everyday provision of wants, the family acquired a new structural significance as an island of ethical values. Familism was the privatized culture celebrating this unit as the sole arena for altruism: women were its 'moral vanguard'" (18). In England capitalism gave rise to the phenomena of women's magazines "which were saturated with the ethos of dependent femininity and familism" (19). In a future work, I hope to study Spanish women's magazines and the social implications of Spain's familism.

Finally, it is important to note that Krausist ideology did much to foster the notion of woman as man's helpmeet. Women had to be educated "to achieve a better society by means of the nuclear family, to contribute to the harmony of society" (Javier María Donézar [unpublished manuscript]; quoted in Cabrera Bosch 35).

18. Even the most theoretical feminists usually acknowledge this danger. On the other hand, some of our most well-known critics continue to deconstruct sado-masochistic art without ever acknowledging its effects. Studies of the film *The Story of O*, by Norman Holland, and of a cartoon version of Pauline Réage's *Story of O* by Roland Barthes ("I hear and I obey") are typical examples.

19. Cepeda argues that the Civil Code of 1889, modeled after the Napoleonic Code of 1810, emphasizes the man's authority (183). She states further that the "main difference betwen the Old Regime and the Liberal Regime with respect to woman consists of her greater freedom in the eighteenth century" (183). In the nineteenth century, a citizen's legal rights depended on his wealth, and woman, "having lost her economic function, remained legally unprotected" (183). The Liberal Regime, concludes Cepeda, severely restricted women's economic independence (192).

20. See Di Febo's article for a cogent discussion of the relation between women's domestic and moral roles and Spain's political and social goals, which she describes as "this attempt

at utopian recomposition of the social and cultural fabric, rent apart by the civil wars and severely put to the test by warring political factions" (60). Some of the conservative appeals to feminine pacifism and women's role as moral guidepost and consoler of men were put forth by otherwise enlightened Krausists who argued for an upgrading of women's education. Among them, Di Febo cites: Fernando de Castro's *Discurso inaugural de las conferencias dominicales sobre la educación de la mujer* [Inaugural speech of the Sunday Conferences on Women's Education], Tomás Tapia's *La religión en la conciencia y en la vida* [Religion in the conscience and in life], and Pi Margall's *La misión de la mujer en la sociedad* [Woman's mission in society]. Paradoxically, many of the most liberal thinkers of the day took quite conservative stances in regard to women's function in society and the family. On the other hand, the not overliberal Pardo Bazán spoke out plainly and forcefully against what she called women's *relative* role: "The error"—she writes in criticism of the marquis del Busto's speech on women— "is to attribute to her a destiny of mere relativity; not to consider her in or of herself, but only in or for others" (*La mujer española* 158).

21. The bourgeois ideal of the domestic angel was applicable only to a small percentage of middle- or upper-class Spanish women. However, Adrian Shubert reports that the number of women in the workforce declined continually between 1877 and 1930, so it is safe to say that during this period working relations were changing along gender lines (38).

22. According to Shubert, when a woman married her legal situation worsened considerably: "she automatically lost most of her legal rights and became an appendage of her husband. She required his permission to be in business and he had the authority to administer her property: she could not sell or mortgage the property she brought to the marriage without his approval, nor could she accept or reject an inheritance by herself" (32).

## CHAPTER 3

1. See Matilde Albert Robatto who notes in *La hija del mar* evidence of Rosalía de Castro's concern for the plight of women in a suffocatingly patriarchal society: "[t]he text makes us think that Rosalía considered the function of women in society to be too unjust and limited and she perceived the meagre power that woman had in making her own decisions." On the other hand Robatto argues that Castro "in her 'feminine' way, accepted as appropriate woman's right to modesty and tears" (68).

2. The irony that male freedom by definition impinges on women's freedom will haunt the nineteenth-century novel for decades to come. In fact, as I discuss in Chapter 4 (132–33), it helps explain the general indifference with which women writers like Pardo Bazán often greeted progressive political regimes.

3. *La hija del mar* restages an Oedipal drama that it would be easy to connect with Castro's own circumstances. Castro forgave or at least came to understand why her mother abandoned her to the care of aunts until she was approximately eight years old. A deepseated resentment, mixed with repressed Oedipal longings for her father (who chose to remain a priest and only cared for her physical well-being) take the form of feminine rage against Alberto, both on the part of Teresa (significantly the name of Castro's mother) and her daughter Esperanza (a clear stand-in for the author).

4. In general this holds true for all of the novels studied here. There are, of course, isolated exceptions in women's fiction. In Sinués's *La amiga íntima* [The intimate friend], for example, the narrator is fascinated by the dark beauty and figure of the sirenlike Blanca. However, any eroticism of the portrait is tempered by an obvious desire to condemn the moral decay hidden behind the mask of feminine beauty.

5. It bears mentioning that in a society with a very low literacy rate among women, the

proletariat, peasant women, and the urban poor were not likely to be readers much less writers of books.

6. As happens with Emilia Pardo Bazán, many critics instead celebrate Castro's ability to overcome "her condition of woman" (Del Barco 513); in other words, to *get it right* by following a masculine example.

7. If we gather together all of *El caballero*'s commented "defects" we would have a good beginning. According to C. Poullain, for example, the novel suffers from a flawed *undecidability* and a mixing of *too many* diverse elements (68).

8. This initiation process was, predictably, not smooth. According to Marina Mayoral, "Rosalía is absolutely pessimistic with respect to the possibility that a woman's talent be accepted by the society in which she lives and was born: no one is a prophet in his own land: 'If even I had been born in France or Madrid! but, here? . . . Oh!'" She confesses that even though in general she scorns such attitudes, 'there are times when, nevertheless this offends me and damages my self esteem'" (*Rosalía* 33).

9. Most critics interpret *El caballero*'s 'novelty' as a new literary form: some call it a new kind of poetry; others, a new novel combining satiric and fantastic elements (Poullain 43).

10. Antonio Risco interprets the Duke as an empty *(vacante)* symbol, "a pitcher that the reader must fill" (129). I would argue, however, that the Duke's semiotic excess guides our interpretation even in a work as open as this to multiple interpretations.

11. Women writers, following a tradition set by María de Zayas, perhaps, told these little romances of horror often. The one produced here brings to mind the scene in Carolina Coronado's *Jarilla* (1851), in which Jarilla is riding bareback on her brave knight's steed. Her breasts are rubbing painfully against his armor until they begin to bleed, causing her to faint (43).

12. Mikhail Liermontov (Lermontov) (1814–1841) was a Russian (Circassian) soldier, poet, playwright, and novelist associated in the Spanish mind with Romantic figures like Byron (whom he knew). His reputation as a Russian Romantic was only exceeded by that of Pushkin. His adventures and travels were widely admired among the Spanish intelligentsia, and his writings on the Caucasus evidently exerted a strong influence on Rosalía de Castro's imagination. It is interesting to note that Lermontov was exiled for criticizing court customs in his famous elegy "The Death of a Poet," written in 1837 upon the death of Pushkin. In it Lermontov summons God's vengeance against the "proud sons of famous fathers," "Vile panderers of lewdness," and "butchers of freedom, genius and renown" who, instead of a garland, give the poet a crown of thorns. The work with the most resonance in Castro's novel is *A Hero of Our Time* (1840), about a dashing Russian soldier, Pechorin, who is the rave among society women, young and old. Pechorin enthralls his female admirers by narrating his exploits in the Caucasus. In *El caballero*, the narrator makes several comparisons such as this one between the Duke and Pechorin: "Por única respuesta, el gran duque se sonrió de la manera que se sonreía Pechorin, el héroe de cierta novela rusa" (742) (as his only reply the great Duke smiled like Pechorin, the hero of a certain Russian novel).

13. This complaint is echoed in Castro's contemporaries. Even the women writers who were conservative in their views about feminine conduct, such as Gimeno de Flaquer, often criticized the lack of respect for women's intellect and recognition of women writers. In 1877 Gimeno de Flaquer complained: "a Spanish man will permit a woman to be frivolous, vain, giddy, silly, superficial, prudish and flirtatious, but not a writer" (211; quoted in Bieder, "Feminine Discourse" 463).

14. The marquise de Sévigné (Marie de Rabutin-Chantal [1626–96]) was a French letter writer and woman of fashion who was a model of the educated woman often cited in Spanish literature. For example, Pardo Bazán mentions her as an example of a learned woman in her

essay "La educación del hombre y la de la mujer" [Man's and woman's education compared] (*La mujer española* 72).

15. Obviously, where all the seamstresses for these mothers of the future would come from is not the issue at this point in the novel's argument about women's occupations. Bourgeois novels that recognize how important it is for women to have freedom from domestic duties, time to write, a room of their own, and so forth, rarely examine the relationship between (some) women's aspirations as writers and an underclass of servants who would necessarily substitute for them in the kitchen or the nursery.

## CHAPTER 4

1. I use the term *feminine* in this chapter as Leslie Rabine does, "in the French poststructuralist sense of an unnameable other excluded from the phallocentric symbolic order" (16). See also the introduction, note 16.

2. Pilar González Martínez divides Pardo Bazán's fiction into three phases. The first, comprising novels written from the beginning of her career to 1890, was the period most steeped in patriarchal values and the one that identifies women with the stereotypes most common in the gender myths of Western culture.

3. Margaret Homans writes that, whether women value maternal language because of cultural dictates or their own interest, "they also always mythologize the subordination of this language to the demands of culture that define women as mothers in the first place" (28).

4. In this sense it is interesting to compare Julián with the equally pusillanimous Bonifacio Reyes in Leopoldo Alas's 1891 novel *Su único hijo* [His only son]. The crisis in Alas's novel comes when Bonifacio recognizes his connection with the "great chain of fathers and sons," as Noël Valis terms it (*The Decadent Vision* 176), and struggles to survive the female threat by avoiding the contact of women altogether (Charnon-Deutsch, *Gender* 63–67). Julián's great moment is also a recognition of his parenthood and his love for a child but he simultaneously recognizes that he forms a unit with the mother whom he must attempt to save from an evil male force. He does not try, as Bonifacio does, to eliminate the mother (the *other* mother) from the scheme of things.

5. In our dominant myth of entry into the symbolic order, as well as other conventional narratives of development, the child is a male and the mother is dead (Homans 81). The mother does not figure as a subject apart from her attributes as mother and we somehow do not connect her with her daughter. As Elizabeth Grosz explains: "The mother/daughter relation is the 'dark continent of the dark continent,' the most obscure area of our social order. To 'enlighten' its blackness would pose a threat to the social order which has taken so much trouble to cover it over" (181). The reciprocal relation between men, based on what Lévi-Strauss imagined was a universal system of the exchange of women was predicated upon a "radical non-reciprocity between men and women and a relation, as it were, of nonrelation between women" (Butler 41). *Los pazos* thus breaks two taboos at once by representing a total reciprocity verging on indistinction between two people of the supposedly "opposite" sex, and by making a space for a mother/daughter relation into which one may only enter by becoming a woman.

6. The mother/daughter taboo also highlights a national obsession with legitimacy, patriliny, and genealogy that has yet to be explored in relation to its discrete social and historical contexts. For example, what difference did it make that Isabel II, literally placed on the throne by her tenacious mother María Cristina, *restored* Spanish monarchy to its traditional line of male kings, or that revisions of the Civil Code, such as those incorporated in the 1880s, repeatedly reinforced the father's legal role in the family while proscribing and limiting women's rights (Nash 19–24).

7. In her book *Aporías de una mujer*, González Martínez states that Pardo Bazán polarizes the notions of male and female, only then to seek ways to "make the masculine and feminine dance together in a chain of signifieds and metaphors" (58). Unfortunately, her structuralist methodology prevents her from studying in depth her most interesting conclusions regarding this gender "dance."

8. A common complaint of feminists is that male authors tend to divide women into two groups, the whore and the spiritualized mother (Modleski 78). What critics sometimes overlook is that women authors often reciprocate by dividing men into two classes, "the omnipotent, domineering, aloof male and the gentle, but passive and fairly ineffectual male" (Modleski 79). Pardo Bazán often does both, especially in her early works like *Los pazos*.

9. A long list of critics have dwelled on these contradictory failures. For example, Maurice Hemingway studies Julián's weakness as one of the novel's principal flaws. See also the curious article by Anthony Gooch who is clearly appalled by Julián's feminization, and the more enlightened studies of Carlos Feal-Deibe and González Martínez, who note the various instances in *Los pazos* when Pardo Bazán describes the feminization of Pedro and his uncle (Nucha's father) as a beneficial, civilizing process.

10. Useful here is the notion of feminine masquerade that Joan Rivière described as a "mask of womanliness to avert anxiety and the retribution feared from men" (quoted in Butler 51).

11. See also Judith Butler who explains how "'being' the phallus is always a 'being for' a masculine subject who seeks to reconfirm and augment his identity through the recognition of that 'being for'" (45).

12. Pardo Bazán's pronouncements on motherhood varied according to her specific ends. When she wanted to argue that women should not be required to stay home to be "trained" for their future roles as mothers, she claimed that mothers were "the masterpiece of natural instinct" (*La mujer* 81) and that consequently maternal love could not be taught. On the other hand, she fought vociferously against the notion that motherhood was a woman's only, or even most noble, destiny: "every woman has ideas, but not all conceive children. A human being is not a fruit tree that only is cultivated for its harvest" (89). Women's reproductive function in no way supersedes any of her other human faculties. Accordingly, sexual attraction and the reproductive instinct should not limit "other social, artistic, political, scientific, or religious ends or motives, nor even the indisputable exercise of individual freedom, implied in the absolute right to remain celibate or sterile" (*La mujer* 159).

13. Julián's list of virgins borders on the absurd, only thinly disguising the author's contempt. The cult of the Virgin was so widespread in nineteenth-century popular fiction and conduct books that Pardo Bazán sometimes balked at its overwhelming influence. Popular literature was especially absorbed with representations of the ideal woman as virgin. Alicia Andreu studies the *Mujer Virtuosa* (Virtuous woman) of popular fiction between the years 1840 and 1890 as a kind of exemplar of the cult of the Virgin: "a chaste, innocent, melancholic, sad being who radiates sweetness" (74). Nucha, though not a perfect match, certainly embodies this ideal of the *Mujer Virtuosa*.

14. Katherine Rogers defines the nineteenth century as the era of women's apotheosis: "they were the nobler half of humanity, whose role was to elevate men's sentiments and inspire their higher impulses. Women were purer than men, more religious, more altruistic, more devoted. As members of the delicate sex, they were absolutely entitled to chivalrous protection" (189).

15. Although Pardo Bazán argued forcefully against the depiction of childbearing as an illness, she recognized that it could be a dangerous undertaking, especially under certain conditions. Lack of exercise, ignorance of hygiene, and women's "fatal sedentarism" account

for their chronic illnesses and hysteria. "It is not nature but society as it is constituted today that perchance throws women off-balance" (*La mujer* 151).

16. Michelle Massé's description of the woman in a Gothic novel as a pawn is relevant here: "she is moved, threatened, discarded, and lost" (*In the Name* 108).

17. For a graphic representation of this, see her short stories, such as "Las medias rojas" [The red stockings], "La dama joven" [The young woman], or "Dos mujeres" [Two women]. It is probable that Pardo Bazán's ambivalence vis-à-vis mother nature will become a topic of critical attention as we become more aware of the myth's implications for female subjectivity.

18. In this respect I disagree with González Martínez's terms for the feminine in Pardo Bazán's early work: "matter-body-life" (26); "nature, instinct and poetry" (9). Julián and Nucha, at least, have no "magic communication with nature" (11) and if Nucha's daughter does it is by virtue of nurture not nature. González-Martínez does briefly recognize the significance of woman as mediator of the civilized (16), but she fails to pursue this paradox. Perhaps her desire to see the evolution of Pardo Bazán's fiction from a more materialistic to a spiritualistic notion of woman leads her to exaggerate the consistency of her categories.

19. The opposite conclusion regarding Julián's appreciation of nature is reached by most critics. See, for example, García Guerra's comments in the chapter "Natura y nutura" [Nature and nurture] (111).

20. For a further discussion of gender and point of view, see Bieder ("Between" 132) who describes the narrative voice of *Los pazos* as fundamentally male-oriented but discovers a subsurface of female voices in the narrative technique of "focalization" ("Between" 133). In Pardo Bazán's other works, the images of nature split on this paradox: sometimes mother nature is recognized (and welcomed) by women as a door to the complex experiences of motherhood. Other times, nature is either something that acts as a surrogate mother for the male character who fixates on women's life-giving capacities or a force that shunts women into unwelcome roles.

21. Later in *La Madre naturaleza*, Pardo Bazán imagines a male version of Pepe Rey in the form of Gabriel. But more than a needed civilizing agent, Gabriel is an unwelcome intruder whose knowledge of the civilized world cannot compensate for his ignorance of the natural.

22. Pardo Bazán's notion was not exaggerated. As Di Febo points out, the 1889 revisions of the Civil Code, modeled after the Napoleonic Code, did little more than consecrate the subjection of wife and daughter to the husband or the father's authority (76).

23. Pardo Bazán frequently carried on such literary gender debates with her male colleagues. See for example, her story "Cuento Primitivo" [An old story] (1893) in which she reverses the gender roles of Adam and Eve in response to Clarín's highly misogynistic "Cuento futuro" [A story of the future] (1892). According to Carmen Bravo Villasante, *Insolación* [Sunstroke] might have been Pardo Bazán's explanation for her brief infidelity to Galdós.

24. Bieder interprets Julián as an androgyne who is "neither wholly integrated into the male experience nor totally excluded from it" ("Between" 134). However, it is also possible to argue that Julián's attempts to "mediate between the female and male spheres, moving freely between them without belonging fully to either" (134) are a failure.

25. See the section entitled "Maternidad como dualismo materia-espíritu y campo-ciudad" [Maternity as a matter-spirit and country-city duality] (44–45), where González Martínez describes in more detail the "good" and "bad" mothers of Pardo Bazán's first period (1879–89).

26. See, for example, "Del amor y la amistad" [Of love and friendship] (*La mujer española*

147) and "La esposición de trabajos de la mujer" (The exposition of feminine labors] (*La mujer española* 165).

27. See Geraldine Scanlon's excellent article for a comprehensive examination of the complex interplay of class and gender in *La Tribuna*. As Scanlon states, Pardo Bazán's attitude toward Amparo's role was ambivalent: she was sympathetic to her gender struggle and aspirations while condemnatory and condescending toward her political goals.

28. In her excellent study of Gómez de Avellaneda's *Sab*, Susan Kirkpatrick describes how Avellaneda used the mulatto Sab to protest indirectly the plight of the bourgeois woman writer. This colonization of the more marginalized by the less marginalized has become an important topic in subaltern studies such as those of Spivak cited here.

29. Sexual desire, predictably, is imagined as a debasing attraction because it is shortlived: it excites and irritates man but does not exalt him or move him (1:200–201).

30. Pardo Bazán's contemporary Concepción Gimeno de Flaquer also depicted passion in her novels as anathema to women's family role, indirectly admonishing characters to "sufrir y abstenerse" (suffer and abstain) (*Suplicio de una coqueta*; quoted in Bieder, "Feminine Discourse" 470).

31. See González Martínez for a discussion of Pardo Bazán's weak, absent, or bad fathers.

## CHAPTER 5

1. For example, in MacPherson de Bremon's *El hilo del destino* [The thread of destiny] the main *tragedy* of the young orphans Julián and María is to have to work, one as a seamstress and the other as a translator, in order to provide for "las necesidades de la vida material" (the necessities of material life). Amid their anguish and exalted sentimentalism they have to think about the crass business of earning money, "tienen por precisión que anteponer su dolor a la dura necesidad que las hace obrar, no como su corazón les pide, sino como ella les exige" (they are forced to put before their sorrow the hard necessity that forces them to work, not at what their hearts desire, but according to their needs) (2:8).

2. Monserdà extends her indictment of the reading of novels to Naturalist authors whose works are full of sadness, pessimism, and passion (157). For Florentina, both traditions have the same effect; they both take her to a world that is "different" than her own (158).

3. In sharp contrast to Antonieta's stellar success (and acceptance) as a *fabricanta*, is the description of the miserable working conditions of Spanish women involved in the textile industry:

> slaves to the century's notion that women should not work, they should zealously hide their shameful poverty and their working conditions are all the more painful for this. Most of them work without light, live with no exercise or fresh air; they iron until dawn, until they gather the few reals a day that permit them to continue in the same miserable situation. Premature blindness, deviations of the vertebral column and especially anemia and tuberculosis, besiege these workers. (González et al. 128–29)

4. In her review (*La mujer española* 141) of the novel Pardo Bazán complains that "*Tristana* prometía otra cosa; que Galdós nos dejó entrever un horizonte nuevo y amplio, y después corrió la cortina" (*Tristana* promised something else; Galdós let us see dimly a new and expansive horizon, and then he closed the curtain). Galdós pulled the curtain not only on Tristana's struggle for independence, but her "lucha por la libre elección amorosa" (struggle for the free election of a partner) (140).

5. I am not suggesting that the notion of the companionate marriage was unknown in

Spain. In *El ángel del hogar*, Bridget Aldaraca points out that as early as 1790, Josefa Amar y Borbón, in her treatise *Discurso sobre la educación física y moral de las mugeres* [Discourse on the physical and moral education of women], challenged the "rigid authority with which the husband controls the wife" (46) and proposed a family structure based on the "harmony born of communication." However, it is only in the latter half of the nineteenth century that characters of the middle classes begin to adapt this ideal and to recognize more fully women's social importance. Aldaraca cites the hero of Galdós's *Tormento* (1884), *El amigo Manso* [Our friend Manso] (1882), and *La familia de León Roch* [León Roch's family] (1878) as examples.

6. According to Rafael Flaquer Montegui, this notion of the "new family" had been promoted in the working-class press since the early 1870s. Against the notion of the bourgeois marriage, corrupted by concerns of economic expediency, the proletariat press proposed an association that both partners would accept freely, free from subjugation, based on mutual respect and equal rights, and dissolvable under certain conditions (280). Montegui is quick to point out, however, that his survey of the working-class press was largely discouraging in regard to women's rights (285).

7. For a discussion of women's legal and social status in Spain vis-à-vis other European countries, see María Isabel Cabrera Bosch's "Las mujeres que lucharon solas" [The women who fought alone]. See also chapter 4, "La situación de la mujer en el siglo XIX hasta 1936" [The situation of women in the nineteenth century until 1936] in González et al.; and section 4, "Cincuenta años de retraso" [Fifty years behind] in Capmany.

8. Elizabeth Ordóñez believes Fe and Mauro are modeled after another couple Pardo Bazán greatly admired: Harriet Taylor and John Stuart Mill. See "Revising Realism" 158–61.

9. Pardo Bazán's reactionary political leanings are summarized in *Historia social de la literatura española* [A social history of spanish literature] by Carlos Blanco Aguinaga, Julio Rodríguez Puértolas, and Iris M. Zavala. Despite her purely decorative Naturalism, argue the writers, Pardo Bazán "turns out to be, in general, just another example of Hispanic traditionalism, conveniently decorated with a cosmopolitan sensibility that only amounts to a slight variance from the bourgeois mentality of the Restoration" (2:150).

10. According to Northrop Frye, this corresponds to Romantic tendencies to exalt only what is individualistically revolutionary or progressive and to designate society and its institutions as "demonic or regressive" (83; quoted in Pratt 181).

11. Sexual equality was obviously becoming an issue in late nineteenth-century Spanish society. The many warnings to women about the possible dire consequences of seeking equality are perhaps indicative of the power that such notions were beginning to enjoy. Most periodical literature geared toward a female readership constantly warned women that it was a mistake to strive for sexual equality.

12. Fe's detailed description of her new image and activities echo the many treatises addressed to Spanish women regarding ways to save money on their personal hygiene and clothing. Henceforth she will keep herself immaculately clean, washing and ironing her own dresses and collars. When she washes her hair, she will be sure to use plenty of water and soda crystals, "porque el *shaampoing [sic]* cuesta un sentido" (because shampoo costs a fortune). If she cleans her nails well *herself*, she won't have to worry about wearing gloves (2:488).

13. Pardo Bazán does not argue that women of all classes should be granted equal educational opportunities. Her argument against extended education of the working classes uses a familiar conservative rationale: if the lower classes are given too much education, they will no longer be content to be servants, farmhands, and factory workers. The level of education should be determined by social conditions (*La mujer española* 73). For members of her own class, Pardo Bazán argued forcefully for fuller academic opportunities, complaining that

women (such as her own daughter who was enrolled in the Instituto del Cardenal Cisneros) were only admitted to institutions of higher learning "por lástima o por excepción" (out of pity or as an exception) (101).

14. By way of showing that men and women conceived of adventure differently, Jane Miller quotes Jane Austen who writes in her diary: "I have read the Corsair, mended my petticoat, and have nothing else to do" (*Women Writing*, 20). By contrast, speaking of that climactic moment in a woman's life when she marries, Pardo Bazán said in her diary: "Three things happened to me that year. I started wearing long dresses, I got married, and the Revolution of September broke out" (Bravo-Villasante 18). It was obviously a momentous year. Doubtless a nineteenth-century man would not have felt comfortable with the irreverent juxtaposition of the revolution and Pardo Bazán's long skirts and marriage, or the Corsair vying for attention with Austen's petticoats.

15. For an exploration of these issues, see Mary Nash's introduction to *Mujer, familia y trabajo en España, 1875–1936* [Woman, family and work in Spain, 1875–1936].

16. It is useful here to compare Mauro's generous "manifesto of equality" with the Civil Code of the same year *Memorias* was published (1889), in which woman's status as second-class citizen to her husband is spelled out in painstaking detail (Nash 159–92). It is also pertinent to recall Pardo Bazán's 1892 article on John Stuart Mill. In her extravagant praise of Mill's relationship with Harriet Taylor, we see the prototype of the couple that *Memorias* celebrates. Quoting, and then commenting on Mill's *The Subjection of Women* (1869), Pardo Bazán writes enviously that not even Dante enjoyed such an ideal reciprocal relationship (*La mujer española* 125).

17. Although not universally shared, Pardo Bazán's complaints about the Spanish husband's lack of solidarity found expression in several contemporary treatises (see Nash 126).

18. Although national congresses like the First International dedicated sessions to women in the workforce, the little progress made in this area reflected the fear that women might become too competitive (Montegui 279).

19. Most women worked in agriculture, Spain's primary sector. The vast majority of women working in the tertiary (service) sector were household servants. In 1877 there were 313,000 female servants and in 1887 there were 322,000 (Shubert 40). The two *dignified* professions open to middle-class women were that of teacher or music instructor (Lobato Villena 275).

## CONCLUSION

1. For a sampling of this see Simón Palmer's *Escritoras españolas*. The thousands of poems, articles, stories, historical and religious novels about saints and virgins compose one of the principal themes of women's literature.

2. See Foucault's *The History of Sexuality*, vol. 1, especially part 2, "The Repressive Hypothesis" 17–49.

# Works Cited

Adams, Parveen. "Of Female Bondage." *Between Feminism and Psychoanalysis*. Ed. Teresa Brennan. London: Routledge, 1989. 247–65.

Alas, Leopoldo ["Clarín"]. "Congreso Pedagógico." *Palique*. Ed. José María Martínez Cachero. Barcelona: Editorial Labor, 1973. 195–99.

———. *La Regenta*. 2 vols. Ed. Gonzalo Sobejano. Madrid: Clásicos Castalia, 1982.

Albert i Paradís, Catalina. *Solitut. Obres completes*. Ed. Manuel Montoliu. Barcelona, Editorial Selecta, 1951.

Aldaraca, Bridget. "El ángel del hogar: The Cult of Domesticity in Nineteenth-Century Spain." *Theory and Practice of Feminist Literary Criticism*. Ed. Gabriela Mora and Karen S. Van Hooft. Ypsilanti, Mich.: Bilingual Press, 1982. 62–87.

———. *El ángel del hogar: Galdós and the Ideology of Domesticity in Spain*. North Carolina Studies in the Romance Languages and Literatures, no. 239. Chapel Hill: University of North Carolina Press, 1991.

Altieri, Charles. "An Idea and Ideal of a Literary Canon." *Critical Inquiry* 10.1 (September 1983): 37–60.

Andreu, Alicia. *Galdós y la literatura popular*. Madrid: Sociedad General Española de Librería, 1982.

Arenal, Electa. "The Convent as Catalyst for Autonomy: Two Hispanic Nuns of the Seventeenth Century." *Women in Hispanic Literature: Icons and Fallen Idols*. Ed. Beth Miller. Berkeley and Los Angeles: University of California Press, 1983. 147–83.

Armstrong, Nancy. *Desire and Domestic Fiction: A Political History of the Novel*. New York: Oxford University Press, 1987.

———. "Some Call It Fiction: On the Politics of Domesticity." *The Other Perspective in Gender and Culture. Rewriting Women and the Symbolic*. Ed. Juliet Flower MacCannell. New York: Columbia University Press, 1990. 59–84.

Auerbach, Nina. *Communities of Women. An Idea in Fiction*. Cambridge: Harvard University Press, 1978.

———. "Magi and Maidens. The Romance of the Victorian Freud." *Writing and Sexual Difference*. Ed. Elizabeth Abel. Chicago: University of Chicago Press, 1982. 111–30.

Barthes, Roland. *The Pleasure of the Text*. Trans. Richard Miller. New York: Hill and Wang, 1975 (*Le Plaisir du texte*. Paris: Seuil, 1973).

Bartky, Sandra Lee. *Femininity and Domination. Studies in the Phenomenology of Oppression*. New York: Routledge, 1990.

Baumeister, Roy E. *Masochism and the Self.* Hillsdale, N.J.: Erlbaum, 1989.

———. "Masochism as Escape from Self." *Journal of Sex Research* 25.1 (February 1988): 28–59.

Belote, Betsy. "Masochistic Syndrome, Hysterical Personality and the Illusion of a Healthy Woman." *Female Psychology. The Emerging Self.* 2d ed. Ed. Sue Cox. New York: St. Martin's, 1981. 320–33.

Benjamin, Jessica. *The Bonds of Love: Psychoanalysis, Feminism, and the Problem of Domination.* New York: Pantheon, 1988.

———. "A Desire of One's Own: Psychoanalytic Feminism and Intersubjective Space." *Feminist Studies: Critical Studies.* Ed. Teresa de Lauretis. Bloomington: Indiana University Press, 1986. 78–101.

Bergler, Edmund. "*Little Dorrit* and Dickens' Intuitive Knowledge of Psychic Masochism." *American Imago* 14 (1957): 371–88.

Berliner, Bernhard. "On Some Psychodynamics of Masochism." *Psychoanalytic Quarterly* 16 (1946): 459–71.

Bersani, Leo. *The Freudian Body: Psychoanalysis and Art.* New York: Columbia University Press, 1986.

———, and Ulysse Dutoit. *Forms of Violence: Narrative in Assyrian Art and Modern Culture.* New York: Shocken, 1985.

Bieber, Irving. *Sadism and Masochism.* Vol. 3 of *American Handbook of Psychiatry.* 6 vols. New York: Basic Books, 1966.

Bieder, Maryellen. "Between Genre and Gender: Emilia Pardo Bazán and *Los pazos de Ulloa.*" *In the Feminine Mode: Essays on Hispanic Women Writers.* Ed. Noël Valis and Carol Maier. Lewisburg: Bucknell University Press, 1990. 131–45.

———. "Feminine Discourse / Feminist Discourse: Concepción Gimeno de Flaquer." *Kentucky Romance Quarterly* 37.4 (1990): 459–77.

———. "A Question of Gender: Narrative Voice in *Los pazos de Ulloa* and *La madre naturaleza.*" Midwest Modern Language Association Annual Meeting. Chicago, 7 November 1986.

Blanco, Alda. "Domesticity, Education and the Woman Writer: Spain 1850–1880." *Cultural and Historical Grounding for Hispanic and Luso-Brazilian Feminist Literary Criticism.* Ed. Hernán Vidal. Literature and Human Rights, no. 4. Minneapolis, Minn., Institute for the Study of Ideologies and Literature, 1989. 371–94.

Blanco Aguinaga, Carlos, Julio Rodríguez Puértolas, and Iris M. Zavala. *Historia social de la literatura española.* 3 vols. Madrid: Castalia, 1978.

Böhl de Faber, Cecilia. *Clemencia.* Ed. Julio Rodríguez-Luis. Madrid: Cátedra, 1985.

———. *Elia.* Madrid: Alianza Editorial, 1968.

———. *La familia de Alvareda.* Ed. Julio Rodríguez-Luis. Madrid: Clásicos Castalia, 1979.

———. *La Gaviota.* Ed. Carmen Bravo-Villasante. Madrid: Clásicos Castalia, 1984.

Bravo-Villasante, Carmen. *Emilia Pardo Bazán.* Barcelona: Círculo de Lectores, 1971.

Brenkman, John. *Culture and Domination.* Ithaca: Cornell University Press, 1987.

Brooke-Rose, Christine. "Dissolution of Character in the Novel." *Reconstructing Individualism.* Ed. Thomas C. Heller et al. Stanford: Stanford University Press, 1986. 184–96.

Brooks, Peter. *Reading for the Plot: Design and Intention in Narrative.* New York: Knopf, 1984.

Brownmiller, Susan. *Against Our Will: Men Women and Rape.* New York: Bantam Books, 1976.

Butler, Judith. *Gender Trouble: Feminism and the Subversion of Identity.* New York: Routledge, 1990.

Cabrera Bosch, María Isabel. "Las mujeres que lucharon solas: Concepción Arenal y Emilia Pardo Bazán." *El feminismo en España: Dos siglos de historia.* Ed. Pilar Folguera. Madrid: Editorial Pablo Iglesias, 1988. 29–50.

Caplan, Paula. *The Myth of Women's Masochism.* New York: Dutton, 1985.

Capmany, Aurèlia, Carmen Alcalde. *El feminismo ibérico.* Barcelona: Oikos-tau, 1970.

Caserio, Robert L. "Mobility and Masochism: Christine Brooke-Rose and J. G. Ballard." *Novel* 21 (Spring/Winter 1988): 292–310.

Castro, Rosalía de. *Obras en prosa.* Madrid: Aguilar, 1988. Vol. 2 of *Obras completas.* 2 vols. 1988.

Cepeda Gómez, Paloma. "La situación jurídica de la mujer en España durante el Antiguo Régimen y régimen liberal." *Ordenamiento jurídico y realidad social de las mujeres. Actas de las cuartas jornadas de investigación interdisciplinaria.* Madrid: Seminario de Estudios de la mujer, 1986. 181–93.

Charnon-Deutsch, Lou. *Gender and Representation: Women in Nineteenth-Century Spanish Realist Fiction.* Lafayette, Ind.: Purdue University Monographs in Romance Languages, 1990.

Chodorow, Nancy J. *Feminism and Psychoanalytic Theory.* New Haven: Yale University Press, 1989.

———. *The Reproduction of Mothering: Psychoanalysis and the Sociology of Gender.* Berkeley and Los Angeles: University of California Press, 1978.

Cixous, Hélène. "Reaching the Point of Wheat, or A Portrait of the Artist as a Maturing Woman." *New Literary History* 19.1 (1987–88): 1–21.

Claret, Father Antonio Maria. *Avisos saludables a las casadas.* Vich: Imp. José Trullás, 1846.

Clayton, Jay. "Narrative and Theories of Desire." *Critical Inquiry* 16.1 (Autumn 1989): 33–53.

Clèmessy, Nelly. *Emilia Pardo Bazán como novelista (De la teoría a la práctica).* 2 vols. Trans. Irene Gambra. Madrid: Fundación Universitaria Española, 1981.

Coronado, Carolina. *Jarilla.* Madrid: Biblioteca Universal, 1851.

Coward, Rosalind. *Patriarchal Precedents: Sexuality and Social Relations.* London: Routledge and Kegan Paul, 1983.

Cuevas de la Cruz, Matilde, and Luis E. Otero. "Prostitución y legislación en el siglo XIX. Aproximación a la consideración social de la prostituta." *Ordenamiento jurídico y realidad social de las mujeres. Actas de las cuartas jornadas de investigación interdisciplinaria.* Madrid: Seminario de Estudios de la mujer, 1986. 247–58.

de Lauretis, Teresa. *Alice Doesn't: Feminism, Semiotics, Cinema.* Bloomington: Indiana University Press, 1984. Chapter 5, "Desire and Narrative."

———. *Technologies of Gender.* Bloomington: University of Indiana Press, 1987.

Del Barco, Pablo. "Caminando con las botas azules." *Cuadernos Hispano-americanos* 425 (1985): 511–15.

Deleuze, Gilles. *Masochism: An Interpretation of Coldness and Cruelty.* New York: Zone Books, 1989.

————, and Félix Guattari. *Anti-Oedipus: Capitalism and Schizophrenia*. Minneapolis: University of Minnesota Press, 1983.

Deutelbaum, Wendy, and Cynthia Huff. "Class, Gender, and Family System: The Case of George Sand." *The (M)other Tongue: Essays in Feminist Psychoanalytic Interpretation*. Ed. Shirley Nelson Garner, Claire Kahane, and Madelon Sprengnether. Ithaca: Cornell University Press, 1985. 260–79.

Deutsch, Hélène. *The Psychology of Women: A Psychoanalytic Interpretation*. 2 vols. New York: Grune and Stratton, 1944–45.

Di Febo, Giuliana. "Orígenes del debate feminista en España. La escuela krausista y la Institución libre de Enseñanza (1870–1890)." *Sistema* 12 (1976): 49–82.

Dijkstra, Bram. *Idols of Perversity: Fantasies of Feminine Evil in Fin-de-siècle Culture*. New York: Oxford University Press, 1986.

El Saffar, Ruth S. "Mother Nature's Nature in *La madre naturaleza*." Midwest MLA Convention. Chicago, 7 November 1986.

Enríquez de Salamanca, Cristina. "¿Quién era la escritora del siglo XIX?" *Letras Peninsulares*. 2.1 (Spring 1989): 81–107.

Feal-Deibe, Carlos. "La voz femenina en *Los pazos de Ulloa*." *Hispania* 70.2 (1987): 214–21.

Flaquer Montegui, Rafael. "La función social de la mujer a través de la prensa obrera madrileña (1868–1874)." *Ordenamiento jurídico y realidad social de las mujeres. Actas de las Cuartas Jornadas de Investigación Interdisciplinaria*. Madrid: Seminario de Estudios de la Mujer, 1986. 279–86.

Foucault, Michel. *Power/Knowledge: Selected Interviews and Other Writings, 1972–1977*. Ed. Colin Gordon. New York: Pantheon, 1980.

————. *History of Sexuality*. Vol. 1. *An Introduction*. Trans. Robert Hurley. New York: Vintage, 1980. Vol. 2. *The Use of Pleasure*. Trans. Robert Hurley. New York: Vintage, 1985.

Fowler, Bridget. *The Alienated Reader: Women and Romantic Literature in the Twentieth Century*. Hemel Hempstead (England): Harvester Wheatsheaf, 1991.

Freud, Sigmund. "A Child is Being Beaten." *Collected Papers*. Vol. 2. New York: Basic Books, 1959, 172–201.

————. "The Economic Problem in Masochism." *Collected Papers*. Vol. 2. New York: Basic Books, 1959. 255–68.

————. "Femininity." *New Introductory Lectures on Psychoanalysis*. Trans. James Strachey. New York: Norton, 1965. 99–119.

————. *On Creativity and the Unconscious*. Trans. I. F. Grant Duff. New York: Harper, 1958.

————. "Three Essays on the Theory of Sexuality." *Standard Edition*. Vol. 7. London: Hogarth, 1981. 133–243.

Frye, Northrop. *The Secular Scripture: A Study of the Structure of Romance*. Boston: Harvard University Press, 1976.

Gallop, Jane. *The Daughter's Seduction*. Ithaca: Cornell University Press, 1982.

————. "Writing and Sexual Difference: The Difference Within." *Writing and Sexual Difference*. Ed. Elizabeth Abel. Chicago: University of Chicago Press, 1982. 283–97.

García Guerra. Delfín. *La condición humana en Emilia Pardo Bazán*. Laracha, La Coruña: Xuntanza, 1990.

García Sánchez, Ramón. "La Mujer." *La mujer. Revista de instrucción general para el bello sexo*. 1.6 (16 July 1871): 6–7.

Garner, Shirley Nelson, Claire Kahane, and Madelon Sprengnether, eds. *The*

*(M)other Tongue: Essays in Feminist Psychoanalytic Interpretation.* Ithaca: Cornell University Press, 1985.

Gilbert, Sandra, and Susan Gubar. *The Madwoman in the Attic. The Woman Writer and the Nineteenth-Century Literary Imagination.* New Haven: Yale University Press, 1979.

———. "Tradition and the Female Talent." *The Poetics of Gender.* Ed. Nancy K. Miller. New York: Columbia University Press, 1986. 183–207.

Gilligan, Carol. *In a Different Voice: Psychological Theory and Women's Development.* Cambridge: Harvard University Press, 1982.

Gimeno de Flaquer, Concepción. *El doctor alemán.* Barcelona: Calisto Ariño, 1880.

———. *La mujer española, estudios acerca a la educación.* Madrid: Guijarro, 1877.

———. *La mujer juzgada por una mujer.* 2d ed. Barcelona: Luis Tasso y Serra, 1882.

———. *Suplicio de una coqueta.* Mexico: Imprenta de Francisco Díaz de León, 1885 (*¿Culpa o expiación?* Mexico: Secretaría de Fomento, 1890).

Gold, Hazel. "Back to the Future: Criticism, the Canon, and the Nineteenth-Century Spanish Novel." *Hispanic Review* 58.2 (Spring 1990): 179–204.

González, Anabel, Amalia López, Ana Mendoz, and Isabel Urueña. *Los orígenes del feminismo en España.* Madrid: Zero, 1980.

González Martínez, Pilar. *Aporías de una mujer. Emilia Pardo Bazán.* Madrid: Siglo XXI de España, 1988.

Gooch, Anthony. "Análisis psico-semántico de un personaje de 'Los pazos de Ulloa' y 'La madre naturaleza' de Emilia Pardo Bazán: Julián." *En torno a Pemán.* Cádiz: Diputación Provincial de Cádiz, 1974. 445–68.

Grassi, Angela. *El bálsamo de las penas.* 4th ed. Madrid: G. Estrada, 1878.

———. *El copo de nieve.* Madrid: G. Estrada, 1876.

Griffin Crowder, Diane. "Amazons and Mothers: Monique Wittic, Hélène Cixous and Theories of Women's Writing." *New Literary History* 24.1 (Spring 1983): 117–44.

Grossman, William I. "Notes on Masochism: A Discussion of the History and Development of a Psychoanalytic Concept." *Psychoanalytic Quarterly* 55 (1986): 379–413.

Grosz, Elizabeth. *Jacques Lacan: A Feminist Introduction.* New York: Routledge, 1990.

Hartsock, Nancy C. M. *Money, Sex and Power: Toward a Feminist Historical Materialism.* Boston: Northeastern University Press, 1983.

Hemingway, Maurice. *Emilia Pardo Bazán: The Making of a Novelist.* Cambridge: Cambridge University Press, 1983.

Herrnstein Smith, Barbara. "Contingencies of Value." *Critical Inquiry* 10.1 (September 1983): 1–35.

Hirsch, Marianne. *The Mother / Daughter Plot. Narrative, Psychoanalysis, Feminism.* Bloomington: Indiana University Press, 1989.

Holland, Norman. "I-ing Film." *Critical Inquiry* 12.4 (Summer 1986): 654–71.

Homans, Margaret. *Bearing the Word: Language and Female Experience in Nineteenth-Century Women's Writing.* Chicago: University of Chicago Press, 1986.

Horney, Karen. *Feminine Psychology.* Ed. Harold Kelman. New York: Norton, 1967.

———. *Neurosis and Human Growth.* New York: Norton, 1950.

Irigaray, Luce. *Speculum of the Other Woman.* Trans. Gillian G. Gill. Ithaca: Cornell University Press, 1985.

Jacobus, Mary. "The Question of Language: Men of Maxims and *The Mill on the Floss.*" *Writing and Sexual Difference.* Ed. Elizabeth Abel. Chicago: University of Chicago Press, 1982. 37–52.

Janeway, Elizabeth. "On the Power of the Weak." *Signs* 1 (1975): 103–9.

Kaplan, Carey, and Ellen Cronan Rose. *The Canon and the Common Reader.* Knoxville: University of Tennessee Press, 1990.

Kaplan, Cora. "Pandora's Box: Subjectivity, Class and Sexuality in Socialist Feminist Criticism." *Making a Difference: Feminist Literary Criticism.* Ed. Gayle Greene and Coppélia Kahn. New York: Methuen, 1985. 146–76.

Kaplan, Louise. *Female Perversions The Temptations of Emma Bovary.* New York: Doubleday, 1991.

Kirkpatrick, Susan. "Gómez de Avellaneda's *Sab:* Gendering the Liberal Romantic Subject." *In the Feminine Mode: Essays on Hispanic Women Writers.* Ed. Noël Valis and Carol Maier. Lewisburg: Bucknell University Press, 1990. 115–30.

———. *Las románticas: Women Writers and Subjectivity in Spain, 1835–1850.* Berkeley and Los Angeles: University of California Press, 1989.

Krafft-Ebing, Richard von. *Psychopathia Sexualis.* Trans. Franklin S. Klaf. New York: Bell, 1965.

Kristeva, Julia. *The Powers of Horror. An Essay on Abjection.* Trans. Leon S. Roudiez. New York: Columbia University Press, 1982.

———. *Revolution in Poetic Language.* Trans. Margaret Waller. New York: Columbia University Press, 1984. (*La révolution du langage poétique.* Paris: Seuil, 1976).

———. "Stabat Mater." *Tales of Love.* Trans. Leon S. Roudiez. New York: Columbia University Press, 1987. 234–63.

———. *Tales of Love.* Trans. Leon S. Roudiez. New York: Columbia University Press, 1987.

Lacan, Jacques. *Feminine Psychology.* Ed. Juliet Mitchell and Jacqueline Rose. Trans. Jacqueline Rose. New York: Norton, 1982.

Laplanche, Jean. *Life and Death in Psychoanalysis.* Trans. Jeffrey Mehlman. Baltimore: Johns Hopkins University Press, 1976.

———, and J.-B. Pontalis, *The Language of Psychoanalysis.* Trans. Donald Nicholson-Smith. New York: Norton, 1973.

Lipking, Lawrence. "Aristotle's Sister: A Poetics of Abandonment." *Critical Inquiry* 10.1 (September 1983): 61–81.

Lobato Villena, María Dolores, and Pisonero García. "Rechazo y obligatoriedad del trabajo de la mujer, en 'El norte de Castilla' del siglo XIX." *Ordenamiento jurídico y realidad social de las mujeres. Actas de las Cuartas Jornadas de Investigación Interdisciplinaria.* Madrid: Seminario de Estudios de la Mujer, 1986. 267–77.

Lowder Newton, Judith. *Women, Power and Subversion: Social Strategies in British Fiction, 1778–1860.* New York: Methuen, 1985.

MacKinnon, Catharine A. "Feminism, Marxism, Method and the State." *Feminist Theory: A Critique of Ideology.* Ed. Nannerl O. Keohane, Michelle Z. Rosaldo, Barbara C. Gelpi. Chicago: University of Chicago Press, 1982. 1–20.

MacPherson, Catherine Bremon. *El hilo del destino.* Madrid: Fortanet, 1876 (Madrid: Ayguals de Izco Hnos, 1853).

Manquer Montegui, Rafael. "La función social de la mujer a través de la prensa obrera madrileña, 1868–1874." In *Ordenamiento jurídico y realidad social de las mujeres. Actas de las Cuartas Jornadas de Investigación Interdisciplinaria.* Madrid: Seminario de Estudios de la Mujer, 1986. 279–86.

Marantz Cohen, Paula. *The Daughter's Dilemma: Family Process and the Nineteenth-Century Domestic Novel.* Ann Arbor: University of Michigan Press, 1991.

Martínez Cuadrado, Miguel. *La Burguesía conservadora 1874–1931*. Vol. 6 of *Historia de España Alfaguara*. 7 vols. 6th ed. Ed. Miguel Artola. Madrid: Alianza Alfaguara, 1980.

Massé, Michelle A. "Gothic Repetition: Husbands, Horrors and Things that Go Bump in the Night." *Signs* 15.4 (1990): 679–709.

———. *In the Name of Love: Women, Masochism, and the Gothic*. Ithaca: Cornell University Press, 1992.

Mayoral, Marina. *Rosalía de Castro*. Madrid: Fundación Juan March/Cátedra, 1986.

———. Introduction. *Emilia Pardo Bazán, Dulce Dueño*. Madrid: Castalia, 1989. 7–44.

Mendus, Susan. "The Marriage of True Minds: The Ideal of Marriage in the Philosophy of John Stuart Mill." *Sexuality and Subordination*. Ed. Susan Mendus and Jane Rendall. New York: Routledge, 1989. 171–91.

Messer-Davidow, Ellen. "The Philosophical Bases of Feminist Literary Criticism." *New Literary History* 19.1 (1987): 63–103.

Meyer Spacks, Patricia. *The Female Imagination*. New York: Avon Books, 1976.

Miller, Jane. *Women Writing About Men*. New York: Pantheon, 1986.

Miller, Nancy. "Changing the Subject." *Coming to Terms. Feminism, Theory, Politics*. Ed. Elizabeth Weed. New York: Routledge, 1989. 3–16.

———. "Emphasis Added: Plots and Plausibilities in Women's Fiction." *The New Feminist Criticism*. Ed. Elaine Showalter. New York: Pantheon, 1985. 339–60.

Modleski, Tania. *Loving With a Vengeance: Mass-produced Fantasies for Women*. New York: Routledge, 1990 repr.

Monserdà i Vidal, Dolors. *La fabricanta*. 4th ed. Barcelona: Editorial Selecta, 1972. (Originally published, Barcelona 1904).

Munich, Adrienne Auslander. *Andromeda's Chains: Gender and Interpretation in Victorian Literature and Art*. New York: Columbia University Press, 1989.

Nash, Mary. *Mujer, Familia y trabajo en España, 1875–1936*. Barcelona: Anthropos, 1983.

Nietzsche, Friedrich. *The Gay Science*. Trans. W. Kaufmann. New York: Random House, 1974.

Ordóñez, Elizabeth. "Paradise Regained, Paradise Lost: Desire and Prohibition in *La madre naturaleza*." *Hispanic Journal* 8.1 (1986): 7–18.

———. "Revising Realism: Pardo Bazán's *Memorias de un Solterón* in Light of Galdós's *Tristana* and John Stuart Mill." *In the Feminine Mode: Essays on Hispanic Women Writers*. Ed. Noël Valis and Carol Maier. Lewisburg: Bucknell University Press, 1990. 146–63.

Pardo Bazán, Emilia. *Cartas a Benito Pérez Galdós (1889–1890)*. Ed. Carmen Bravo-Villasante. Madrid: Ediciones Turner, 1975.

———. *Dulce Dueño*. Ed. Marina Mayoral. Madrid: Castalia. Biblioteca de Escritoras, 1989.

———. *Insolación*. Barcelona: Bruguera, 1981.

———. *La mujer española y otros artículos feministas*. Prologue by Leda Schiavo. Madrid: Editora Nacional, 1976.

———. *Obras completas. Novelas*. Ed. Federico Carlos Saínz de Robles. 2 vols. Madrid: Aguilar (Vol. 1, 4th ed., 1964; Vol. 2, 3d ed. 1973 rpr.).

Pérez Escrich, Enrique. *La esposa mártir*. 2 vols. Madrid: Librería de Miguel Guijarro, 1865.

Pérez Galdós, Benito. *Doña Perfecta. Novelas.* Ed. Federico Carlos Saínz de Robles. Madrid: Aguilar, 1981 rpr.

———. *Tristana.* Vol. 5. *Obras completas.* Ed. Federico Carlos Saínz de Robles. 6 vols. Madrid: Aguilar, 1967.

Pi Margal, Franciso. *La misión de la mujer en la sociedad.* Madrid: Rivadeneyra, 1869.

Poovey, Mary. *Uneven Developments: The Ideological Work of Gender in Mid-Victorian England.* Chicago: University of Chicago Press, 1988.

Poullain, Claude H. "Valor y sentido de la novela de Rosalía Castro de Murguía, *El caballero de las botas azules.*" *Cuadernos de Estudios Gallegos* 25 (1970): 37–69.

Pratt, Annis. *Archetypal Patterns in Women's Fiction.* Bloomington: Indiana University Press, 1981.

Rabine, Leslie W. *Reading the Romantic Heroine: Text, History, Ideology.* Ann Arbor: University of Michigan Press, 1985.

Reik, Theodor. *Masochism in Modern Man.* Trans. Margaret H. Beigel and Gertrud M. Kruth. New York: Farrar, Straus, and Giroux, 1941.

Riffaterre, Michael. *Fictional Truth.* Baltimore: Johns Hopkins University Press, 1990.

Risco, Antonio. "*El caballero de las botas azules* de Rosalía, una obra abierta." *Papeles de San Armadans* 77 (1975): 113–30.

Rivière, Joan. "Womanliness as Masquerade." *Formations of Fantasy.* Ed. Victor Burgin, James Donald, and Cora Kaplan. London: Methuen, 1986. 35–44. (Originally published, *International Journal of Psychoanalysis* 10 [1929]).

Robatto, Matilde Albert. *Rosalía de Castro y la condición femenina.* Madrid: Ediciones, Partenon, 1981.

Rogers, Katherine. *The Troublesome Helpmeet: A History of Misogyny in Literature.* Seattle: University of Washington Press, 1966.

Rose, Jacqueline. "Kristeva, Take Two." *Coming to Terms: Feminism, Theory, Politics.* Ed. Elizabeth Weed. New York: Routledge, 1989. 17–33.

———. *Sexuality and the Field of Vision.* London: Verso, 1986.

———. "Where Does the Misery Come From? Psychoanalysis, Feminism, and the Event." *Feminism and Psychoanalysis.* Ed. Richard Feldstein and Judith Roof. Ithaca: Cornell University Press, 1989. 25–39.

Saez de Melgar, Faustina. "La mujer de ayer, la de hoy y la de mañana." *La mujer. Revista de Instrucción General Para el Bello Sexo.* 1.2 (June 1871): 2–3.

Saínz de Robles, Federico Carlos, ed. *Obras completas.* By Benito Pérez Galdós. Vol. 5. 5th ed. Madrid: Aguilar, 1967.

Sáiz, Concepción. *La revolución del 68 y la cultura femenina.* Madrid: Librería de Victoriano Suárez, 1929.

Sawicki. Jana. *Disciplining Foucault. Feminism, Power, and the Body.* New York: Routledge, 1991.

Scanlon, Geraldine. "Class and Gender in Pardo Bazán's *La Tribuna.*" *Bulletin of Hispanic Studies* 67.2 (April 1990): 137–50.

———. *La polémica feminista en la España contemporánea (1864–1974).* Madrid: Siglo XXI, 1976.

Schor, Naomi. "Dreaming Dissymmetry: Barthes, Foucault and Sexual Difference." *Coming to Terms: Feminism, Theory, Politics.* Ed. Elizabeth Weed. New York: Routledge, 1989. 47–58.

———. "Reading Double: Sand's Difference." *The Poetics of Gender.* Ed. Nancy K. Miller. New York: Columbia University Press, 1986. 248–69.

Scott, Joan W. "Gender: A Useful Category of Historical Analysis." *Coming to*

*Terms: Feminism, Theory, Politics.* Ed. Elizabeth Weed. New York: Routledge, 1989. 81–100. (Also in *Gender and the Politics of History*)

———. *Gender and the Politics of History.* New York: Columbia University Press, 1988.

Showalter, Elaine. "Toward a Feminist Poetics." *The New Feminist Criticism.* Ed. Elaine Showalter. New York: Pantheon, 1985. 125–43.

Shubert, Adrian. *A Social History of Modern Spain.* London: Unwin Hyman, 1990.

Silverman, Kaja. "Masochism and Male Subjectivity." *Camera Obscura* 17 (Fall 1988): 31–67.

Simón Palmer, María del Carmen. "Escritoras españolas del siglo XIX o el miedo a la marginación." *Anales de Literatura Española de la Universidad de Alicante* 2 (1983): 477–90.

———. *Escritoras españolas del siglo XIX. Manual bio-bliográfico.* Madrid: Castalia, 1991.

Sinués de Marco, María del Pilar. *La abuela.* Madrid: Ilustración Española y Americana, 1878.

———. *La amiga íntima.* Madrid: Victoriano Suárez, 1908.

———. [untitled article]. *El Imparcial.* (Madrid: 30 July 1877): 4.

———. *Morir sola.* Madrid: Administración, 1890.

———. *La mujer de nuestros días.* Madrid: Agustín Jubera, 1878.

———. *El sol de invierno.* 2d ed. Madrid: La Moda Elegante Ilustrada. 1879.

Spivak, Gayatri. "Three Women's Texts and a Critique of Imperialism." *The Feminist Reader: Essays in Gender and the Politics of Literary Criticism.* Ed. Catherine Belsey and Jane Moore. New York: Basil Blackwell, 1989. 175–95.

Stanton, Domna C. "Difference on Trial: A Critique of the Maternal Metaphor in Cixous, Irigaray, and Kristeva." *The Poetics of Gender.* Ed. Nancy K. Miller. Columbia University Press, 1986. 157–82.

Studlar, Gaylyn. *In the Realm of Pleasure.* Urbana: University of Illinois Press, 1988.

Tapia, Tomás. *La religión en la conciencia y en la vida.* Madrid: Rivadeneyra, 1869.

Thompson, Clara M. *On Women.* New York: Mentor Books, 1971.

Urey, Diane. "The Incestual Difference in *Los pazos de Ulloa* and *La madre naturaleza.*" Midwest MLA Convention. Chicago. 7 November 1986.

Valis, Noël. *The Decadent Vision in Leopoldo Alas: A Study of "La Regenta" and "Su único hijo."* Baton Rouge: Louisiana State University Press, 1981.

———. "Eden and the Tree of Knowledge in Fernán Caballero's *Clemencia.*" *Kentucky Romance Quarterly* 29 (1982): 251–60.

———. "The Language of Treasure: Carolina Coronado, Casta Esteban, and Marina Romero." *In the Feminine Mode: Essays on Hispanic Women Writers.* Ed. Noël Valis and Carole Maier. Lewisburg, Pa.: Bucknell University Press, 1990. 246–72.

"Variations of Some Common Themes." (By the editors of *Questions Féministes*) *Feminist Issues* 1 (1980): 15–17.

Vicuña, G. "La gran industria y la industral doméstica." *Instrucción para la mujer* 1.6 (16 May 1882): 81–82.

Winders, James A. *Gender, Theory, and the Canon.* Madison: University of Wisconsin Press, 1991.

Winnett, Susan. "Coming Unstrung: Women, Men, Narrative and Principles of Pleasure." *PMLA* (May 1990): 505–18.

Wyatt, Jean. *Reconstructing Desire: The Role of the Unconscious in Women's Reading and Writing.* Chapel Hill: University of North Carolina Press, 1990.

# Index